The Will of the Many

Anthropology, Culture and Society

Series Editors:
Professor Vered Amit, Concordia University
and
Dr Jon P. Mitchell, University of Sussex

Published titles include:

The Will of the Many

How the Alterglobalisation Movement
is Changing the Face of Democracy

MARIANNE MAECKELBERGH

PLUTO PRESS
www.plutobooks.com

First published 2009 by Pluto Press
345 Archway Road, London N6 5AA and
175 Fifth Avenue, New York, NY 10010

www.plutobooks.com

Distributed in the United States of America exclusively by
Palgrave Macmillan, a division of St. Martin's Press LLC,
175 Fifth Avenue, New York, NY 10010

British Library Cataloguing in Publication Data
A catalogue record for this book is available from the British Library

ISBN   978 0 7453 2926 0   Hardback
ISBN   978 0 7453 2925 3   Paperback

Library of Congress Cataloging in Publication Data applied for

This book is printed on paper suitable for recycling and made from
fully managed and sustained forest sources. Logging, pulping and
manufacturing processes are expected to conform to the environmental
standards of the country of origin. The paper may contain up to
70 per cent post consumer waste.

10 9 8 7 6 5 4 3 2 1

Designed and produced for Pluto Press by
Chase Publishing Services Ltd, 33 Livonia Road, Sidmouth, EX10 9JB, England
Typeset from disk by Stanford DTP Services, Northampton, England
Printed and bound in the European Union by
CPI Antony Rowe, Chippenham and Eastbourne

CONTENTS

SERIES PREFACE

Anthropology is a discipline based upon in-depth ethnographic works that deal with wider theoretical issues in the context of particular, local conditions – to paraphrase an important volume from the series: *large issues* explored in *small places*. The series has a particular mission: to publish work that moves away from old-style descriptive ethnography – that is strongly area-studies oriented – and offer genuine theoretical arguments that are of interest to a much wider readership but which are nevertheless located and grounded in solid ethnographic research. If anthropology is to argue itself a place in the contemporary intellectual world then it must surely be through such research.

We start from the question: 'what can this ethnographic material tell us about the bigger theoretical issues that concern the social sciences'; rather than 'what can these theoretical ideas tell us about the ethnographic context'. Put this way round, such work becomes *about* large issues, *set in* a (relatively) small place, rather than detailed description of a small place for its own sake. As Clifford Geertz once said: 'anthropologists don't study villages; they study *in* villages'.

By place we mean not only geographical locale, but also other types of 'place' – within political, economic, religious or other social systems. We therefore publish work based on ethnography within political and religious movements, occupational or class groups, youth, development agencies, nationalists; but also work that is more thematically based – on kinship, landscape, the state, violence, corruption, the self. The series publishes four kinds of volume – ethnographic monographs; comparative texts; edited collections; and shorter, polemic essays.

We publish work from all traditions of anthropology, and all parts of the world, which combines theoretical debate with empirical evidence to demonstrate anthropology's unique position in contemporary scholarship and the contemporary world.

Professor Vered Amit
Dr Jon P. Mitchell

ACKNOWLEDGEMENTS

Trying to list all the people who help to make a book is a task akin to counting trees in a forest. No matter how much inspiration they provide, you can never mention them all, and when you do, you risk not seeing the wood for the trees. Those who contributed most to this book did not do so as individuals or directly, but they did so collectively and indirectly through their actions. This book tells a story of a social movement that is trying to change the world as we know it. There is nothing so motivating as being surrounded, every day, by people who are putting such ambitious aspirations into practice. I believe that change comes primarily through action, that knowledge is created through struggle, and that when knowledge is not acted upon, it is wasted. The ideas developed in this book, the implications and analyses, are given meaning only in so far as they reflect actions that are already happening and actions that are yet to come. My aim is not to create knowledge for knowledge's sake, nor is it to create knowledge 'for' the movement as a way to 'help'. The movement actors I have met over the past decades create so much knowledge every day, practical knowledge given meaning through action, that each addition is at best only a drop in the bucket. The most I can hope for is that this book can explain the significance of these already existing actions to those who have not had the good fortune to be a part of creating them. My years of research and activism have brought me into contact with people whose commitment moves mountains and whose actions inspire storms, and it seems unfair to keep this pleasure for myself. Still, there is an inherent tension in writing about activism and social movements, in becoming the commentator rather than (or in addition to) the actor; it requires humility on the part of the author and an acceptance of how little the written word can accomplish without the actor. The most important thanks, then, go to the movement actors themselves. Not only those I have met, not only those that I call friends, but even those I have never met and never will meet. Thank you, not just for sharing these ideas, not just for helping in producing this text, but for surprising and inspiring me and many others every day. There is no end to the ideas that flow out of every conversation in an activist environment. My heartfelt gratitude to all who have contributed in this way.

That the ideas expressed here became a book and not a series of action trainings is due to the incredible opportunity I have had to meet and work with others who know how to inspire their students and their colleagues. Among these many, a few deserve specific mention. Without the academic insight, activist understanding and general support of Neil Stammers and Jeff Pratt this book would quite simply not exist. For their unwavering faith in me and dedication to this project, I am infinitely grateful. Thanks to David Graeber, Jane Cowan and the anonymous reviewers who provided me with crucial comments, insightful questions and much appreciated enthusiasm. Thanks to Oscar Reyes for his acutely academic yet nevertheless activist perspectives that permeate this entire book; thanks to Pieter Baets who helped shape these ideas through years of fruitful conversations; thanks to Christian Scholl for his indispensable advice on the first draft and after; and thanks to Hema Kotecha for her continuous support and reading of draft chapters. Perspectives, mistakes, and the fact that this can only ever be a partial story, however, reflect my shortcomings only.

If it was not for my mother's considerable patience with my radical philosophies, and the simple and singular request she made, so many years ago, for me to *please* give university a chance, I would probably be living in a tree today and not writing books – for better or for worse. As always, my deepest thanks, for everything, belong to her. Others, however, were also essential – my aunt Lucrèce, uncle Aimé and grandparents, Moeke, Vader, Bonma and Bonpa – for all the time and care they offered me while writing, and the entire Kotecha family for being my home away from home. Over the years it took to complete this project, I relied not so much on having money as on being given things for free. I would like to thank the many people who have offered me food, given me free tea and coffee, those who have housed me for weeks, months, years, those who gave me computers to work on and those who helped me get from point A to point B.

The exceptionally efficient folks at Pluto Press also made this process a pleasure. Particular thanks to David Castle for his enthusiastic encouragement, to the series editor Jon Mitchell and to Sophie Richmond for her dedication to detail.

Despite all the support and help I received from these people and many others, I choose to dedicate this book not to those who helped me, but to one who kept me from it, one who dragged me away from the computer, first to struggle by his side and later to fight for his freedom. The risk that activism entails does not feature in the pages of this book. This, however, does not make it any less real. Daniel, your laughs, hugs and practical dedication are dearly missed every single day and I hope this book will help you fill a few of the empty hours that lie ahead.

Marianne Maeckelbergh
May 2009

LIST OF ABBREVIATIONS

ATTAC	Association pour la Taxation des Transactions financières pour l'Aide aux Citoyen(ne)s
Babels	International Network of Volunteer Interpreters and Translators
BOC	Brazilian Organising Committee of the WSF
CIRCA	Clandestine Insurgent Rebel Clown Army
CND	Committee for Nuclear Disarmament
DAN	Direct Action Network
DIY	Do-It-Yourself
DNC	Democratic National Convention
EPA	European Preparatory Assembly
ERAP	Economic and Research Action Project
ESF	European Social Forum
EU	European Union
EZLN	Ejercito Zapatista de Liberación Nacional
FIOM	Federazione impiegati operai metallurgici
FSU	Fédération Syndicale Unitaire
FTAA	Free Trade Area of the Americas
G8	Group of Eight. The G8 summit is a meeting between the leaders of the UK, US, Germany, France, Italy, Japan, Canada and, since 1997, also Russia.
GLA	Greater London Authority (London mayor's office)
GPJC	Georgia Peace and Justice Coalition
GR	Globalise Resistance
IC	International Council of the WSF
IGC	Indian General Council of the WSF
IMF	International Monetary Fund
Indymedia	an independent alternative media network
IOC	Indian Organising Committee of the WSF
IST	International Socialist Tendency
IYC	Intercontinental Youth Camp
LCR	League Communiste Révolutionnaire
LSF	London Social Forum

MPH	Make Poverty History
MST	Movimento dos Trabalhadores Rurais Sem Terra
NBA	Narmada Bachao Andolan
NGOs	non-governmental organisations
NSMs	New Social Movements
OC	Organising Committee
PGA	Peoples' Global Action
PMOs	Peace Movement Organisations
RNC	Republican National Convention
RTS	Reclaim the Streets
SCLC	Southern Christian Leadership Conference
SDS	Students for a Democratic Society
SEA	South East Assembly (UK)
SNCC	Student Non-violent Coordinating Committee
SUD	Solidaire Unitaire Démocratique
SWP	Socialist Workers Party
TAZ	Temporary Autonomous Zone
UFPJ	United For Peace and Justice
UKCC	United Kingdom Coordinating Committee of the ESF
UKOC	United Kingdom Organising Committee of the ESF
WB	World Bank
WOMBLES	White Overalls Movement Building Libertarian Effective Struggles
WSF	World Social Forum
WTO	World Trade Organisation

INTRODUCTION:
THE UNGLAMOROUS SIDE OF GLORY

How to *exist with the other* in a planetary world is the moral challenge of our time. (Melucci 1992: 53)

The Road to Seattle

Wetlands Social Justice Centre

This story starts in an unexpected corner of a forgotten basement in a dingy nightclub. It is an activist nightclub called Wetlands located in an old warehouse district of New York City. By the entrance the walls are covered in posters and there are tables piled with leaflets: 'Boycott Mitsubishi', 'Heineken out of Burma', 'Stop Animal Testing'. Downstairs there is a big room with couches and chairs which, most nights, serves as a lounge for pot-smoking hippies, but once a week it becomes a meeting space for an odd mix of old unionists and young vegans. A small group of paid and unpaid staff work hard to put together the meetings and the letter-writing campaigns while also organising protests and civil disobedience actions. Every week the meeting takes on a different topic; one week it is federal lands; the next, human rights; the week after it is rainforests; and the fourth, animal rights. The people who attend are almost the same each week and the overlap between topics and issues is intentional and political; the guiding philosophy at Wetlands is that all struggles are linked and all oppression is rooted in the same structural problems.

The year is 1995 and the fame of the 'Battle of Seattle' is still an impossible dream. I am 'animal rights campaign coordinator' at Wetlands but I need to know much more than simply animal rights issues; the phone calls I receive each day are about the military dictatorship in Burma, the rainforest destruction carried out by Mitsubishi corporation, the Dineh people's struggle against forced relocation from their holy lands to a nuclear waste site, to name but a few. All the worries that eventually brought activists to the streets of Seattle to confront the World Trade Organisation (WTO) exist here in these meetings already. Just one look around the room confirms the diversity of the activists too. There are almost as many women as men. There are some older men and women who have been active in trade unions and environmental movements since the 1960s, offering the advice of hardened experience. There is a group of school children with all the time and energy of those who have only just discovered the problems of the world, and there are the young adults in their twenties and thirties with varying degrees of activist experience, some who wear the crusty clout of many arrests on their sleeves and others whose revolution is in their art ... or both. From my vantage point in 1995, this was already a very diverse struggle of interconnected, yet different, issues.

In four years' time some of these people will be among the tens of thousands who flood the streets of Seattle to shut down the World Trade Organisation. Those who stay behind will hold their breath as they watch the news of 30 November 1999 – the day that the WTO is successfully shut down and global trade agreements are derailed. Eyes glued to their TV screens, hearts pounding in their chests, they will know, for one brief moment, that this political victory was not won by some world power or through military might, but by us, by our friends, by the thousands of faces barely visible through the cloud of tear gas that hung over Seattle for five unforgettable days. These images of suffering and success will inspire instant support meetings at Wetlands and across the world by what, in that moment, came to be known as the 'anti-globalisation movement'.

Seattle, N30 1999

As I wandered, at times ran, through the streets of Seattle, the thought went through my head over and over again, 'What happened to make this possible?' We had been saying for so many years that the different struggles were related and that the era of single-issue activism was over, but for many of us it was not until the WTO protests in Seattle that we saw this idea enacted on a large scale. The massive protests that took place on the streets of Seattle in 1999 were not the result of a new idea or even a new circumstance (other multilateral organisations had been protested by a variety of groups before) but for many of us it represented a new stage of activism. Suddenly, out of years of campaigning, talking, protesting, getting arrested, trying to make the links between seemingly disparate problems to no avail ... 'Seattle' happened ... and it brought with it, at long last, the beginning of the end for single-issue and 'identity'-based politics.

The alterglobalisation movement did not arise out of thin air; it had predecessors everywhere from the famous Zapatista uprising in Chiapas, Mexico in 1994 to the anonymous basement of Wetlands, and it took the world stage in a visibly united form during the Seattle WTO protests.[1] All the arguments we had spent years trying to resolve so that straight-edge vegans would work with pot-smoking hippies, as mundane as it may sound, were part of the transformation that led to Seattle. Wetlands, like so many other sites of activism in the 1980s and 1990s, was a bridge. Even though we did not know it, we were building links that would take us from the identity politics of the 1980s into the new millennium as the alterglobalisation movement. We were part of a collective learning process on how to negotiate our different beliefs and identities. It took time and hard work to build these connections, but we were not starting from scratch. We had tools, ideas and experiences that helped us learn. We had consensus decision-making, participatory democracy, non-violent direct action and civil disobedience; we had theories about which interpersonal dynamics strengthen or weaken our movements – and we had been working on improving these skills for decades. When the World Trade Organisation came to Seattle in 1999 – we were ready.

The Unglamorous Side of Glory

Movement actors often say that the alterglobalisation movement is everywhere and nowhere. No matter where you look, it is there, they say, but you may not always see it. The glimpses of this movement that I offer in the coming pages are to be read against this backdrop of permeation. Social movements tend to get recorded as if they were nothing more than flashes of brilliance that emerge and submerge. Stories of glory are told, famous figures are revered, and unforgettable moments are made more unforgettable by repeated transformation into words. Social movements become the images they leave behind, images tied to particular places and particular times. Many social movements would not enter our field of vision without these star-studded reveries. These moments are transforming for those who live them and often leave lasting impressions on the movements that created them. However, as significant as these stories are, they are told at the expense of other tales, much less glamorous perhaps, but equally important. This book tells the story of these famous collective spaces of movement activity – not of the events themselves, but rather the processes that went into making these events. I offer an ethnography of the decision-making processes of alterglobalisation movement actors in the preparatory meetings for the European Social Forum (ESF), the World Social Forum (WSF) and the autonomous sections of the anti-G8 summit mobilisations. These events have captured much media attention and been written about in detail by activists and scholars alike, but there exists little ethnographic material on the decision-making processes that determine these events.

The belief underlying this book is that the answer to the ever-pending question, 'What is the movement for?' lies not in any text about movement principles or intentions, but lies instead in movement practices. The people who make up the alterglobalisation movement, the movement actors, are intentionally prefigurative of the 'other world(s)' they would like to see and, as such, if one wants to know what the alterglobalisation movement is for, one must look at what the alterglobalisation movement *does*.[2] Once our gaze is thus shifted, we find that what this movement is doing is radically changing the meaning of democracy and simultaneously constructing a democratic world based on principles of diversity and horizontality. Much of the literature emerging from this movement demonstrates clearly the central place given to democracy in the 'goals' of the alterglobalisation movement, but what is not clear from this literature is what that democracy might look like. Taking an ethnographic approach to the movement allows for an exploration of the actual decision-making practices already in place, which make visible the beginnings of an emerging democratic alternative.

The Alterglobalisation Movement

This book cannot tell the story of the alterglobalisation movement as a whole, but offers instead a description of decision-making processes found in the collective spaces of the global networks of movement organising so as to extrapolate from these the beginnings of an alternative democratic praxis. The collective spaces of the global networks of movement activity are limited to moments when movement actors from diverse groups and networks come together. Many processes take place in these moments of collective movement activity, but the subject of this book is limited to one such process – collective decision-making. Six inextricable practices will be explored here – prefiguration, consensus/conflict, horizontality, diversity, democracy and connectivity.

These collective spaces of movement activity are essential to understanding the alterglobalisation movement as a whole and the processes described here certainly have a broader significance, but the alterglobalisation movement is first and foremost highly diverse and heterogeneous and it is impossible to speak of any six categories that can explain the movement entirely. There are many spaces and moments of the alterglobalisation movement in which, and many actors for whom, the values emphasised here would not appear as central. I choose to focus on these practices due to their importance to decision-making in the alterglobalisation movement and because they aid an understanding of that which is unique about the democratic praxis of this movement. However, choosing this focus necessarily obscures other movement practices which are of central importance to movement actors, particularly those of protest, direct action, confrontation and 'resistance' more broadly.[3] What I offer here is a partial and conflictive view and, consequently, I continuously use my ethnography (including examples from outside these global networks) to emphasise the limits of my own framework. I demonstrate conflict, diversity and lack of unanimity within the alterglobalisation movement, even though at times it may seem to undermine my argument. In Chapter 2, for example, when I argue for the centrality of 'process', I do so by presenting a conflict about 'process' and offer voices both for and against its importance to avoid creating the impression that *central* values are equivalent to *universal* values.

The presence of conflict within the alterglobalisation movement raises the important question of whether we can speak of *one* movement. The very term 'movement of movements' points to the alterglobalisation movement being at once a single movement and multiple movements and this renders any simple claim to singularity impossible.[4] Indeed, referring to the alterglobalisation movement as a single movement requires a redefinition of 'singularity' to accommodate a great deal of diversity. This is by no means a revolutionary idea; few anthropologists today would argue that speaking of any group of people as one ought to lead to the assumption that those people are homogeneous. Although there are certainly grounds for arguing that the alterglobalisation movement is not a single movement, I choose to understand the diverse practices and beliefs of the alterglobalisation movement as a single movement because part of the political project outlined here is precisely to overcome the assumption that difference precludes unity.

This relationship between diversity and singularity raises the question, however, of the form such diversity must take in order to be understood as unified and not just as an unrelated set of simultaneous activities. What is of interest to me is not only that the movement actors are so diverse, but that they nevertheless come together within a structure that makes collective decision-making possible despite deep divisions. Ultimately, this relates to how we understand a social movement to be constituted. Many definitions have been proposed in the past and I will not attempt to propose a general definition of social movements here, but rather describe briefly how this movement seems to constitute unity through/despite differences. The alterglobalisation movement is one movement not because those involved form 'a network of informal interactions ... engaged in a political or cultural conflict on the basis of a shared collective identity' (Diani 1992: 13, cf. Stammers and Eschle 2005: 54), but rather because the network of formal and informal interactions constituted by movement actors ties them together through a series of overlapping unities. The focus of this book is unity constructed between movement actors around practices of decision-making, but this unity represents only one of many unities that bring movement actors together.[5] Other sources of unity include an opposition to neoliberal globalisation and multilateral organisations, the abolition of capitalism, anti-corporatism, anti-war, the 'reclaiming of the commons' (Klein 2000, 2005), direct action, a general ethos of 'resistance', among others. Indeed, there are so many sources of unity that they cannot possibly be mentioned here. Nevertheless, it is important to note that for the alterglobalisation movement there is no *one* unity that applies to all movement actors.[6] There is no *single* 'vision'/'goal', no *single* 'adversary', and no *single* 'identity' (cf. Castells 1997, Touraine 1985) shared by all movement actors. There is, however, enough overlap between the various goals, adversaries and identities to tie all the movement actors together and to ensure that these actors with various goals, adversaries and identities often find themselves partaking in the same processes. Activists of very diverse backgrounds and beliefs will work together on a project for a brief period of time, their interests will temporarily overlap, and once the project, action, event is over, they will start another project with others and re-create the overlapping in a new form.[7] The alterglobalisation movement is unbounded, with no clear delineations across space and time, and one could easily argue that the WOMBLES and the Socialist Workers Party (SWP) are not part of the same movement (and indeed many of these movement actors would argue this themselves). However, I repeatedly found these actors in the same rooms, discussing the same ideas and organising around the same events. Their perspectives differed greatly, but they were part of the same process. From a movement actor's point of view, someone is considered to be included only if they can be understood to in some way overlap with one's own politics, ideals, or practices. From an external viewpoint, however, these overlapping unities can be seen structurally, and although the WOMBLES may not self-identify as part of the same movement as the SWP, their involvement in the same projects and mutual rejection of multilateral organisations (to mention just one overlapping unity) nevertheless links them.

Getting over the 1960s: From Hopes to Practices

The journey that led to Seattle is a political trajectory that 'begins' in the 1960s. In the decades since the 1960s, many commentators have declared the 1960s movements a failure and others have credited them only with lasting cultural changes (see Daniels 1989: 3–15), but perhaps the most important effect of the 1960s movements will turn out to be their role in shaping the alterglobalisation movement. Some of the most important political values, structures and practices of the alterglobalisation movement – participation, an aversion to representation, horizontality, diversity, decentralised notions of power, *autogestion*, consensus, carnival as subversion, rejecting individualism, an acceptance of conflict as constructive, critical reflexivity, non-reified approach to knowledge, an emphasis on the importance of the 'grassroots', an internationalism based on strong solidarity and communication between activists all over the world – are all characteristics for which the seeds were sown, if not grown, in the 1960s.

The six practices central to this book can all be traced back to the movements of the 1960s. These practices, however, have undergone considerable evolutions and have slowly adopted different forms and meanings. The new and unfamiliar ideas that the movement actors of the 1960s struggled with are today not only familiar to movement actors, but improved by decades of experimentation. This evolution within the movement, together with changes outside of the movement, has resulted in important differences between 1960s movements and the alterglobalisation movement. In this section I briefly address three such differences which I deem most significant: the movement actors' perception of a global world; the more elaborately structured and effective consensus decision-making procedures; and the decline of identity politics.

A Global Perspective

There can be no doubt that the movements of the 1960s were global in scope, with significant uprisings on every continent except Antarctica. There was exchange of information across national boundaries, resulting in solidarity between movements and a ripple, or 'eros' effect of protest (Katsiaficas 1987). In the alterglobalisation movement today, however, there is a shift from solidarity and support between people in different places to a struggle that is waged globally and constituted globally. George (2004: xiii) declares that:

> we face an historically unprecedented moment. No one has ever tried to democratise the international space before, or to ensure a decent existence for everyone on earth. These goals are no longer utopian but have become practical prospects; whence the declaration another world is possible, because it is.

When alterglobalisation movement actors call for action, they often do so on a global scale and the actions and gatherings take place all over the world. The WTO protests in Seattle in November and December 1999 and the protests against the International Monetary Fund (IMF)/World Bank (WB) in April 2000, were quickly followed up with the IMF/WB protests in Prague in September 2000. In the year 2001 movement actors organised five major international mobilisations on three different continents and Peoples' Global Action (PGA) held international planning conferences in the US, Italy and Bolivia. These mobilisations included the first ever World Social Forum in Porto Alegre, Brazil which brought together over 20,000 movement actors from nearly every part of the world. In April 2001, Canadian and US activists worked together to stop the Free Trade Area of the Americas (FTAA) summit from meeting in Quebec City. That same summer activists in Europe were on the road (often accompanied by North

Americans) headed from one massive mobilisation to the next; first they confronted the European Union (EU) in Gothenburg, Sweden in mid June, then they took on the World Bank at the end of the same month, and only a few weeks later they faced the wrath of the various Italian police forces at the G8 summit in Genoa, Italy, where one young man was shot and killed by police and many more were hospitalised. The violence in Genoa was dwarfed a few months later by the attacks on the World Trade Center in the US the following September, which almost instantly made organising against global centres of power more difficult in the US and around the world due to the consequent restrictions on civil liberties, heightened security at global summits and anti-terror legislation that can be, and in some cases has been, used against social movement actors. Still, movement actors continue to organise massive gatherings like the WSF, having brought together nearly 125,000 people in India in 2004 and 150,000 people in Brazil in 2005. Mobilisations against multilateral organisations also continued in places as geographically dispersed as Cancun, Mexico, in 2003, St Petersburg, Russia, in 2006 and Lake Toya, Japan, in 2008.

The choice to organise against multilateral institutions, and to do so by mobilising internationally, is a recognition of the shifting balance of power in global decision-making. Movement actors realise that sites of decision-making are less and less the formal democratic structures of nation-states, that nation-states are increasingly becoming dependent on international corporations for their economic survival, that the executive branch of government is gaining in relative importance as part of a reconfiguration of state power which allows state power to be increasingly exercised through institutions and structures of global governance. This reconfiguration has exaggerated the problems of democratic governance, particularly of state-based representative structures, and has rendered forms of protest that appeal to these representative structures less appealing to movement actors. Rather than challenge the policies of multilateral organisations through political parties or unified organisations that influence national governments, the alterglobalisation movement attempts to link as many different people as possible on a global level through horizontal structures based on diversity. Movement actors today are not just resisting all over the world; this resistance grows out of and helps to constitute the global connections they build with each other (Juris 2008b).

What were once mutually supportive separate struggles for democracy are now *also* a single democratic project for a radically different world. This shift in perspective has consequences for the way movement actors understand 'solidarity' (see Chapter 4) and the nature of the connections they build with each other (see Chapter 5). The perception of a global community is possible today partially because of the increased connectivity of the world, but this does not provide sufficient grounds for a social movement to dare to claim global change as a possibility. What makes 'another world possible' in this context of increased connectivity are the practices and ideas inherited from the 1960s and 1970s movements. It is through the combination of these practices with today's increased connectivity that change on a global scale becomes thinkable. These practices provide the constitutive meaning for the connections made possible through modern technology.[8] The specific details of these practices as they exist in the alterglobalisation movement will be developed in the chapters to come, but before embarking on this description, it is necessary to first establish an historical context for these practices.

Structuring Participatory Democracy

This shift away from political parties as the overarching framework through which different struggles are united towards 'the party' as only one movement actor among many, is only partially in response to the crisis of representative politics. Equally important were the lessons learned about participatory democracy within the movements of the 1960s and 1970s. Movements of the 1960s were developing radically 'new' democratic structures and practices, and they were doing so in a context of distrust for centralised communist organisation and any 'vision of sweeping social change' (Miller 1994: 66). Many of those active in student movements of the 1960s in Europe, the US and Latin America had been expelled from their respective communist parties. The growing distrust of Communism after the uprising and subsequent Soviet invasion of Hungary in 1956 laid the foundation for an almost universal condemnation of the Soviet invasion of Czechoslovakia in 1968: 'Soviet contempt for the world movement was shocking, and world Communist unanimity had dissolved' (Eley 2002: 361). For some movement actors in Europe, this dissolution represented a complete rejection of communist politics, and for others only a rejection of Stalinism (Lynd 1969: 2), often in favour of Mao and the revolutionary ideals of the contemporaneous Chinese cultural revolution, or rather, European imaginings thereof (Ross 2002: 90–113).[9] These divisions represented attempts to horizontalise the political practices of the movements and resulted in the creation of new democratic practices. At the Conference of European Communist Parties (in East Berlin, 1976) 'diversity was institutionalized' and a document was written that called for 'respect for free choice of different roads' (Eley 2002: 361). But 1976 was very late in the fast-moving politics of the 1960s, and by the time this official step had been taken, distrust of Communism in western European movements was widespread.

This distrust of Communism and traditional political parties remains today. Although there are alterglobalisation movement actors striving for a communist revolution, this political ideology no longer delimits the movement. In the 1960s, activists were developing new practices in a context where the left was dominated by communism for which, 'centralized, bureaucratic organization with a pyramidal chain of command [was] efficient, rational, proper, and a sign that the organization [was] mature and effectively able to mobilize its members and accomplish its objectives' (Gerlach 1983: 133, cf. Dalton et al. 1990: 13). It is against this pyramidal, centralised structure that many of the movement actors were rebelling in the 1960s. Today, the movements of the 1960s and 1970s are themselves the backdrop, and many of the older movement actors bring this scepticism of traditional left politics with them. Even those who advocate highly structured and organised approaches or are themselves involved in political parties will often refuse centralised hierarchy.

In Europe, post-1989, the malevolence of an already discredited Stalinism has been confirmed and this has (almost) entirely silenced those movement actors who were referred to as 'Communists with a capital C' in the 1960s.[10] The failure of Communism, furthermore, 'led to a delegitimizing of representative systems and undermined the hope that representation was possible in a different form' (Hardt and Negri 2004: 249). Even in movement spaces where there are many self-proclaimed communists, like the ESF and WSF, the planning process is infused with discussions about what constitutes a democratic way to organise meetings; there is an aversion to fixed structures of authority; there are no officers or positions of power; and there is a deep distrust of representation. Communists in the alterglobalisation movement today (whether they are 15 or 60 years old) grew up in a political climate influenced by the 1960s and many are open to non-hierarchical, fluid, indeterminate structures and 'participatory democracy'.

In the US, the term 'participatory democracy' was popularised in 1962 by the Students for Democratic Society (SDS) in their famous 'Port Huron Statement' (1962). This statement did not define participatory democracy in terms of horizontality or consensus; this interpretation of participatory democracy was created over time by SDS members as they challenged the centralisation and sexism of the organisational structure of SDS itself in search of the 'authenticity' alluded to in the Port Huron statement (Miller 1994: 204–06).[11] Participatory democracy quickly came to 'capture the essence of the New Left' (Miller 1994: 142), receiving its meaning slowly through the insistence, especially by women and 'minorities', that the means used to organise within the movement should reflect the ideals desired outside the movement (see Evans 1980, Gitlin 1993 [1987]: 362–76, Mansbridge 1983: 21, Miller 1994: 204–06). This prefigurative aspect of the 1960s and 1970s movements has often been ignored or understated, but many authors have argued that prefiguration was nevertheless widespread (Breines 1989, Epstein 1991, Eschle 2001, Fuller 1989, Polletta 2002).

The practice of prefiguration and the development of participatory democracy were intricately linked. In Mexico the calls for democracy took place in the context of a totalitarian regime and were mainly aimed at the state, but students were nevertheless adamant that democracy was possible in their own organising structures while they struggled for *Libertad democrática*. Mexican students prefigured the democratic Mexico they were fighting for by setting up local assemblies at different universities across Mexico City, linked to each other through a National Strike Council (Berman 1996: 49). Students also set up smaller groups called 'brigades' (Soldatenko 2005: 112) which bore similarities to the *comités d'action* set up in France. According to Denise, a member of one such *comité d'action* quoted in Daum (1988: 144): 'Our functioning was very different from that of the traditional parties of the "groupuscules" that some of us had known. We had no imposed ideology, something that permitted people, whoever they were, to participate in its elaboration.'[12] In Nanterre le mouvement de 22 mars was, 'without formal leaders, without common theoretical positions ... divided by their different political beliefs but united by a common will to act, and a pact that all decisions would be taken by general assembly' (quoted in Eley 2002: 343).[13] In the Censier building of the occupied Sorbonne University in Paris in May 1968, student imaginings of the Paris Commune took on a concrete character as students started to build on their unprecedented autonomy by reaching out to workers in an attempt to create workers' councils based on a 'tradition of direct democracy' and 'self-management' (see 'Paris: May 1968' n.d.). In Germany, the Netherlands and Italy too, movement actors were trying to prefigure 'workers' councils' as a response to bureaucratic governments and unions, while in the Eastern Bloc, 'pluralist forms of communism' were emerging (Berman 1996: 48–49, Caute 1988, Eley 2002: 361–65).

In the US, the Student Non-violent Coordinating Committee (SNCC) reacted to the top-down bureaucratic organising structures of the Southern Christian Leadership Conference (SCLC) to democratise internal movement practices. SNCC activists felt that if they were asking people to put their lives on the line for the struggle, then those people should have a say in the decisions made by the organisation (Evans 1980, Polletta 2002). Students from SDS were among those who put their lives on the line, and they were deeply inspired by the participatory ethos of SNCC:

> Particpatory democracy came from the gap between the grassroots activism Hayden observed in Mississippi and the sterility of mainstream politics ... participatory democracy as a commitment to surmount the usual barriers of status, a commitment on the part of participants to treat each other as equals, not by dividing up power equally, but by fostering each person's self-development. And it came, Hayden says, directly from SNCC. (Polletta 2002: 127–28)

The specific meaning of participatory democracy was continuously evolving, however, and the meaning that stuck, the one that we still find today, lies in the conflation of participatory democracy with consensus decision-making. This conflation is one of the most important innovations carried on since the movements of the 1960s. The growing sense that existing movement power structures were 'hopelessly "inflexible" and "unresponsive"' (Ross 1983: 182), combined with a large influx of new students into the movement after the April 1965 March on Washington against the Vietnam War, fundamentally changed the character of the New Left and brought about what was 'semifacetiously' referred to as the 'new New Left' (Ross 1983: 185, Sale 1973). By 1965, in the SDS-run Economic and Research Action Project (ERAP), 'it was taken for granted that the Oakland project would be run by consensus' (Booth quoted in Miller 1994: 243, see also Polletta 2002: 132–34).

These early practices of consensus, however, were riddled with problems of structurelessness (see Freeman 1970), which often led to the demise of groups and projects. The necessary organisational structure only began to develop in the 1970s after the introduction of Quaker consensus decision-making methods into the peace, anti-nuclear and women's movements. The role of feminism and feminists on the subsequent centrality of consensus decision-making cannot be overstated. So central was the role of women that consensus process has often been referred to as 'feminist process'. The anti-nuclear and peace movements of the 1970s and 1980s, under the influence of anarcha-feminists, became an important learning process for consensus decision-making in the US and Europe (Epstein 1991, Kitschelt 1989, Mushaben 1989, Rochon 1988). It is largely due to the conflation made by these movements between participation and consensus decision-making that consensus and the notion of horizontality are central to the alterglobalisation movement today.

This development of participatory democracy as a practice based on consensus coincided with a near universal emphasis on democracy as a goal within so-called 'new social movements' (Castells 1997, Cohen 1983, Hirsch 1988, Laclau 1985, Melucci 1989, Mouffe 1988) and peace movements (Hegedus 1989). Especially movements in Asia, the Middle East, Africa, Latin America and Eastern Europe had a demand for democracy and self-determination as 'the overriding issue of protest' (Braungart and Braungart 1990: 177). In the UK, as demands for more democracy were unequivocally ignored throughout the 1990s, movement actors began to 'concentrate on fighting schemes politically by building local opposition outside the formal decision-making process' (Doherty et al. 2000: 7). The growing disillusionment with the potential to change government policy across Europe in the 1990s (combined with the failure of Soviet Communism and the totalitarianism of many postcolonial 'democracies') reinforced the importance of constructing alternatives within movements and influenced the rise of movements based on autonomy and a Do-It-Yourself (DIY) 'culture'.

These 1980s and 1990s movements further developed the democratic structures we find in the alterglobalisation movement today, and did so in an explicitly decentralised manner. In Germany, autonomous movements were larger, more radical, more diverse and more unpredictable that those of the 1960s, and were characterised by anti-authoritarianism, independence from political parties, decentralised organisational forms and an emphasis on direct action (Katsiaficas 2006: 3, cf. Grauwacke 2004). DIY movements and squatter movements were centred around the idea of prefiguration at the level of lifestyle based

on a philosophy of autonomy and the rejection of political representation through an emphasis on direct involvement in all
aspects of life, including decision-making (see McKay 1998,
Poldervaart 2004). These autonomous movements, and the anti-
nuclear, feminist and peace movements, developed the structure
of affinity groups and spokescouncils into a functioning system
for consensus decision-making at a large scale, with the result that
these practices have dominated the independent left ever since
(especially in the US) and were at the heart of the Direct Action
Network (DAN) largely responsible for the success of 'Seattle'.

The form consensus decision-making took in Seattle was,
nevertheless, different. The anti-nuclear and feminist movements
of the 1970s linked these practices with the envisioning of politics
as 'culture', and consequently the practice of consensus came to
be about changing oneself and creating 'real community' based
on love, trust and friendship, often with spiritual overtones,
which posed serious obstacles to the inclusivity of participatory
democracy (Breines 1989: 46–66, Epstein 1991, Mansbridge
1983: 21, Polletta 2002: 218–30, Rootes 1982: 35). A deep
commitment to strategic non-violence was also conflated with
consensus decision-making and civil disobedience, and consensus
began to be seen as a 'non-violent' form of decision-making.
These ideals brought with them the assumption that human beings
would be genuinely good if given the chance. This culture of non-
violence led to an aversion to conflict and the ideal of creating a
conflict-free society (Epstein 1991: 32). Consensus also became
about unanimity of opinion and differences between participants
were suppressed in the interest of unity.

While this vision of conflict-free consensus was developing,
many organisations of the New Left had deteriorated into
increasingly conflictual relationships. The circumstance was
such that movement actors were trying to learn to use consensus
decision-making with the goal of a conflict-free society in a
context of high levels of conflict between movement actors who
felt that they were being discriminated against. This contributed
to the creation of a poor learning environment and several
commentators and activists concluded that consensus was only

viable in small groups of like-minded people. Many movement actors rejected participatory democracy altogether as a 'product of a naïve early state of protest' (Lynd quoted in Breines 1989: 121). Nevertheless, as movement actors began to focus more and more on struggles around various 'identities', consensus decision-making continued to be important, but on a smaller scale where it often went unnoticed. This was especially true in the women's movement, where 'plurality and flexibility were the rule' (Eley 2002: 372). This period, from the late 1970s to the 1990s, was a crucial incubation period for consensus decision-making. The smaller scale and the emphasis on friendship within consensus-based groups made it possible for movement actors to be innovative and take risks with the process until they developed structures that really worked.

This period is also marked by a decentralisation of movement activity. The fragmentation resulting from conflict over identity in the movements in the 1970s and 1980s, although detrimental in certain ways, was also a positive step required to break free from the perceived need for 'unity as sameness' and laid the groundwork for the decentralised structure that lies at the heart of the democratic practice of the alterglobalisation movement. Although the value of horizontality stems from 1960s and 1970s movements, the structure of networked decentralisation essential to the alterglobalisation movement is owed primarily to the movements of the 1980s and 1990s. Groups as diverse as the Zapatistas, the Narmada Bachao Andolan, Food not Bombs, ACT UP! and Friends of the Earth created structures of decentralised groups and subgroups (intentionally and unintentionally) first across nations and then globally. And, perhaps most importantly, they built links between these groups not only through shared ideas and mutual support, but through networks of communication. This communication received a crucial boost in speed and reach as the Internet became available to more and more movement actors, and the alterglobalisation movement achieved an unprecedented scale of connectivity, developing a 'networking logic' in the process that allowed for a much more inclusive and structured democracy (Juris 2008b) even though the Internet itself was not very useful as a tool for decision-making (Graeber forthcoming 2009). As Polletta (2002: 190–91) remarks:

> A 1960s activist would be surprised by the procedural paraphernalia that accompanies democratic decision making [in movements] today. There are formal roles in the process … and sophisticated hand signals … models for egalitarian forms and deliberative styles are simply available to activists today in a way that they were not for 1960s activists.

But, of course, these models and structures are not 'simply available'; today's decision-making practices and the increased connectivity of global networks have been actively built by activists and are being continuously and intentionally developed.

Overcoming Identity Politics

This increased networking was near impossible, however, as long as conflicts between movement actors from different groups and movements continued to be divisive. The identity politics that characterised many of the 'new social movements' in the 1970s and 1980s represented a politicisation of the personal, as embodied in the feminist slogan: 'The personal is political'. At the level of lived movement experience, this politicisation enacted a conflation between individual behaviour and structural discrimination to the extent that personal dynamics became political problems. Evans (1980) offers a lengthy description of this dynamic at work in SNCC, where sexual relationships between black men and white women created politically charged conflicts in which these relationships functioned as symbols of racial and patriarchal oppression within the movement. This politicisation of the personal was necessary to improve the power relations within movement structures and was essential to the development of both prefigurative politics and inclusive democratic practices. In the 1980s, however, the interpretation of personal dynamics in political terms made meetings between diverse movements nearly impossible.

The change that was required for the alterglobalisation movement to emerge was the depoliticisation of the personal, but without depoliticising the problem of power inequalities and categorical discrimination between movement actors. This delicate manoeuvre required a rejection of identity-based politics *as the main field of struggle* and the transformation of difference as division into difference as unity. Kruks (2001: 85) describes identity politics as follows:

> What makes identity politics a significant departure from earlier, pre-identarian forms of the politics of recognition is its demand for recognition on the basis of the very grounds on which recognition has previously been denied: it is *qua* women, *qua* blacks, *qua* lesbians that groups demand recognition. The demand is not for inclusion within the fold of 'universal humankind' on the basis of shared human attributes; nor is it for respect 'in spite of' one's differences. Rather, what is demanded is respect for oneself *as* different ...[14]

The respect shown between movement actors for each person '*as* different' is a necessary prerequisite for the functioning of the alterglobalisation movement. While participatory democracy is the mother of 'horizontality', identity politics is responsible for the absolute centrality of 'diversity'. Without the fights waged around gender, race, ethnicity and sexuality over the past 30 years, the 'anti-oppression' principles of most alterglobalisation movement spaces would not exist. Today, meetings between many different groups and actors are possible because structural discriminations *have been* recognised and meeting structures are put into place to limit them, but it is no longer 'identity politics' because some shared identity is not the basis upon which alterglobalisation movement actors are demanding recognition. Rather than insisting that the movement should not focus on the WTO because it is not the quickest means of achieving women's liberation, the fight against the WTO is carried out *while* incorporating an awareness of the power hierarchies that exclude women, not only from the WTO, but also from the movement.

The rendering visible of oppression along identity lines was an essential step, but as 'identity politics' became the basis for political unity, a singular homogeneous unity, it led many movement actors into a trap where 'identities' became fixed and predetermined (Eschle 2001: 128). Movement actors who had multiple identities began to see the oppressive nature of identity politics itself (Crosby 1992: 131, Evans 1995, Mirza 1997: 8–9). The incongruity between identity and interests, opinions and ideas also challenged the stability of identity politics (Young 2000: 126). These 'group-based movements ... have sometimes exhibited ... essentializing tendencies' (Young 2000: 87) which have been thoroughly critiqued by movement actors themselves (Dyson 1994, Spelman 1988).[15] Over the years, movement actors realised that, although it was liberating to construct/discover and assert an identity, that same identity could be imposed upon them from the outside (Morin 1982, in van Boeschoten 2000: 29, cf. Barth 1969), turning the advantages of essentialism into a constraining discourse.

Movement actors like those at Wetlands saw the divisive effect of identity-based politics as damaging to the success of all single-issue social movements and spent most of the 1990s trying to overcome these rigid distinctions without undermining the politics that these distinctions represented.[16] While acknowledging the practical reality of these oppressions they challenged the 'supremely stubborn thesis that everyone is principally and irreducibly a member of some race or category' (Said 1991: 178). Today in the alterglobalisation movement, identity 'takes shape while trying out practices; [the] participants' identity is not pre-set but rather it is shaped by actions' (Levidow 2004).[17] Understanding the alterglobalisation movement no longer rests on the 'new social movement' analytical category of 'identity' and the exploration of how it is constructed (see Castells 1997, Touraine 1985), but rather on *process* – where process is a practice, a fluid action, an ongoing activity.[18]

Ethnography of a Global Social Movement

Following a Process

The difficulties we are confronted with when constructing a history of the alterglobalisation movement are dwarfed only by comparison with the challenges this movement poses to ethnographic methods. How can we do ethnography of a global network that is not clearly delineated in time or space and has no singular identity, adversary or goal? It was when I began to answer this question that I realised that if I wanted to research this movement I had to follow not the ideas or the goals (for these would have taken me in myriad different directions), but to follow the process. This process took me to three distinguishable spaces of collective movement activity which became six specific case studies: the ESF in 2003 and 2004, the WSF in 2004 and anti-G8 protests in 2003, 2004 and 2005. Due to the global nature of the alterglobalisation movement, this research was carried out in five different languages – English, French, Dutch, Hindi and German.[19] In the end two sites stood out as the most interesting, the ESF in London in 2004 and the anti-G8 protests in Scotland in 2005. There are many reasons these two sites became the main focus, but perhaps the most important influence was the long-term access I had to them, having lived in the UK for several years. Despite the centrality of the UK, due to my focus on the collective decision-making spaces of the alterglobalisation movement which exist not in the UK per se, but rather in a 'global' disembedded space, it was necessary to supplement the UK case studies with research from other sites to distinguish what was particular to the UK from what was characteristic of the movement more widely. One of the problems of researching these global, temporary sites is that there is little time to establish oneself and to soak up the level of detail necessary to give ethnography its meaning and its context, because these communities come together for only a few days a month (for meetings) and only a few months out of the year (in the months prior to the planned event). Consequently, I had different levels of engagement with the 'field' at various times throughout my research. At times I was completely immersed, working and living with activists 24 hours a day, and at other times 'fieldwork' consisted only of going to a weekend of meetings or reading emails. In the case of both the ESF and the anti-G8 mobilisations, the UK was not originally meant to be my main case study; I had already carried out research at the Paris ESF

2003 and the anti-G8 protests in Switzerland and the US prior to commencing my research in the UK. I was, therefore, embedded not only in the UK context but also the 'global' context of the ESF and the anti-G8 mobilisations before beginning my research in my two main case studies.

Throughout my research I took on many different participatory roles. In the case of the ESF and the WSF I worked in the offices of the social forum on a daily basis, working and living with other volunteers. This 'office work' included frequent after-office chats at home or in the pub, and going out for dinner or going on short excursions together. In the course of the stressful yet invigorating process of putting together a social forum for tens of thousands or hundreds of thousands of people, strong bonds were built and some of the people I met are now among my dearest friends.

In the anti-summit mobilisations, my role changed from year to year. In Switzerland, I spent most of my time with my affinity group planning actions, but was first involved in the *village autogéré* in Geneva. In the US I worked as a street medic, and in Scotland I took on many different roles, including action medic, trainer, meeting facilitator, warehouse cleaner, and affinity group member.[20] In the preparatory process for both the ESF and the anti-G8 mobilisations I was active in local groups in the UK and Belgium, including the UK mobilisation to the Paris ESF in 2003 and Dissent! België. The most important site for this research, however, was meetings. In the case of the ESF, these meetings continuously moved from one locality to another, but took on the same shape, with mostly the same people irrespective of locality. For the ESF, I travelled to meetings in Germany, France, Italy, Belgium and the UK. All the meetings I attended as part of my research of the WSF, on the other hand, were in Mumbai. For the anti-G8 mobilisations, I travelled to meetings in several UK cities, Switzerland, the US, Germany, Belgium and the Netherlands.

Engaged Anthropology

By now it should be clear that this ethnography is in the tradition of 'engaged anthropology' (Gledhill 2000, Scheper-Hughes 1995,

Walter 1995) or 'activist anthropology' (Hale 2006, Lyon-Callo and Hyatt 2003, Speed 2006). What I offer here is an anthropology written at least partially from the 'inside' and this position allows me to practise what Wood (1998) has called 'participant comprehension' (in Mosse 2002: 6). My role has continuously been a double role, where I have not only been interpreting the cultural practices of the alterglobalisation movement, but have simultaneously been actively involved in creating these practices (cf. Mosse 2002). Despite the open nature of the alterglobalisation movement, there remains a great deal of distrust for the 'police, media and anthropologists', who have been declared officially unwelcome. Despite being an anthropologist, I am able to gain access to these movement spaces, quite simply because I am already a part of these movement spaces – because I am also an 'activist'. Being an activist is about taking action, not only on the streets, but also in meetings, in offices, at home, in the pub – everywhere. When Nancy Scheper-Hughes (1995: 410–11) explained to her research subjects that she could not participate in their political work because she 'could not be an anthropologist and a *companheira* at the same time', the response she received was unequivocal:

> They gave me an ultimatum: the next time I came back to the Alto do Curuzeiro it would be on their terms, that is, as a *companheira*, 'accompanying' them as I had before in the struggle and not just sitting idly by taking field notes.

This same ultimatum exists silently in the alterglobalisation movement. As Juris (2008b: 6) writes of the alterglobalisation movement actors: 'what impressed me most about so many of those I came to know and respect during my time in the field was their fierce dedication to egalitarian, collaborative process, which demanded of me a politically engaged mode of ethnographic research'. Gaining access to many of the spaces of the alterglobalisation movement depended on having this engagement. Anyone can take part in meetings and activities of the alterglobalisation movement, but activism is not a spectator sport, and to gain access to spaces of movement activity that are otherwise kept private, the anthropologist has to tip the balance between participant-observer in favour of participating.

Since access to many movement spaces is negotiated through *doing*, the more I did, the more connected I became, and the more opportunities arose to do more and become more connected. My ability to take on many different tasks was due to certain skills I had. In the ESF the skills that gained me access to movement spaces and actors who would otherwise have ignored me, were my language skills. While at first I had to argue my way into small back-room meetings of the key players in the ESF process, I ended up being quite a welcome sight there because they often needed an interpreter. In the ESF offices too, my language skills were very useful. In the anti-summit mobilisations other skills were more important, and here my position as activist was essential for gaining access. My familiarity with public order situations, my knowledge of consensus decision-making and my ability to facilitate meetings were skills that communicated who I was in a way that words could not. They were skills that only activists have, that only experience gains.

As a result of these skills, I also learned that different kinds of doing gain different kinds of access. When I spent two weeks cleaning toilets and scrubbing pigeon droppings off an old warehouse floor in Glasgow, I got a chance to spend a lot of time with practically oriented activists whom I had not met at national meetings before. Through this type of work I got to know those who took on important roles in the practical setting-up of the various housing sites/alternative living spaces and could observe this process taking place. When I went to open meetings and participated like everyone else, I gained access to what was said during the meeting and perhaps in the pub afterwards, but when I facilitated the meetings myself, I gained insight into how the agenda was constructed, how movement actors perceived the ideal meeting and what kinds of compromises were made in the negotiation between real and ideal. I also realised quickly that by taking on the more visible tasks, like facilitating meetings or giving trainings, I became more recognised and connected within the wider movement network. These tasks also brought me into contact with many of the most highly connected people, and, due to the way networks function, where the more connected you are the more connected you get, I often found myself among the 'hyperconnected'.

My role as someone engaged in a process and not just observing it was the key to gaining access to most of the ideas and practices described in the chapters to come. However, this position also had some limitations. When I arrived in London to research the London ESF, it quickly became clear that my politics was at once the mechanism through which I gained access to many otherwise disguised movement spaces and the reason for which I was denied access to other movement spaces. Once I was labeled a 'horizontal' by the UK ESF 'bid group' (see Chapter 2), my chances of being hired as office staff for the London ESF became non-existent and those within the Socialist Workers Party who had, up to then, included me in several 'insider' discussions, seemed to decide that I was not to be trusted. As my own politics became more exposed (by the company I was keeping and the ideas I expressed in meetings), I watched myself shift from the category of 'insider' to 'outsider' for some of the members of the UK Coordinating Committee (UKCC).[21] Kuper (1995: 423) argues that 'there are many situations in which political activism will inevitably close off various avenues of information and cloud judgement' and there is no question that this is the case. Without engaging I would have had much less access to movement actors, but by engaging, 'I had to accept that there were places where I was not welcome ... that were irrevocably closed to me and consequently to anthropology' (Scheper-Hughes 1995: 411).[22] Nevertheless, I hope I managed to limit these drawbacks to the engaged approach by being aware of these limitations, and by observing which avenues became closed to me and why.

Gaining adequate access to write an ethnography of the alter-globalisation movement was in my case much less a question about gaining access to the physical spheres of movement activity, but rather about positioning myself within those spheres. For me, gaining access to the subject of my research in a way that made ethnography possible almost required me to take a step *out* of the field. I often had to take a step away from the field and the habitual way I interacted with it, re-adjust my mind, and then step forward again on new terms. This continuous effort to remain 'objective', to remain in some way at a distance despite my engagement, was necessary to render visible some of the aspects of movement culture that I would otherwise have taken for granted as an insider. Too many of the assumptions movement actors made were also my assumptions and at times it became hard to see them. I had to reconceptualise the field not as a place, but as an approach. Gupta and Ferguson (1997a: 35) ask if 'perhaps we should say that, in an interconnected world, we are never really "out of the field." Yet, if this is true, what does change when anthropologists go from (usually) First World universities to various destinations around the world?' In my case, turning the interconnectedness I already had into a 'field' was enacted by a shift in perspective.

The Global Field

My research not only breaks with the 'traditional' anthropological mould due to my position as an insider, but also because the research sites I chose to examine are more global than local. Anthropologists have often acknowledged the interconnectedness of cultures and the impossibility of understanding culture in isolation from external influences, especially since the 1980s, but the approach taken to the construction of the research subject and the research field has been slow to change accordingly. Appadurai (1991: 191–92) argues that 'groups are no longer tightly territorialised, spatially bounded, historically unselfconscious, or culturally homogenous' and concludes that there is, 'an urgent need to focus on the cultural dynamic of what is now called *deterritorialization*' (cf. Escobar 2001). He argues that, 'the task of ethnography now becomes the unravelling of a conundrum: what is the nature of locality as lived experience, in a globalized, deterritorialized world?' (Appadurai 1991: 196). Robertson (1995: 34) has argued:

it makes no good sense to define the global as if it excludes the local. In somewhat technical terms, defining the global in such a way suggests that the global lies beyond all localities, as having system properties over and beyond the attributes of units within a global system.

The alterglobalisation movement exists, of course, primarily in many localities, but by choosing to research the decision-making practices of the global networks, my research became biased towards global spaces of movement activity. My research was a 'multi-sited ethnography' (Marcus 1995), but the alterglobalisation movement is not only multi-sited, it is also deterritorialised, or as I prefer, disembedded, removed in certain moments from all locality. Hannerz (2003: 21) argues that:

the field is not only *multi-local*, it is also *translocal*, in the sense that it is necessary to clarify the nature of relations *between* localities. Some people might claim that while the analytical entity is translocal, the fieldwork is multi-local, quite simply because one is always somewhere.

The idea that one is always somewhere seems self-evident, but as I read this sentence I was sitting in Paris (my 'field'), with my laptop beside me displaying an email about the London ESF that came from one of the coordinators of the Indian Intercontinental Youth Camp, on the Rede de Resistencia global network e-list. Although I intuitively knew that I must be *somewhere*, I wondered for a moment where that was exactly. The greater diversity of source materials being used in ethnography today (see Eriksen 2003: 14), challenges even this apparent truism that we are always somewhere, because we may be in one locality, drawing on sources produced in a second locality about a third locality. Throughout my research, I supplemented every conversation I had with information from virtual conversations taking place on email, as well as movement actors' projections of their networks through websites and other written sources. The mix between geographical subject, source, route and destination of these emails often diminished the importance of the local.

This increased connectivity and deterritorialisation has challenged the notion of the field in anthropology. Gupta and

Ferguson (1997a: 38), citing Gordon (1991), offer a history of the construction of the anthropological notion of the field and argue that what constitutes 'the field' in anthropology is changing considerably due to the increasing influence of the global on the local:

> Practicing decolonized anthropology in a deterritorialized world means as a first step doing away with the distancing and exoticization of the conventional anthropological 'field,' and foregrounding the ways in which we anthropologists are historically and socially (not just biographically) linked with the areas we study.

The reconceptualisation of the field as a result of global changes, also opens the door to a more engaged anthropology that 'abandons the outmoded conception of its objects of study as localised and separate from the researcher' (Mosse 2002: 7).

The field in my research was global not only because I chose to research a global social movement, but also because the particular subject of collective decision-making and the particular sites (ESF, WSF and anti-G8 mobilisations) continuously move from one locality to another with very little change to the basic organisation of the practices that are examined in this book. My interest in finding similarities across movement spaces, the driving question of what holds this movement together, further biased my research towards the global over the local because it is often in the global spaces that this commonality can best be seen. Consequently, it must be said that at the centre of my research are the privileged movement actors, those who can afford the time, money and energy to go to these international meetings and enter the global space. Scheper-Hughes (1995: 417) equates the 'global' with an 'imagined postmodern, borderless world (Appadurai 1991)' in which:

> The flight from the local in hot pursuit of a transnational, borderless anthropology implies a parallel flight from local engagements, local commitments, and local accountability. Once the circuits of power are seen as capillary, diffuse, global and difficult to trace to their sources, the idea of resistance becomes meaningless ... The idea of an anthropology

without borders, although it has a progressive ring to it, ignores the reality of the very real borders that confront and oppress 'our' anthropological subjects and encroach on our liberty as well.

Although I hope to have avoided 'whimsical postmodernism' (Scheper-Hughes 1995: 417) in my analysis, the picture painted in the coming pages does obscure the fact that most of the alter-globalisation movement actors cannot be present in the movement spaces I am describing because of the 'reality of the very real borders that confront and oppress'. This fact, however, in no way fosters a 'flight from local engagements' and does not diminish the potential for a more 'global' but nevertheless engaged anthropology.

Democracy in Social Movements

An ethnography of democracy within the alterglobalisation movement is an ethnography of an evolving political process and it consequently requires that we understand the alterglobalisation movement not as resting on a common identifiable element that remains fixed over time, but as a confluence of diverse elements that are in perpetual motion. Political anthropology has often stressed this processual dimension of politics, exploring non-state-based political practices, understanding political systems as 'belonging to all social formations' and not just to clearly defined organisations and institutions (Balandier 2004 [1967]: viii). In this sense anthropology is an ideal lens for understanding democracy within the alterglobalisation movement because it emphasises, 'a "becoming" rather than a "being"' (Swartz et al. 2002 [1966]: 102) and looks at political process as constructed and contested. The analysis of these political processes by the Manchester School made conflict a central analytical category because these anthro-pologists 'worked in plural societies, characterised by ethnic diversity, sharp economic inequalities between ethnic groups, religious differences, political and legal heterogeneity' (Swartz et al. 2002 [1966]: 104, cf. Gluckman 1954, 1965, Llewellyn and Hoebel 1941). Due to the diverse nature of the alterglobalisation movement, we need a similar analysis that allows for a social system to be understood not as a coherently integrated whole, but as multi-dimensional, with constituent parts that can be highly integrated, loosely integrated or largely independent from each other (cf. Epstein 1958, Furnivall 1948, Mitchell 1960, Wilson 1968 [1942]), or as Appadurai (1996) more recently formulated it, as 'fractal' and 'overlapping'.

Despite this seemingly perfect fit, very few anthropologists have taken up 'democracy' as a research subject. Decision-making systems have long been of central interest to anthropologists, but these descriptions have not always used the term 'democracy', even though comparisons between democracy and tribal political systems were common, especially before the export of 'western' liberal democracy into the fields of anthropology.[23] Paley (2002: 471) has classified anthropological approaches to democracy into five 'lenses anthropologists have used for viewing democracy: cultures and meanings, circulating discourses, qualities of citizenship, civil society and governmentality, and alternative democracies'. What most of these approaches share in common is the analysis of democracy in terms of constructed and contested meaning. Anthropologists examining the construction of 'citizenship' have pointed to the ways it can be exclusively constructed along lines of gender (Gutmann 2002), ethnicity (Hayden 1992, Verdery 1998) or discourses of multiculturalism that define only certain cultural rights as acceptable (Hale 2002, Povinelli 2002, Warren 1998) and only certain citizens as worthy of the protections and benefits of the state (Holston and Caldeira 1998). Anthropologists have also analysed the way the term 'democracy' has been used as a means to 'involve citizens in service provision' (Paley 2002: 483), particularly in discourses of 'participation' and 'development', in which 'the people' are expected to take on the responsibility for providing services which the state no longer provides (Paley 2001, Rose 1996). Finally, perhaps the most interesting theme that emerges is the role of democracy in the legitimation of authoritarian practices. Aretxaga (1999: 48), in her study of post-Franco Spain, argues that democracy has become a 'fetish', which 'became under the socialist government the legitimizing discourse for a wide variety of authoritarian state practices'. Paley (2002: 476) cites Coronil (1997) to demonstrate the way military dictatorship in Venezuela legitimates its abuse of power by 'labelling' itself a democracy, and quotes Warren (2002) and Poole and Rénique (1992), who have shown that 'militaries exercise their power through procedural democracy itself, meaning that even after official regime transitions, the armed forces – and correspondingly, violence and authoritarianism – continue to be embedded in the subsequent democracy' (Paley 2002: 476, see also Gledhill 2000: 110–19, Schirmer 1998). In most of this literature, the violence is attributed to the legacy of the preceding authoritarian regime and not considered to be directly linked to democracy as such. However, Tambiah (1996) argues that in South Asia the competitive procedures of democracy themselves result in violence and Graeber (2008) has argued that as long as democracy is defined as a system of majority rule it necessarily requires an apparatus of coercive force to ensure that those in the minority will succumb to the majority's will. This relationship between democracy and violence is part of what leads many movement actors to question the desirability of democracy and to insist that if democracy is to survive in the twenty-first century, it must do so in a radically different form.

Thus far most of the ethnographies described have been concerned primarily with democratic systems rather than democratic values, which biases the focus towards institutions of democracy and how democracy is experienced by 'the people' when it is exercised by institutions, allocating the enactment of democracy to the state. It is only in Paley's final lens of 'alternative democracies' that we see the forms democratic values can take outside of these state-based institutions. It is in this last category of alternative democracies, that 'the meanings attributed to democracy in various contexts and struggles do not necessarily match hegemonic definitions in actually existing systems or even normative liberal democracy ideals' (Paley 2002: 485). And it is here that the anthropology of democracy meets the anthropology of social movements, and is consequently the category to which an ethnography of the alterglobalisation movement would belong.

While anthropology is a useful tool for analysing both democracy and social movements, it is perhaps even more useful when analysing democracy within social movements precisely for its focus on the construction and contestation of 'meaning'. But anthropology goes beyond mere examination of 'meaning' and provides 'a coherent attempt to overcome the material/symbolic divide' (Wade 1999: 450), where social movements are viewed 'equally and inseparably as struggles over meaning as well as material conditions' (Escobar 1992: 69, see also Comaroff and Comaroff 1991, 1992, Mintz 1985). This approach represents an attempt to 'construct a synthesis of the two approaches that treats social movements as both expressive and instrumental' (Foweraker 1995: 13) to bridge the perceived gap between 'postmodern theoretical innovation and materialist reassertion' (Hale 1997: 570). Many anthropologists have warned against a 'postmodern' approach that emphasises 'struggles over meanings, symbols, collective identities, and rights to 'specificity and difference' (Edelman 2002 [1999]: 417), stressing instead the need to historically contextualise these meanings in material processes. Edelman (2002 [1999]: 417) argues that 'NSMs' [New Social Movements] version of identity politics and postmodern scholarship ... resonate with some of the more dehumanizing aspects of contemporary neoliberal economics' and that 'NSMs have "helped reproduce the fragmentation of the popular classes sought by the state and the market" (Vilas 1993: 42)'.

The ethnography I offer here is very much an ethnography about contested 'meaning', where movement actors challenge prevailing interpretations of 'democracy' and 'strategically and selectively appropriate and transform transnationally circulating discourses, sometimes filling foreign words with their own meaning' (Paley 2002: 485, cf. Nash 2001). This practice of appropriation is often written about in literature on development projects. Edelman (2002 [1999]: 412) describes how in Costa Rica the word 'development', 'could be appropriated and infused with new meaning' as part of a strategy of 'resistance'. This is part of a wider trend in the anthropology of development to argue that, 'locating power does not show that it is determinant or that a particular discourse is not appropriable for other purposes' (Cooper and Packard 1997: 3) and is influenced by the post-Foucault assumption that power and resistance are interconnected processes (Foucault 1983). The concept of 'resistance' in anthropological literature has itself been subjected to many different meanings and appropriations, the nuances of which cannot be explored here, but a frequent use of the term focuses on resistance in 'everyday life' (de Certeau 1984, Scott 1985, 1998), which includes not only social movements, but also the smaller-scale daily measures taken by 'those-to-be-developed' (Hobart 1993) to subvert, circumnavigate and appropriate development projects (see Crewe and Harrison 1998, Li 1999, Marglin and Marglin 1990, Moore 2000).[24] This level of 'daily life' is central in anthropological analysis of social movements 'because it is at this level ... that many of today's forms of protest emerge and exert their influence' (Escobar and Alvarez 1992a: 4). Establishing the site of resistance in 'daily life' allows anthropologists to put their unique skills to use by focusing on locality, which is presumably where 'daily life' takes place. And indeed, many studies of social movements examine the way local struggles react to the fragmentation and/or homogenisation of 'globalization' by reinforcing 'their own culture, ideas and traditions' (Escobar and Alvarez 1992a: 10), emphasising ties to imagined cultures or communities (in the past, present and future) and asserting particular identities or differences through notions of 'autonomy' (see Calderón et al. 1992, Doane 2005, Findji 1992, Nash 2005b, Pratt 2003, Sylvain 2005).

But the alterglobalisation movement has resisted the temptation to create a single imagined community or to assert divisive identities; they are trying to overcome this fragmentation without losing the right to 'specificity and difference'. The movement is 'global' and dispersed, diverse but not fragmented. I therefore offer a slightly different approach based not on 'local' research of 'daily life', but 'global' research of temporary moments and spaces that give form to daily, continuous processes. These are processes that link, that connect, that bind us together through difference. And, as we shall see, one of the ways that movement actors keep this right to difference open to them is by appropriating the term 'democracy' and then infusing it with new meanings, continuously bringing it into question. As Polletta (2002: 230) has argued:

Democracy in social movements does not produce dutiful citizens. It produces people who question the conventional categories and responsibilities of citizenship – and who question the boundaries of the political, the limits of equality, and the line between the people and their representatives.

It is especially this line between people and their representatives that alterglobalisation movement actors are bringing into question by building global networks that make decisions democratically without recourse to fixed representative structures thereby rendering representation redundant (see Graeber forthcoming 2009, Juris 2008b). As Graeber (forthcoming 2009) argues, 'what goes on in meetings, the structures of decision-making is critical to the [alterglobalisation] movement. Perhaps more than anything else, this is a movement about creating new forms of democracy' and he demonstrates how developing democratic structures goes hand in hand with challenging force and violence as powers of control by the state (Graeber forthcoming 2009). Juris (2008a: 360) describes how alterglobalisation movement actors have developed a 'cultural politics of networking' that shapes 'the way specific networks are produced, how they develop, and how they relate to one another within broader social movement fields', arguing that:

emerging networking logics [are] changing how grassroots movements organize, and [are] inspiring new utopian imaginaries involving directly democratic models of social, economic and political organization coordinated at local, regional and global scales. (2008b: 3)

These 'new forms of democracy' and 'directly democratic models of … political organization' are the focus of this book. In the pages to come I use my ethnography of these democratic processes to critically examine political philosophy on democracy in order to draw out the theoretical and practical implications of this emerging form of alternative global democracy.

Network Democracy

Democracy is everywhere a contested notion, and nowhere more so than in the fluid, networked world of the alterglobalisation movement, where even a basic definition of democracy can only be a work in progress. At the risk of hindering this perpetual evolution of democratic praxis, this book attempts to identify the democratic values that underlie the decision-making practices of the alterglobalisation movement actors. Underlying this project is a perceived need to address two lines of inquiry: an exploration into the democratic praxis of the alterglobalisation movement ought first to partially answer the accusatory question, 'What is the alterglobalisation movement for?', and, second, provide an insight into the prefigurative method through which the alterglobalisation movement *presents*, brings into the present moment, the 'other world(s)' for which it struggles.

In Chapter 1 I start by mapping out the different types of movement spaces, structures and actors I met, focusing on the roles people play and the relationships they build with each other, specifically on the conflict between the 'verticals' and the 'horizontals' – between those who advocate purely horizontal networks and those who prefer more hierarchical modes of organising. These two complex and unstable categories of movement actors were often in conflict over the concept of *process* and what its role ought to be in movement decision-making. In Chapter 2 I take this conflict about process as the ethnographic lens through which to answer the question 'What is prefiguration?' I address the question of *how* this movement organises, as well as the implications of prefiguration as a political practice for under-standings of movement strategy and goals. The link between two seemingly separate political positions – the importance of process and the fact that the alterglobalisation movement intentionally has no *single* 'goal' – is addressed here to argue that prefiguration is in fact a strategic movement practice.

Chapter 3 shifts from the question 'What is prefiguration?' to address the question 'Prefiguration of what?' and once again takes conflict as the starting point for a discussion of two central values being prefigured by the alterglobalisation movement –

horizontality and diversity – as well as the relationship between these two concepts and movement approaches to power. I argue that for movement actors conflict is not something to be avoided, but something to be desired for its constructive potential. Movement actors believe that conflict is necessary if diversity is to be possible, but conflict has to be transformed from adversarial to constructive. This transformation is a continuous process, reinforced by practices of horizontality. Horizontality requires the active decentralisation of various forms of power so that there may be many loci of power. It reflects a desire for diversity and a rejection of discourses of unity. I demonstrate that although diversity leads to conflict, *adversarial* conflict is not caused by this flow of diversity. Adversarial conflict arises when these flows are blocked. Movement actors, therefore, often approach conflict as something that can be productive if it is given space for expression.

In Chapter 4 I bring my ethnography into dialogue with political theory to describe how the movement's decision-making practices challenge and radically upset many of the assumptions we hold about what democracy is and what it ought to be. I argue that movement actors' practices expose very different interpretations of central democratic values, such as liberty, equality, participation and representation. Movement actors assume equality to be something that must be continually created and constructed and not a natural state of affairs that needs merely to be acknowledged or declared by some authority. This has several consequences for the way democracy is practised, the most important of which is the rejection of voting as a decision-making method. Because movement actors assume that an equality of *inputs* is impossible (due to inevitable power inequalities) the *outcomes* of decision-making are of central importance. Voting, therefore, cannot lead to equality because it always results in unequal outcomes – outcomes which favour one group over another. I argue that the significance of diversity as a value is not that it understands 'the people' to be diverse and complex, although it does, but that it allows this diversity in 'the people' to be translated into a diversity of *outcomes*. This shift in interpretation of democratic values brings with it a need for different democratic structures based on networks instead of nation-states. The role these network structures play in facilitating the prefiguration of this democratic process as a strategy for social change is addressed in Chapter 5, where I use biological complexity theory in combination with cross-disciplinary work on networks and an anthropologically informed notion of agency to explore the activist ideal of *connectivity* as a form of communication based on reciprocal contamination and mutual feedback rather than one-way speaker–listener (command–obey) communication.

The alterglobalisation movement confronts us with a radical democratic alternative based on a decentralised network structure and principles of horizontality and diversity, and it intends to turn this alternative into reality through prefiguration and connectivity. The decision-making praxis of the alterglobalisation movement points to the urgent need to radically rethink (and re-practise) democracy in the context of the highly diverse, globalised world we find ourselves in today. Some of the fundamental democratic questions that arise are: what happens when democracy is practised through a network structure instead of the nation-state? What happens to 'the people' when the constituency is a network and not a clearly delineated geographical space? Or, in other words, can we have democracy without universal suffrage? What happens when democracy is practised without the assumption of 'free and equal' individuals? What happens when the goal of democracy is no longer agreement? I offer potential answers to these and other questions by describing ethnographically a form of democratic decision-making already being practised on a global scale. I argue that implicit in consensus decision-making and horizontality is the assumption that if there is a clear and highly structured procedure in place for *how* to decide, then there need not be an agreement on *who* decides. Movement actors therefore displace one of the central questions of democratic theory, the classic question of 'Who rules?' and develop instead a set of principles for *how* to rule that challenges both the individualism and homogeneity of liberal representative democracy. In so doing, movement actors open up the possibility for a much more diverse democracy in which conflicting identities and opinions flourish.

1

HORIZONTAL ARMIES AND VERTICAL NETWORKS

We, the international working group on resistance against the next G8, are just a group of people sitting in a field, wanting to change the world. (International Working Group on Resistance Against the G8 2007)

Anti-summit Mobilisations

An Army Descends

I am stood with an umbrella, holding it above the head of an activist who is 'locked on' outside the Faslane Nuclear Submarine Base. We have been here for over five hours in the burning sun, and everyone is starting to wonder why. I am the one holding the umbrella because the person locked on has both of his arms locked inside two metal tubes through which he is attached to five other people. Together they form a circle, lying on the ground, chained to each other in front of the Faslane Nuclear Submarine Base. It is day one of a week of protests organised against the 2005 G8 summit in Scotland.

The blockades have been scheduled to last until 5 p.m., but there is still an hour to go and many people have already gone home. We would really like to go home too and are thinking of giving up, but just before the pressure of the day takes its toll, we are swept away to an alternative universe. Suddenly, as if out of thin air, an army appears. Yes, an army, but this is not your average army. This army has red noses and is wearing mismatched furry pink and green fatigues. They stand in formation in front of the blockade announcing that they have come as part of operation 'HA, HA, HAA' (Helping Authorities House Arrest

Half-witted Authoritarian Androids) as they laugh in unison. General Mayhem (or was it Kolonel Klepto?) rings his whistle and the troops stand tall, saluting him with their thumbs to their nose and wiggling their fingers. Then, they break formation and start to run everywhere chaotically. These clown-soldiers each take an umbrella and hold it above the activists lying on the ground, telling jokes and making everyone laugh. Other clowns are performing a military stand-up comedy act as the deep sound of drums swells in the distance. Slowly, the rhythm of the 'samba band' draws nearer. When they finally arrive at the gate, the pink-and-silver clad dancers swirl through the clown army, and the pink, camouflaged clowns dance with the samba band to the Brazilian beats in an unchoreographed but synchronised routine. The entire space is transformed from a hot, empty, exhausted moment to the centre of an absurdly surreal world of laughter and music.

In this chapter I present a small portion of some of the actors I met during my fieldwork, focusing on the relationships they create. The main aim of this chapter is to map out the dynamics between these diverse groups of people and to offer a sense of how the various groups relate to one another and to the democratic praxis outlined in this book. To this end, I describe the people I worked with primarily in terms of the roles they fulfilled and how these activities placed them in relation to one another. I begin with the Clown Army as a semiotic tool for introducing some of the ideas underlying the autonomous strands of the alterglobalisation movement. I then briefly introduce the Dissent! network and the movement structure of 'affinity groups'. Using examples from G8 mobilisations in 2003, 2004 and 2005, I outline the relationships between the various networks in anti-G8 mobilisations, highlighting both commonalities to all settings and peculiarities to each setting. I argue that in social fora organising processes we find divisions and tensions within a singular process, while in anti-summit mobilisations, we see the coming together of diverse networks in parallel processes. Below I describe the political backgrounds of movement actors that will underlie the descriptions of conflict in the chapters to come, especially, the conflict between the 'verticals' and the 'horizontals'. Finally, although not directly relevant to a discussion of the collective spaces of global networks which are the subject of this book, I briefly introduce and locate the Narmada Bachao Andolan (NBA) within the framework of the alterglobalisation movement to highlight the relationship between the alterglobalisation movement itself and the many movements that constitute it.

The Clown Army

I start with the Clown Army, not because they are the most important or the largest section of the alterglobalisation movement, but because they are hilarious. Conveniently, they also embody many of the most important values of the alterglobalisation movement. In the UK the Clown Army's official name is the Clandestine Insurgent Rebel Clown Army (CIRCA). The significance of this name, in their own words, is as follows:

> We are **clandestine** because we refuse the spectacle of celebrity and we are everyone ...
>
> We are **insurgent** because we have risen up from nowhere and are everywhere ...
>
> We are **rebels** because we love life and happiness more than 'revolution'. Because no revolution is ever complete and rebellion continues forever. Because we will dismantle the ghost-machine of abstraction with means that are indistinguishable from ends. Because we don't want to change 'the' world, but 'our' world. Because we will always desert and disobey those who abuse and accumulate power. Because rebels transform everything – the way they live, create, love, eat, laugh, play, learn, trade, listen, think and most of all the way they rebel.
>
> We are **clowns** because what else can one be in such a stupid world ... Because buffoons always succeed in failing, always say yes, always hope and always feel things deeply ...
>
> We are an **army** because we live on a planet in permanent war – a war of money against life, of profit against dignity, of progress against the future ...

> We are **circa** because we are approximate and ambivalent, neither here nor there, but in the most powerful of all places, the place in-between order and chaos. (Clown Army n.d.)

The Clown Army's sentiment is echoed in many other sections of the movement. In this abbreviated version of their *raison d'être*, we see some of the major ideas underlying the autonomous sections of the anti-summit mobilisations: the refusal of fame, leadership and uniformity; the idea that they come from nowhere and are now everywhere as symbolic for the unpredictability and open, indeterminate nature of the struggle; the replacement of 'revolution' with prefigurative rebellion in which the accumulation of power is undermined through refusal to acknowledge it; the element of mockery as a way to undermine authority; and the idea that despite valuing unpredictability and chaos, some form of order or organisation is necessary. In all of these aspects they are very much in tune with other autonomous movements.

Dissent!

During the 2005 anti-G8 mobilisations, the Clown Army worked in loose connection with the Dissent! network. The Dissent! network was started in 2003 by movement actors involved in radical environmental and anti-roads actions, Reclaim the Streets, PGA, the anti-war movement and 'the global anti-capitalist movement which has emerged around meetings of those that rule over us':

> The Network has no central office, no spokespeople, no membership list and no paid staff. It's a mechanism for communication and co-ordination between local groups and working groups involved in building resistance to the G8, and capitalism in general. It hopes to exist long after the world leaders have returned home in the early summer of 2005. (Dissent! 2004a)

There is intentionally no clear statement on the Dissent! website as to what exactly Dissent! is or believes. This elusiveness has a functional motivation – to keep the network as open, diverse and inclusive as possible. This vagueness is also a political statement. Dissent! follows in the footsteps of many movement networks, and even the 'alterglobalisation' movement as a whole, by refusing to be defined, refusing to succumb to one clear definition. Despite this lack of unitary definition, the Dissent! network still acts in unison; where there is no definitional unity there is still operational congruency. During the 2004 G8 protests, Dissent! released a statement of solidarity with the US protest groups, in which they defined themselves as 'a UK-wide anti-capitalist network that operates by the People's Global Action hallmarks' (Dissent! 2004b; see also PGA n.d.).

While there is no single definition of what Dissent! is, everyone involved has an opinion on the matter. One of my personal favourites is 'dissent is nothing and it was always nothing, it is made by what anticapitalists do within and everywhere'. The word 'nothing' is not meant to be derisive; this was a positive statement almost advocating that Dissent! *ought* to be 'nothing' in a conversation about avoiding a unitary purpose for the network. Allowing dissent to be 'nothing' (*read* nothing-in-particular) is in this case akin to allowing it to be many different things.

Affinity Groups and Action Groups

The autonomous sections of the alterglobalisation movement often organise themselves into 'affinity groups'. An affinity group is a small group of people (six to twelve people roughly) who build strong relationships of trust and friendship with each other and take action together. Normally, an affinity group will work together for many years on several different actions. In the alterglobalisation movement the close 'affinity' which was once a defining characteristic has diminished in favour of privileging action. Although there are still some who are part of long-term affinity groups that intentionally build friendship and community among their members, today most affinity groups are ad hoc and fleeting, being formed only a few days before a major blockade. Activists are aware of this difference and often call these last-minute affinity groups not 'affinity groups' but 'action groups'.

This shift is partially due to the fact that movement actors often travel long distances and are accustomed to different political practices, and not all of them have the habit of working in affinity groups. Even for those who do have an affinity group at home, action groups are often a practical necessity because many people who come to these mobilisations take one to four weeks off from work or school to participate, and it is rare that an entire group of six to twelve people can do this together. The large scale of these mobilisations, and temporary, short time-frame, also leads to the diminishing importance of personal trust and friendship and an increase in the importance of having common action goals and wanting to employ the same action tactics. As Polletta (2002: 192) points out in the case of DAN, there is also a political aim behind this shift; affinity groups for direct actions are used as 'an opportunity to "go outside [one's comfort zone]" by joining people with different backgrounds' and not people one already knows and trusts.[1]

Switzerland: Transient Affinity

This was certainly true of my affinity group during the 2003 G8 protests, which was a random selection of people, most of whom I had never met before. The G8 was meeting in Evian, France and protests were being organised in three different locations – Annemasse (France), Geneva and Lausanne (Switzerland). When I first arrived, I went to Geneva where I met with those setting up the autonomous village (*village autogéré*). I pitched my tent in the village and started to help welcome new arrivals at the information stand in the *parc des bastions*. In the *village autogéré* I met a Scottish woman with whom I later travelled to Lausanne. In Lausanne we randomly ran into an old friend of mine from the US and together with two of his friends we formed an affinity group. We intended to blockade the port in Lausanne and we quickly found others, mostly anglophones, who were interested in joining us. There were ten of us all together, but only one that I had known for more than two weeks. It was an affinity group of travellers. Two out of the ten were from Lausanne and the others were from the US or the UK. After the G8 protests, many of them travelled to Thessaloniki to protest the EU summit in Greece. The path that led them to Lausanne was often random. One man in the group never intended to come to the G8 protests, but he had been travelling across Europe, staying in squats along the way, and ended up at a gathering on squatting and autonomous lifestyles where he ran into a friend who convinced him to come to Lausanne. Two of the women were taking the summer off and travelling from one protest to another. One of the women, a 32-year-old single mother, had her twelve-year-old son with her. They were all either students or intentionally unemployed, living off of money they had saved and surviving by not spending very much, using tactics like hitch-hiking and 'skipping' food.[2]

The US: Just Not a Sexy Place

For the G8 protests in 2004, I did not have an affinity group. It was difficult to get information ahead of time about the actions and logistics being planned. Perhaps I was just ill informed because I did not live in the US, but there were certainly fewer e-lists and websites than for the 2003 mobilisation, and nothing compared to 2005 and 2007. There were many reasons for the small size of the mobilisation in the US, but the main reasons were the upcoming Democratic National Convention (DNC) and the Republican National Convention (RNC) against which massive demonstrations were being planned. The location of the G8 summit was no help either. The summit itself was held on Sea Island, which was entirely off limits to protesters, dubbed a 'red zone'. The protesters had no choice but to go to Brunswick, Georgia on the mainland across from Sea Island. The small town of Brunswick was not a hotbed of political activity, although there were plenty of reasons why it should be. Racial segregation was still unofficially in place, separate toilets and all. There were so many toxic chemicals in the ground and water that it was impossible to open the tap without suffering from the smell. As one of the protesters put it: 'It's just not a sexy place.'[3]

When I first arrived in Georgia, I first went to the Indymedia centre in Atlanta. The Indymedia centre, located in an abandoned church, was also home to four adults and one teenager. One woman living there who was involved in organising the protests was a single mother who had at one time been homeless with her now teenage daughter. During the protests she was working full time for the Georgia Peace and Justice Coalition (GPJC) for a small stipend. She spent most of her time on the phone worrying that 'There are only eleven days to go and we still have no venues, no permits, no housing. One minute they tell us we can have a park or the college, the next we can't.' While in Atlanta I went to a street medic training and decided to 'run' as a medic during the protests. After the training, another medic and I travelled down to Brunswick together and stayed at the house of a local activist who had offered her property as a campsite. This woman was a 'veteran' of the 1970s women's movement and had supported campaigns for indigenous rights, but was no longer involved in political activism. She lived with her husband and three children in a medium-size house outside of Brunswick. She was very welcoming and friendly to all the protesters who came to stay, taking on a motherly role. She was less welcoming, however, to unwanted guests, including 'rednecks' (a 'classist term' not often used by activists, I was told) and 'authorities'. She kept a shotgun on the porch and in a conversation about potential trouble, she took her shotgun in her hands and comforted us by saying: 'Don't y'all worry now, if theys come even close to that fence there, I'll git rid of 'em.' The medics and I who stayed at her house grew close to her, but the contrast between us and her could not have been stronger. The medics were *über* politically correct and very careful in their use of language so as not to offend anyone. They were all highly educated, middle- to upper-middle-class urbanites from northern US or from abroad, mostly in their twenties and early thirties. She was older and settled in the countryside with a family, and in many ways the stereotype of a Southern woman, albeit a somewhat unconventional version thereof.

Despite these differences, working together went very smoothly. The 2004 G8 mobilisation was so small that literally all the different groups could easily come together and discuss how to proceed. Some of the main contingents were United For Peace and Justice (UFPJ), GPJC, the Gullah/Geeche march for reparations, Fix Shit Up!, the pagan cluster, the Fair World Fair, the medics and Indymedia.[4] UFPJ is one of the largest mainstream anti-war organisations in the US, consisting of 650 local and international groups, but they were not very well represented in the lead-up to the G8 protests, with only one or two members arriving before the protests. Fix Shit Up! was an anarchist project that was aimed at showing the constructive side of anarchism. These activists worked together with local people to 'work on local projects, such as renovating houses and environmental clean-up' with the intention 'to arm ourselves with hammers instead of bricks. To count our victories in the relationships we build, rather than what we tear down' (Fix Shit Up! collective 2004). The Fix Shit Up! project started before the protests and was meant as a long-term commitment to the local community.

The pagan cluster also worked on long-term projects that would outlast the G8 summit. They worked with the local Glynn County Environmental Coalition to teach and learn bioremediation techniques to make 'living soil again'. The local air and soil were deeply polluted and many areas were permanently cordoned off due to toxic levels of formaldehyde, chromium, acetadehyde, acroline and benzine. Many other toxic chemicals were also present, but were unmonitored and toxicity levels were not known; but there was no mistaking the smell in the air and water in Brunswick. According to the pamphlet put out by the Fix Shit Up! collective, cancer rates in Glynn County were among the highest in the country with '1 in 5 residents developing the disease'.[5]

Widespread carcinogenic chemical contamination was not even the biggest political problem in Brunswick. This honour was reserved for the segregative, violent racism that pervaded the town. When another medic and I were going to explore town we were warned by a local activist not to go to the black side of town because white people never go there and they would probably shoot us. One of the aims of the G8 protests was to bring the local black and white communities together, but this was no small task.

Among the white protesters there was a guilty sense of privilege in knowing that we would leave after the protests, and that although the police were unpredictable and potentially dangerous, at least our neighbours were unlikely to murder/lynch us. As I was told one evening while sitting in the Indymedia centre:

> After all we white activists go, who will protect them? This is still the Deep South. There's a redneck with a shotgun around every corner and whose gonna care or even find out if they kill the most hated man in Brunswick?

The most hated man in Brunswick was, apparently, a local Baptist preacher and civil rights activist organising against the G8 and leading the struggle for slavery reparations.

Despite these tensions and difficulties unique to the American context, the G8 protesters mimicked the usual organising structure of anti-summit mobilisations and were able to organise in parallel in such a way that the actions and activities of the various groups, after extensive discussion and some negotiation, did not conflict with one another. The small number of people present led to a more personal method of coordination, where decisions could be taken and communicated outside of large meetings, and the large meetings became more communicative than decisive. This type of relaxed organising structure is very different from those used at the G8 in 2005.

Scotland: The Next Generation

By the time the G8 came back to Europe in 2005 the protest preparations had been under way for nearly two years. The UK has a long tradition of decentralised autonomous direct action and when these activists heard that the G8 summit was coming to the UK, they started a process of formal and informal meetings that led to the creation of the Dissent! network. I eventually took on several different roles as part of the Dissent! mobilisation in the UK, but the affinity group I joined was based in Belgium. At the beginning of 2005, a Dissent! network was set up in Belgium to mobilise people to go to Scotland for the protests. I was living in the UK, but was frequently returning home to Belgium and participating in the Dissent! network there. I gave direct action trainings at the first 'Actie weekend' held in Belgium in April 2005. The aim of this weekend was to start building affinity groups, so Belgium became the context within which I formed an affinity group. My entire affinity group in 2005 consisted of Belgian students. Some were studying social work, others sociology. All of them were deeply engaged in political organising at home and were actively involved in the Dissent! network in Belgium. Most were inexperienced with international mobilisations and direct action. They were the generation that watched Seattle, Genoa and even Lausanne (Evian) on the living room television, dreaming about one day being there themselves. When I first met one of them and told him that I had been in 'Seattle', I could see the hint of jealousy and admiration in his eyes that only stories of mythical proportions can inspire as he said: 'You are probably the only Belgian who was there!'

The Bigger Picture

Despite contextual differences, a common structure repeatedly emerges at anti-summit mobilisations. The process is roughly as follows: the powers that be announce the location of the next WTO/G8/IMF etc. meeting, movement actors near that location contact friends and meetings are held. Through these meetings they communicate with a larger circle of activists than before. Emails go out and websites are constructed. In the autonomous sections of the movement, the settings for many of these meetings are squatted buildings and social centres. Large rooms full of people either sitting on the floor or on chairs, but always in a circle. The format for these meetings is usually the 'spokescouncil' format, in which large meetings (even hundreds to thousands of people) can be organised on the basis of small group discussions that feed into larger group discussions. The principle underlying the spokescouncil is that everyone has to have the opportunity to speak *and* be heard – to have an input into the discussion – without everyone having to listen to everyone else speak. To achieve this, large meetings begin with a topic of discussion which is outlined at the beginning, the meeting is then split up into many small groups, and the topic is discussed for a short time (maybe 15 minutes). Once each group has had a chance to gather the different opinions and ideas, and merge them where possible and highlight points of incommensurability if they arise, each group sends one person (known in movement lingo as a 'spoke' – a temporary representative in a purely informational, non-decision-making capacity) to the middle of the room to relay the information, ideas and concerns that their group raised. Once this information has been exchanged, and all groups have heard the short condensed version of what everyone in the room had to say, discussion in small groups resumes and the groups try to decide what they think on the basis of not only what their group thinks, but also what everyone else in the room had to say. Sometimes everyone from the small groups is present at the larger meetings and sometimes only the spoke, but no decisions are taken without discussion in both large and small groups. This process of small group to large group discussion, is repeated until ideas are turned into a proposal and consensus can be reached, first within the small groups and then within the large group – the spokescouncil. In this way, everyone can participate in the discussion without the spokescouncil meeting becoming unwieldy or never ending.

Smaller planning meetings often start with a 'go around', in which everyone in the room says their name and where they are from or what they do (as an activist). For example, 'George, Bristol Dissent! and Action Trainers Collective'. There are usually one or two facilitators who help the consensus process function smoothly. Anyone who wants to speak raises their hand and the facilitator puts their name on a list and calls upon them when it is their turn. An extensive set of hand signals has been developed to express different sentiments non-verbally. The most common are raising one hand or finger to speak and raising both hands with the index fingers in the air to make a *direct* response to the previous comment. The two-index-finger hand signal moves the person to the top of the speaker's list. This technique, when used correctly, improves the flow of conversation and helps meetings that are addressing several different topics deal with one topic at a time. Another useful hand signal, which was met with varying degrees of enthusiasm by movement actors, is 'twinkling'. This is a shaking, 'twinkling', of the fingers in the air and it signifies agreement. This hand signal is used to allow everyone to actively agree without taking up meeting time by repeating the point or saying 'I agree'. The same signal with the hands facing downwards signifies disagreement. Finally, there is the fist, which indicates that the proposal being discussed violates the person's most deeply held values and that the person intends to block the decision. Blocks are an important part of the democratic process and crucial to keeping it inclusive (see Chapter 4), but I have never seen them actually accepted. Usually what happens in practice is that the blocker gets a chance to explain his or her particular concerns and the group agrees to make adjustments to the proposal taking these into consideration, or the group may decide to split and take two or more courses of action. These are the basic hand signals usually explained at the beginning of consensus meetings in the autonomous sections of the anti-summit mobilisations. The 'time out' or 'technical point' signal, which is a two-handed T shape and is used when someone wants to make a practical and relevant announcement – that, for example, dinner is ready or that the room will need to be vacated in 20 minutes – is sometimes used, but not often explained. Although these hand signals are not universally applied and many activists do not use them, during the 2005 G8 protests these hand signals were even painted on the wall of the Glasgow convergence space in the form of large blue diagrams to help facilitate communication at the spokescouncil meetings.

These meeting practices are most common among the more autonomous movement actors, but they are not the only ones who mobilise against multilateral organisations. There are many different groups mobilising simultaneously and they do not all use consensus. Typically, three different strands emerge: (1) the autonomous networks (including some non-governmental organisations [NGOs]); (2) a coalition consisting of some social movement organisations and socialist/communist groups: (3) the NGOs.[6] The trade unions, who constitute a fourth strand, tend to associate themselves either with the communists or the NGOs.[7] There is only limited contact between the various groups and they may work in ways that complement or contradict each other. The three main strands present during the anti-G8 mobilisation in 2005 were the Dissent! network, G8 Alternatives and the Make Poverty History (MPH) coalition. G8 Alternatives was a broad coalition of different organisations with many socialist and communist organisations, including the Socialist Workers Party (SWP). When the Hori-Zone camp was being planned, originally G8 Alternatives, Dissent!, the Campaign for Nuclear Disarmament (CND) and People and Planet were going to camp together. In the end this was not possible due to difficulties getting an appropriate piece of land, but it demonstrates one way in which these very different groups work together. The idea was that these different contingents would occupy different neighbourhoods of the camp and employ whichever organisational structure they preferred in their own neighbourhood, but the daily camp-wide meetings would use consensus. The SWP could vote in their own neighbourhood, but the camp as a whole would not make decisions by vote or create a fixed elected elite.

The MPH coalition of large NGOs was further removed from these movement activities. MPH was the largest mainstream force in the 2005 mobilisation. It was through this massive campaign under the banner of 'Make Poverty History' that the average person in the UK came to know about the G8. MPH counted among its members many rock stars and consequently surged to fame and popularity quite quickly. They organised a 'million'-person march (to which several hundred thousand people came) in Edinburgh on the weekend before the G8 summit. In the Dissent! network there was much discussion about whether or not to join the MPH march. Bono, the public face of MPH, was working together with the British government and supported the G8 by applauding the cancellation of African debt and urging the G8 to do even more for Africa. MPH was therefore generally viewed disfavourably by most people within the Dissent! network. This book does not explore the inner workings of MPH or G8 Alternatives. As a research strategy, I decided to focus on the

Dissent! network and see if this would lead me into contact with these other groups, which, interestingly, it did not. At a spokescouncil meeting organised by the Dissent! network, many movement actors did decide to attend the MPH march, but they did not decide to do so in communication or cooperation with those organising it.

ESF and WSF

The four categories of movement actors (often organised into three strands in the anti-summit mobilisations) – autonomous, political parties, trade unions and NGOs – are also present in the social forum processes. The autonomous groups usually focus on the Intercontinental Youth Camp (IYC) or the autonomous spaces outside the main forum, while the communists, socialists, trade unions, social movement organisations and NGOs tend to be at the centre of the national Organising Committee and European Preparatory Assembly (EPA) of the ESF or the International Council of the WSF.[8] The relationships between these different groups are not always amicable, but due to the centralised committees and assemblies, the different movement actors are obliged to work together. Consequently the relationships between movement actors within the social forum are sometimes strained.

Playing Bingo

'Quick, pass me a piece of paper; Chris is next in the queue.'
'OK, but let's do phrases and not just words this time. It's getting too easy.'

A hurried exchange between two of the participants at the EPA in Paris as they each take a pen and paper and start to jot down some phrases: 'massive movement', 'great success', 'end to imperialism', 'great opportunity', 'very serious', as part of a game they called *Bingo*. This game consists of writing down four or five phrases or words one predicts the speaker will use and then crossing them out as the speaker uses them. The one who manages to cross out all the phrases wins. Bingo was used as a way to cope with boredom, but the game represents much more than a means of distraction. There are several levels at which Bingo exposes the underlying relationships of movement actors in the ESF. The bingo players did not play this game with every speaker, but only with the speakers from certain traditional left political parties, especially the International Socialist Tendency (IST).[9] Bingo exposes the lack of agreement among the actors present at an EPA while also showing the outright disdain, disrespect and mockery in which this disagreement sometimes results. This mockery was felt to be justified because those being ridiculed had abused the ESF process by using it as a place to gain power for themselves and their organisation. Bingo was a small attempt at undermining the dominant position of the political parties in the ESF process.

This form of mockery is also revealing when we examine what is being mocked. Bingo mocks the repetitiveness and predictability of the traditional left. The division between 'old' and 'new' is being reflected in this game as the division between 'boring' and 'funny'. There is disdain among these movement actors for the 'party line', especially when it is disguised in non-party political language. By playing Bingo, they expose the fact that no matter what country the speaker is from or what the topic of discussion is, members of the IST will express not only the same ideas but use the exact same language to do so. The bingo players are simultaneously revealing and ridiculing this uniformity of opinion; a unitary party line in the ESF context is considered laughable – at least by some. Bingo represents a rejection of political practices that are aimed at unity and grand narratives of linear history, where bigger equals better. The phrases being mocked, phrases such as 'massive mobilisation' and 'big success' are not only narratives of unity but they represent a theory of change where change occurs through the accumulation of people and size becomes the key factor in bringing about the revolutionary moment. This 'size matters theory of social change', as one activist put it, is rejected by many of the movement actors and the presence of these beliefs in the ESF, therefore, becomes a joke to those who do not believe in such theories of social change.

The ESF: The Key Players

The ESF organising context does not change from one year to the next as in the anti-summit mobilisations. As the ESF moves from one country to another, the relative centrality of certain people shifts, but many of the key people remain the same, especially at the level of the EPA. Anti-summit mobilisations are organised almost entirely in the country where they take place; the role of the international community is to organise themselves and to organise their movements, unions, networks and organisations to do outreach at the local level to encourage people to go to the protests for one week or even a few days. Movement actors from all over Europe do not come together to decide how the French and the Swiss should organise the G8 protests, but they do come together to discuss how the French should organise the Paris ESF. Movement actors from across Europe feel they have a say in the process and content of the ESF and those in the host country cannot simply do as they please. This results in more centralised process where there is one European-wide decision-making space – the EPA.

The WSF, by contrast, tends to be more nationally organised than the ESF, with a semi-official representative structure where the members of the national Organising Committee (OC) are representatives of networks or organisations affiliated to the WSF. The International Council (IC) ensures a continuous international involvement in determining the direction, process and content of the WSF without being a decision-making body. Due to the EPA and the IC, many of the same people are involved in the ESF and WSF year after year. The EPA and the existing process inherited from year to year by each OC ensure a structural continuity that is not present in anti-summit mobilisations.

Access to the central core of EPA organisers is greatly helped by (but not limited to) membership in a national Organising Committee past, present or future. The Italian and the French ESF coordinating committees are still at the centre of the organising process at the European level and have relative power compared to those who have never been part of an ESF coordinating committee. When the decision was taken as to where the 2004 ESF would take place, some of the British and Greek 'delegates' gained in relative power as it became clear that both countries would host the ESF, one in 2004 and one in 2005.[10] The two main French figures at the EPA are both are affiliated with ATTAC France and are both trade unionists. Sophie Zafari is a school teacher active with the Fédération Syndicale Unitaire (FSU) and Pierre Khalfa, who is scientific advisor to ATTAC and member of the ATTAC office, used to be active in Solidaire Unitaire Démocratique (SUD). Sophie and Pierre often 'chaired' the EPAs, especially when the ESF was in Paris and London. The central role played by Sophie and Pierre is even more pronounced in smaller meetings where proposals and statements are forged. They often take on the role of summarising or presenting the proposals from small group meetings to the larger EPA and consequently end up central to important decisions. Sophie's role was neatly summarised when some people were joking at a meeting of 'le petit groupe de travail' in Brussels that the decisions being taken would be confusing to anyone who was not present. The jovial response was that we shouldn't worry, everyone would just 'call Sophie if they don't understand'.

Almost all the key figures in the ESF process are associated with trade unions and many are also members of political parties. When the process to decide the location of the ESF 2004 started, it was these people that invited different countries to put together a bid to host the ESF and who attended the 'secret' small meetings. The authority of these actors was often reinforced (intentionally and unintentionally) by the fact that they chaired the EPA, and when they were not chairing, they often sat in the front row. Those who presented the bid for London were Chris Nineham of Globalise Resistance (GR) and SWP, Liz Hutchinson of the CND, Claire Williams from the public service trade union UNISON and SWP, and Dominic Hurley from the Greater London Authority (GLA, London mayor's office). The Greek delegates included Harry Golemis of the Greek Party Synaspismos, director of the Nicos Poulantzas Institute and a founding member of Transform!, Panyotis Yulis of the Greek Social Forum, Natacha Theodorakopoulou from Synaspismos and Party of the European Left, and Petros Constantinou from the Campaign Genoa 2001 and the IST. Together, these and a few other movement actors made up what came to be sarcastically referred to as the 'international elite' by the bingo players.

Exacerbating Divisions

The two years from 2003 to 2004 were especially apt for observing this continuity of constituency. I started my fieldwork in Paris before the ESF in 2003 and followed the process until several months after the ESF 2004 in London. As we shall see in detail in the coming chapters, the decision to bring the ESF to London was not unanimous, and there was much debate about the trustworthiness of those who appointed themselves the coordinating committee and worries about the determining role the GLA was playing. This distrust led to a protectiveness of the ESF principles on the part of the French and Italian delegates, who often took a patronising tone. The format of the EPA did not help to minimise this distrust. EPA meetings took place in a large room with rows of chairs for the audience and a table at the front, sometimes on a podium, where the 'chair(s)' of the meeting sat. Sometimes there was only one chair, other times there were up to four or five – usually from a few different countries. The only people who introduced themselves at the beginning of the meeting were the chairs; everyone else introduced themselves when and if they spoke. The standard introduction included the speaker's name, organisational affiliation, country and language s/he speaks. There was a microphone at the front of the room where people from the floor could queue to speak. Sometimes the chair made attempts at gender parity by deciding to 'alternate the speakers male/female' to which a 'why not female/male?' was once shouted from the audience. The list of men wanting to speak was always longer than the list of women, so this system did not always work. Discussion consisted of people making long queues and interventions on various topics on a first come first served basis. Sometimes the chair intervened and insisted that people stay on topic, but this was rarely successful. In this meeting style there is no way to respond to and build upon previous interventions. In order to reply, one has to join the queue and by the time one can reply, sometimes an hour later, the intervention often seems entirely irrelevant and out of context. This meeting style exacerbated existing divisions between movement actors and represented a break with the meeting style of both the WSF and the autonomous sections of the anti-summit mobilisations. In the WSF meetings I observed, the Indian Organising Committee sat around a table facing each other, with no one on a podium. In the UK, this division caused by differences over organisational process was very strong and the two sides came to be known as the 'verticals' and the 'horizontals' – with a few 'diagonals' on the side.

The Verticals and the Horizontals

There is a great deal to say about the categories 'horizontal' and 'vertical' in terms of movement beliefs and practices, and we will explore some of these in the chapters to come, but for now the most interesting aspect of these categories is their near momentary fluidity. Who is considered vertical and who horizontal is not determined by fixed factors. When these labels are written or spoken about, even by movement actors, they are often assumed to refer to traditional political parties, socialists, trade unionists, some NGOs on the vertical side, and autonomous networks and other NGOs on the horizontal side. These distinctions hold on the theoretical level, but in practice, there is a constant negotiation and re-negotiation of these relationships. Horizontality is something that one *does,* and if one acts like a horizontal, one is a horizontal.[11]

The categories of horizontal and vertical were employed by the horizontals to describe the differences between themselves and the coordinating committee, which was originally made up of the SWP, the GLA, some social movement organisations such as CND, and several trade unionists. The term 'vertical' was meant to refer to the hierarchical organising structure set up by these organisations. However, in practice it referred more often to a perceived attitude of superiority. The horizontals felt that the SWP and GLA were intentionally dominating the organising process. Due to this secondary definition of vertical, and the adversarial, dichotomous nature of the vertical/horizontal distinction, anyone who acted or spoke out against the SWP or the GLA, became by default a horizontal. To advocate horizontality was to be a horizontal, but it was not always so clear what exactly constituted the advocacy of horizontality.

At any given meeting of the horizontals, those present included the autonomous activists and anarchists, as well as communists, several representatives of large British NGOs like the World Development Movement and Friends of the Earth, editors of *Red Pepper* magazine, and many other people who referred to themselves as 'independents'.[12] The alliances between these activists were based largely on their opposition to the verticals. A commitment to principles of horizontality was only true for some of those present. These less horizontal movement actors were often referred to as 'diagonals'. The diagonals were the strategic allies of the horizontals, but they only advocated more openness and horizontality because they felt excluded. The horizontal/ diagonal relationship was a relationship of convenience, but it was nevertheless a strong and mutually supportive bond. The role of exclusion in forging these alliances influenced the ambiguity of these dichotomous categories of vertical and horizontal. One's sense of exclusion greatly affected the alliances made, and the extent of exclusion often shifted between different contexts and moments.

At the European level, allegiance was equally susceptible to the effects of exclusion or loss of control. The relationships between actors were perpetually shifting. As the tensions grew between horizontals and verticals in the UK, the key figures across Europe had to mediate to keep the UK ESF process going. These European actors also had their own political motivations, including a desire to maintain the power of influence they had over the ESF process. They continuously re-aligned themselves according to their own interests and what they believed was in the best interest of the ESF. They were simultaneously maintaining a diplomatic relationship with the SWP and GLA while arguing on the side of the horizontals that the process must be open, participatory and 'horizontal'. Defending the 'openness' of the ESF was important to everyone involved, vertical, horizontal and diagonal, but this defence was not always part of an ideological commitment to horizontality.

The International Non-elites

The social forum organising processes also creates another group of social forum regulars. This group was in many ways the opposite of the above 'international elite' group in that these movement actors took very few official decisions and almost never played the diplomatic games of the political party and trade union types. They were the office lackeys, paper pushers and administrators who focused on the practical side of the social forum. Through my work in the offices of the ESF and WSF, I became one of these international non-elites that travelled all over the world and turned up at the office of whichever social forum, wherever in the world, ready to volunteer her time and her skills. The background and circumstances under which these actors made this journey and commitment were different for each one, but together they created a sort of mobile social forum administration. Most of these people were in their twenties or early thirties; they were unemployed, partly intentionally, partly as a result of a precarious labour market in which finding stable long-term contract work is unusual even for the highly educated. This international team of forum administrators was composed of skilled, intelligent people, often with Master's degrees or business management degrees and experience working in social movement contexts or in the non-profit sector. They either came from Europe (or to a lesser degree the US or Canada) or from the upper echelons of society in the global south. In the case of the WSF India, many of these volunteers were working at the WSF office as part of a cultural exchange programme or a work experience abroad scheme. Some volunteers in India had never been engaged in the social forum process, but through their experience in the office they became a part of this inner circle of social forum administrators and started to turn up at the ESF, the Mediterranean Social Forum and even the WSF in Porto Alegre the next year. In London, even before the ESF was over, these movement actors held late-night discussions (after a long day of work at the London ESF office) planning all the work they could do for the WSF in Porto Alegre.

The Movements within the Movement

This book is about global networks as collective spaces of movement activity – spaces where the different movements and groups and organisations come together. The Narmada Bachao Andolan is one of the many movements within this 'movement of movements' that plays an important role in these collective spaces of movement activity, but the overlap between the NBA and the alterglobalisation movement is often small. Before we can continue to examine these global networks, a few words must be said about the relationship between the alterglobalisation movement as a diverse but singular entity and the many movements that constitute it – each of which has an existence that is partly independent of the larger movement of movements. The global networks examined here, although highly significant for a discussion of decentralised network democracy, represent an out-of-the-ordinary practice for the many of movements within the alterglobalisation movement, and the way this relationship functions needs to be addressed briefly to add the final touch to the picture I am trying to paint of when these practices are crucial to understanding the alterglobalisation movement as well as when and where they might not be so important.

The Narmada Bachao Andolan (NBA)

The struggle of the adivasi people in the Narmada valley in India has taken on a mythical character in the alterglobalisation movement as a quintessential example of the struggles waged by this movement.[13] It is a 40-year-old conflict for indigenous land rights against the paradigm of 'development as modernisation'. The Narmada hydro-electric dam project is one of the biggest river valley projects in the world; it consists of 30 major dams, 135 medium dams and 3000 minor dams (Sheth 1991: 7). According to the Institute of Urban Affairs in New Delhi, the entire project will lead to the displacement of 1 million people. The World Bank says it will be 'the world's largest river basin population resettlement to date' (Alvares and Billorey 1988: 15). The NBA opposes the dam on environmental grounds, human rights grounds, and ultimately unites many different groups around an opposition to the entire mode of development that the dam represents.[14] The struggle for indigenous land rights already constitutes one overlapping unity with many other movements in the 'movement of movements', but by bringing in environmental elements and by challenging the entire paradigm of development, the NBA increased the number of overlapping unities they had with the rest of the alterglobalisation movement and quickly became a symbol of what the alterglobalisation movement as a whole stands for. The NBA is today, together with the Zapatistas and the Movimento dos Trabalhadores Rurais Sem Terra (MST) one of the most well-known movements.

The NBA was founded and is led by a woman named Medha Patkar. She first travelled to the Narmada valley to do research for a PhD on social inequality, which she abandoned when she took on the Narmada valley struggle as her life's work. 'Medhaji', as she is called by everyone in the NBA, treats the Narmada as her calling, 'my family background was such that doing something for society – social, political, economic issues – was very natural for me. I couldn't have selected anything else but that. I was made for that' (in D'Souza 1995). Over the past 25 years, Medhaji has grown into an international icon, at least within movement circles.

During my fieldwork in the valley and the office of the NBA, some of the other activists I met were Philip Matthew, Prakash Lakra, Raman Dala and 'Raijikaka'. Raman Dala and Raijikaka are adivasi farmers from the Narmada valley who were displaced by the dam in the 1980s. During my fieldwork, they were both living in resettlement sites in Gujarat and were active with the NBA trying to get their resettlement packages while fighting the continued construction of the dam. Raman Dala speaks of 'feeling defeated' and Raijikaka has returned to his home village of Gadher in Maharashtra with his wife, children and grandchildren because his life in the resettlement site was unsustainable. The alterglobalisation movement, however, gives them new hope. Both Raijikaka and Raman Dala are active in the NBA protests and *satyagrahas* and they travelled to Bombay by train together with Medhaji and 30 others as part of the NBA's delegation to the WSF.[15] Raijikaka said, reflecting on the WSF:

> We have a new faith in ourselves, a self-confidence and understanding that poor people are fighting everywhere. We are not alone. There are people supporting us from all over the world and they know about our struggle. That gives us strength.

The NBA used the presence of the global movement, and the WSF especially, to reinvigorate their struggle: they organised a large delegation of adivasis to attend the WSF; they held a tour of the Narmada valley for foreign WSFers; and after the closing ceremony of the WSF, they started a *dharna* at the offices of the Maharashtran government which was attended by many of the WSF office staff, volunteers and participants.[16]

From the Outside In

The Narmada Bachao Andolan is an important part of the alterglobalisation movement and appears from time to time in the chapters to come. This book, however, explores the global networks created by the connections between many different movements, people and groups (from the international working group sitting in a field to the WSF participants, adivasis and office staff alike) as part of a process that is redefining the way we understand what constitutes democracy. The NBA as an 'individual' movement within the larger 'movement of movements' is not the focus of this book because this democratic process, and the role that the adivasis play in this process, is not obvious when viewed from within the NBA. Once within the immediacy of the

Narmada valley, the concerns of the adivasis are paramount. The importance of the Narmada movement to the alterglobalisation movement only becomes visible when we look from the vantage point of the alterglobalisation movement, where we can see the overlapping unities that are created, and where the Narmada struggle takes on a symbolic meaning as a struggle against capitalist notions of 'progress' (a meaning of which many adivasis are not aware). This 'progress' was determined to be beneficial without any involvement from those who are most affected by it and this disenfranchisement underlies the motivation of many movement actors and certainly constitutes one overlapping unity. Even though this sense of exclusion does not always manifest itself in a conscious struggle for democracy, and this ideological level of meaning may not appear relevant for many of the displaced people struggling against the Narmada dam project, the link remains. Still, it is important to remember that the NBA and the alterglobalisation movement are not synonymous. Rather, they have perpetually shifting degrees of overlap; sometimes the NBA appears entirely disconnected from the alterglobalisation movement, sometimes partially connected, and at other times so central that it is symbolic of the entire movement. An adivasi living in the Narmada valley may not experience the alterglobalisation movement as part of his or her struggle, but at the analytical level we can see the links made between the NBA and the alterglobalisation movement. What is important for the analysis is that the link between the Narmada movement and the alterglobalisation movement is much more visible when one looks from the outside in than from the inside out.

In the chapters to come I describe only the view from the outside in, through an examination of the way the global networks of the alterglobalisation movement function. But this brief discussion of the NBA is meant to draw attention to the fact that this movement is very diverse and rests on complex connections and communications that are neither universal nor stable. Links between the various movements that constitute this 'movement of movements' are shifting over time, are often temporary or partial, and they look very different from different vantage points at any given moment. The descriptions that follow reflect the view from the collective movement spaces, the global networks, spaces that exist in a certain sense beyond the particular movements that constitute them, and it should be assumed that the view often looks quite different from within each one of these constitutive movements.

2

TURNING DREAMS INTO REALITY

Neoliberalism, like most historical oppressive systems, takes the approach of the 'means justify the ends.' They negate the damage that is created in the process, pay little attention to process outcomes, and focus on short-term goals ... In the autonomous methodology, the process in many cases is more important than the direct goal. (Flores, in Flores and Tanka 2001)

We need not conquer the world. It is enough to make it anew. (Subcomandante Marcos 1996)

What is Prefiguration?

As an activist, I have always had a sense of what prefiguration is, but it was not until university that I first heard the word *prefiguration*. At first I was reluctant to use the word because it seemed so cold and lifeless. Could 'prefiguration' capture what it felt like to turn dreams into a living reality? Could it possibly describe the process of trying to create in this imperfect world structures and practices that are consistent with visions of a perfect world? Before I turn to the academic and activist literature on prefiguration, I would like to briefly describe what it has meant to me as an activist. My intention is not only to provide a description of what prefigurative politics is, but also to offer my own position vis-à-vis the subject of this chapter. In my experience as an activist, practising prefiguration has meant always trying to make the processes we use to achieve our immediate goals an embodiment of our ultimate goals, so that there is no distinction between how we fight and what we fight for, at least not where the ultimate goal of a radically different society is concerned. In this sense, practising prefigurative politics means removing the temporal distinction between the struggle in the *present* towards a goal in the *future*; instead, the struggle and the goal, the real and the ideal, become one in the present. Prefiguration is a practice through which movement actors create a conflation of their ends with their means. It is an enactment of the ultimate values of an ideal society within the very means of struggle for that society.

The academic literature offers a similar notion of what prefiguration is. Franks (2003: 17) argues that direct action should be considered prefigurative because 'what is desired must also be involved in the methods of reaching that aim'. Fuller (1989) describes the presence of prefigurative politics in what she calls 'Peace Movement Organizations' (PMOs):

> In these movements organizational structures and processes are an 'action form,' a method of protest in itself rather than simply a means to mobilize resources.

Similar working notions of prefigurative politics can also be found in much activist literature. Nomadlab (2002) writes:

> Prefigurative politics is based on the notion that the 'future society' is how we act in the present, what kinds of interactions, processes, structures, institutions, and associations we create right now, and how we live our lives.

Two coordinators from Babels, the international network of volunteer interpreters and translators that was set up in 2002 for the first ESF in Florence and has grown from several hundred in 2002 to over 7000 in 2004 (Boéri and Hodkinson 2005), describe the significance of the Babels network as follows:

> the real story of Babels lies in its embodiment of the innovatory but difficult process of 'pre-figurative politics'. By attempting to put into practice the principles of solidarity, pluralism, equality, and horizontality, Babels is creating not only alternative systems and practices to free-market capitalist society, but also the social counter-power needed to defend and embed them permanently. (Boéri and Hodkinson 2005)

Babels is only one example of many ways in which the alterglobalisation movement employs prefiguration. Several scholars writing on the alterglobalisation movement have realised the need to understand movement practice as a reflection of movement ideals. Smith (2008: 213–15) writes of 'experiments in global democracy' arguing that alterglobalisation movement actors 'model and enact a different vision of how the world might be organized, thereby inspiring hope that another world is possible' (2008: 203). Polletta (2002: 177) also acknowledges this relationship in her work on the US-based Communities Organized for Public Service and the Direct Action Network. She argues that 'both groups see democracy within the group as vital to building democracy outside it'. Polletta (2002: 199) points out that for DAN, participatory democracy has a 'normative' aspect in which 'participatory democratic decision-making is at once a means and an end'. Juris (2008b: 295) argues that 'radical anti-corporate globalization activists are not only seeking to intervene within dominant public spheres; they are also challenging representative democracy, in part by developing their own directly democratic forms of organizing and decision making'.

Prefiguration is, above all, something people *do*; it is not a theory of social change that first analyses the current state of affairs, then establishes an ideal goal and then sets out a five-year plan for achieving these goals. It is a different kind of theory, one that theorises through action, a 'direct theory' (Sturgeon 1995: 36). Prefigurative movements are 'movements that are creating the future in their present social relationships ... social change isn't deferred to a later date by demanding reforms from the state, or by taking state power and eventually instituting these reforms' (Sitrin 2006: 4).

Prefiguring Horizontality

In the alterglobalisation movement one finds prefiguration of a plurality of values and ideals. Heavily influenced by DIY tendencies and squatter movements in the US and Europe and by *autogestion* and land rights movements elsewhere (see Corr 1999, 2005), the alterglobalisation movement stems from many movements that have a common practice of taking matters into their own hands and constructing the type of world, community, project they desire without the intermediary of a government or corporate representative.[1] These prefigurative practices, however, cannot all be explored here. Instead I examine the prefiguration of one particular practice that lies at the heart of democratic praxis in the alterglobalisation movement – *horizontality*. Horizontality is a term used by movement actors to refer to less hierarchical, networked relationships of decision-making and organising structures that actively attempt to limit power inequalities. As such it is intentionally democratic and prefigurative. Sitrin (2006: 3), describing the Argentinian uprising of December 2001, introduces *Horizontalidad* as 'democratic communication on a level plane' that:

> involves – or at least intentionally strives towards – non-hierarchical and anti-authoritarian creation rather than reaction ... *Horizontalidad* is a living world that reflects an ever-changing experience.

Horizontality as a movement concept and practice will be explored thoroughly in the next chapter; here it is sufficient to understand the role this general principle plays in the process of movement decision-making as an intentional prefiguration of an egalitarian democratic praxis. In the alterglobalisation movement, the importance of horizontal prefiguration emerges most clearly in discussions of 'process'. Conflicts around *process* expose the importance of prefigurative practices and highlight some significant internal differences in the way movement actors approach consensus and horizontality. In this chapter, I explore the role of prefiguration in social forum spaces and in the 'autonomous' sections of the anti-G8 mobilisations. If it had been possible to research the entire anti-G8 mobilisation, and not just the autonomous networks, I would presumably have found more similarities between these two movement spaces, but the contrasts are perhaps more telling than the similarities. The contrast allows us to see that although most movement actors are in some way prefiguring less hierarchy, they are not all doing so to the same degree. This discussion of prefiguration in the alterglo-balisation movement is followed by a brief outline of the influence of anarchism on this horizontal prefiguration. In the final section, I engage critically with the argument that prefiguration is the antonym of strategy to shed light both on the way prefiguration is understood and the way the alterglobalisation movement is understood, arguing that prefiguration is itself a strategic practice, but represents only one among many strategic practices, each aimed at different types of movement goals.

The Social Forum

- The World Social Forum is an open meeting place for reflective thinking, democratic debate of ideas, formulation of proposals, free exchange of experiences and interlinking for effective action, by groups and movements of civil society that are opposed to neoliberalism and to domination of the world by capital and any form of imperialism, and are committed to building a planetary society directed towards fruitful relationships among Mankind and between it and the Earth.

- The World Social Forum at Porto Alegre [in 2001] was an event localised in time and place. From now on, in the certainty proclaimed at Porto Alegre that 'another world is possible', it becomes a permanent process of seeking and building alternatives, which cannot be reduced to the events supporting it.

(WSF Brazilian Organising Committee [BOC] and IC 2001, The WSF Charter of Principles)

The European Social Forum is an annual convention hosted by a major European city ... It's [sic] purpose is to discuss a range of issues in a non-party political, informed and committed context, providing an opportunity for policy makers and specialists to meet with concerned citizens in a socially-inclusive framework.

The ESF will produce significant benefits for London. It will:

1. present London as a forward-looking and vibrant city and marketed [sic] as such throughout Europe and around the world, making the city an attractive destination of choice, particularly amongst young people;

2. provide direct economic benefits to the tourism industry with up to 60,000 people from Britain and abroad spending four days in London – the demand for accommodation across a range of prices would be considerable;

3. promote cultural initiatives, display the diversity and vibrancy of London's culture and show London to be a modern world cultural capital;

4. promote a wide range of indirect economic benefits to outlets ranging from restaurants and bars to bookshops, cinemas and theatres;

5. encourage the development of a coordinated yet broad and diverse not-for-profit sector across the capital.

(Letter written by the London ESF 'bid group', November 2003)

The above two quotes are taken from official documents released by two separate social forum mobilisations for two very different purposes. The first quote comes directly from the social forum's Charter of Principles, written by the Brazilian WSF Organising Committee amended by the International Council of the WSF shortly after the first WSF in Porto Alegre in 2001.[2] It was written as an explanation of the organisers' intentions as a guide to all future social forum mobilisations. The second quote was taken from a letter written by the London bid group of the ESF 2004. They wrote this letter to potential funders as part of their attempt to make the London ESF an economically and politically viable event. The intended audience of the two documents is therefore very different, and I chose these two quotes intentionally to draw out the large gap between the 'official' political practices of the ESF as outlined in the charter of principles and the actual practices often found in the organising process on the local level. This gap is of particular importance because prefiguration requires, by definition, the closing of the space between rhetoric and practice. The juxtaposition of these two quotes functions better than any abstract argument to show the fickle nature of prefiguration in the social forum movement. Prefiguration is embedded deeply in the ideology of the social forum and for many actors it is an essential characteristic. However, in the practice of social fora we find that practical (and monetary) concerns quickly override the importance of *process*.

The Charter of Principles

It seems unimaginable that the authors of the Charter of Principles could have realised the fire they were igniting with the simple words, 'a permanent process of seeking and building alternatives, which cannot be reduced to the events supporting it'. This half sentence has created a battleground between various political tendencies. Coalitions have been built, friendships won and lost, massive political differences buried and forgotten, others exaggerated into explosion, all because this sentence would – indeed, should – mean that the *process* that goes into organising a social forum should be consistent with the ultimate aim of a more participatory democracy. The Charter of Principles is a document that holds a great deal of power as the basic set of values, the common denominator by which anyone wanting to take part in a social forum must abide. The interpretation of the charter of principles being that the organising *process* is more important than the event itself is, therefore, no small detail.

Even actors who would have rather ignored the existence of prefigurative politics have had to take it into account because those who insist upon prefiguration have the power of 'the charter' behind them. The movement actors in favour of prefiguration, with the charter behind them, are able to place prefiguration at the centre of the social forum process, despite the fact that, for many social forum actors, prefiguration remains at the level of rhetoric. Consequently, there is a tension within the ESF that results from the gap between movement actors who employ a rhetoric about 'openness' and 'transparency' and in some cases even 'non-hierarchy', but do so only to gain credentials vis-à-vis the charter, and those who actively practise these principles. Despite this gap, the very use of the rhetoric exposes the central importance of prefiguration in the social forum; one cannot stake a legitimate claim to involvement in the social forum movement without demonstrating, even if only verbally, one's commitment to *process*.

The Politics of Process

> If people can't be held accountable for their actions in lack of organisation, consultation, openness & transparency then we are doing a diservice [sic] to the very concept of the esf. I make no apologies for that. Ignoring the process needs to be criticised when ever & where ever it occurs. (Dean 2004)

Process-oriented Consensus versus Decision-oriented Consensus

Movement actors in global movement networks claim to be making decisions through consensus. Good *process* is based on consensus. How consensus is practised and understood by those using it, however, differs from one context to the next. In the social forum organising process the use of consensus has changed over time. Although there is a strong rhetorical adherence to consensus, in social forum spaces there are some actors who do not believe in consensus, and many who do not understand how it works. The 'horizontals' tend to interpret consensus primarily as a holistic *process*, while many of the other actors view it merely as a decision-making mechanism that allows everyone to say what they think. Much of the conflict that existed in the ESF process in 2004 evolved around these different approaches to consensus. Interventions at the preparatory meetings about *process* insisted that the process ought to be more 'inclusive' and 'open' with more 'participation':

> *The process is as important as the ESF itself* and we cannot have a different world if we don't force ourselves to practice a different way of working together, based not on self-appointed representation but on a wider inclusive process in which all the differences can express themselves and reclaim the right to participate. (UK Social Forum Network 2004, emphasis original)

The use of abstract language allowed for a great deal of agreement because everyone in the room supported being more inclusive and open and participatory. How those involved understood these words, however, was worlds apart. There were many different visions of what inclusion entailed or what constituted an open meeting and an open process. For everyone involved *process* was about how decisions are made, but some actors were privileging the *how* and others the *decision*. In an ironic twist, the assumption of prefiguration was partially responsible for creating this misunderstanding by conflating the how (means) and the what (ends).

This divide that emerged within the social forum process, is representative of a divergence within the movement more broadly between those stemming from political parties and trade unions and those from autonomous (or even 'new social movement') networks. Because I researched the autonomous section of the anti-G8 mobilisations, the type of consensus practised there was similar to that preferred by the more horizontal side of the social forum spectrum. The theory of participation that prevails in social forum settings is one that creates a space for opinions to be heard as part of making a decision, but participation in the autonomous sections of the anti-summit mobilisations means being a part of the process to determine not only what is decided but also *how* it is decided. A distinction develops, therefore, between decision-oriented consensus and process-oriented consensus, where the former takes centre stage in social forum organising and the latter in the autonomous strands of the anti-summit mobilisations:

> There are a lot of people angry about the way the process had been organised, and I would say get over it. We need to have this discussion about neoliberalism and we need to get on in organising it. (Alex Gordon of the National Union of Rail, Maritime & Transport Workers, EPA, 13 December 2003, London)

> Rather than setting up an endpoint as to where we are going, we should set up a process through which we can get to whatever end. (Dissent! national gathering, Sheffield, 15 October 2005)

These two quotes demonstrate two different approaches to *process*. In some cases, such as the second quote above, the *process* becomes more important than 'whatever end' in question. Defining the *process* was essential for this person, but defining the specific goal was irrelevant. To understand this apparent oddity, it is necessary to understand that prefiguration renders the *process* and the goal inseparable; the *process* becomes the goal. Nevertheless, Alex Gordon's comment received a great deal of applause from others at the meeting, and he was not the only one to make comments about the irrelevance of *process*.[3]

Process and the Politics of a Unified Goal

On 11 October 2003, Alex Callinicos of the SWP and Project K wrote the following in an email:

> I've been reading the debate about the London Social Forum with some bemusement. Most of the discussions by focussing on process rather than substance, miss the point. The important question is: What is the politics of the London Social Forum? (email, Callinicos 2003)[4]

The reply to Alex's email was:

> What Alex doesn't seem to understand is that for many people, this movement is PRECISELY and primarily about process. The movement towards another world must be democratic, transparent and accessible, lest we become what we are fighting against. (email, Sellwood 2003, capital letters original)

As was pointed out in many email replies, Alex 'misses the point' with his statement in several ways. Although Alex's content-over-process position seems to be a minority opinion, it is significant because it exposes a link between two seemingly separate political positions. To fail to understand why a social forum has no single 'goal' is to misunderstand why the process is important. Alex says forget the process, and asks, what is the politics? He assumes the London Social Forum has, or should have, one particular politics. He asks this question in the context of extensive discussion about the spirit and the meaning of the social forum. The social forum, it was repeatedly stated, is one for which the 'central value' is that social fora do not have a platform, they do not take decisions, they do not have clearly defined politics – they are open spaces for people with many different kinds of politics to come together (around basic shared guidelines). Alex and many other movement actors from the traditional left, who favour political practices like setting up political parties to struggle for a communist revolution, do not value consensus decision-making over other methods. In fact, when the ESF did finally come to London there was a gradual but significant change in the connotation of the word 'consensus' due to the central role that the traditional left (the SWP, some trade unions and Socialist Action) and the London local authority (the GLA) played in the UKCC. During the Paris ESF 2003, consensus was used to refer to good process (even if it was not always achieved), but in London consensus almost became a four-letter word to be avoided. The traditional left political parties prefer to mobilise around a singular goal and this leads them to place less value on the idea of multiple goals and consequently to devalue the importance of *process* as a unifying element among people whose specific goals may differ. The important relationship being indirectly exposed here is that as the diversity of values and goals goes up, so does the importance of *process*; there is a direct relationship between valuing diversity and attention to *process*.

Practising Consensus

The consensus practised by the ESF organising process is not always prefigurative of less hierarchical, diverse democracy. In rhetoric about what the ESF is and should be, the intention to practise consensus is certainly present, but practice does not always follow rhetoric. At the EPA held in London on 13 December 2003, Claire of the trade union UNISON and the SWP, acting as chair, began the meeting as follows:

> The way we try and reach decisions is through consensus. We all need to be aware and to understand this. We hope to be able to have lots

of discussion and debate. Looking at our experience in the past, sharing our positive experiences from that. It is important for those of us from the UK to understand what we need to do to be able to organise a good social forum next year. Part of that will be about the process we use. Part of the discussion that will lead from that is that we do need to come to a consensus about where the next ESF will be held, and it is important because of the work that has to be done to set up networks to organise that. Part of the discussion was to look at how these meetings were organised in the past and how to work on that. That's for the working groups for this afternoon. Later on we're planning to bring everyone back together to share what was done during the working groups. Tomorrow, we'll have discussion about process and this morning there will be a discussion about that, particularly important for the UK Social Forums. We need to reach consensus on where the next European Assembly will be held. We want the maximum number of people to be able to participate. Are people happy with this?

The meeting that ensued was perhaps the worst example of consensus I have ever witnessed. The meeting that day concluded as follows:

Dave (Tobin Tax Network, co-chair with Claire): I am sorry to all who did not get a chance to speak, there is a plenary session tomorrow to discuss. I'll summarise the decision:
[He doesn't know what the decision is.]
Redmond O'Neill (Policy Director at the London mayor's office): I think the decision was to hold the ESF in London, however, not to make a final decision until March by which time financial aspects will have to be resolved.
Javier (Indymedia) asks again: What exactly are we deciding?
[Chaos]
Claire: We will have another general assembly meeting in March to make a decision. And if not London, see if there are any other viable possibilities. After that we will have to take a decision after that.
[Chaos]
Leo (Austrian SF): I support the proposal of Pierre and others. That in 2004 in Britain there will be the forum, however, I think it would be wise to have a worst case scenario in case we don't have the possibility to do the forum in UK. We should come with the possibility of discussion to have it take

place somewhere else. [unrest] We need the security that it will take place in one place or another. What are we going to do from here until the next meeting the first of March? Raise money is only one activity. We have to engage in a process reflection of how to build, to modify, to construct the ESF happening wherever it should happen at the time it should happen. The Austrian SF has been in charge for making a proposal for a process. We envision a process based on the different structures on a regional and national level that integrate ...

Claire interrupts: [to the crowd] Can we please be quiet?

Leo continues: There has been a proposal to structure this process in a way where people are sitting together in a way that people can make a proposal. [the microphone gets taken out of his hands by Dave]

Dave: I'm sorry you have to stop this. [referring to the noise and unrest in the room]

Sound technician: Interpreters have to leave now. They were only supposed to be here until 1.30 [it's after 3 p.m.].

Oscar (Red Pepper): There are too many people and problems.

Announcement: Artists against the war at clockhouse pub at 82 Leather Lane at 7 p.m. Comedy and music and booze.

Oscar: The situation is that we no longer have translation. We can discuss many of the issues raised in the workshops. That's the point on the agenda now.

[SUPER chaos]

[Mariangela of the LSF wants to speak and is trying to get the microphone from the chair, but is not succeeding. There is a mini queue of people wanting to speak behind her. She finally gets the microphone.]

Mariangela: There was no consensus!

[Some people are shouting: 'Sit down!']

[Sophie is given the microphone for a moment. But there is no translation and she speaks French. Lots of people are saying 'Shhh! Shhh! Shhh!' Finally there is a little less noise. Sophie throws her hands up in the air and shrugs as she passes the microphone back to Claire.]

Claire: It seems to me that the clear feeling of the meeting is that we have reached consensus.

[Cries from the floor: 'No we did not ever reach consensus!']

Sophie: I suggest that until the first of March we leave for UK to find a solution, but we don't have a solution for after. We wait until the first of

March to see if it is London or not or 2004 or not. I think right now it is not very useful to have a working group because it is not very useful for the Europeans. It is not useful for us. What would be useful would be have a discussion on process and mobilisation, because tomorrow will not be enough. Let's stop this discussion and now have another discussion about mobilisation and the proposal that the German people have to explain.

Oscar: I suggest taking one person to voice the objection to the consensus.

Mariangela: My proposal is that there is no consensus on ESF London. We are going to explore what other possibilities. This finding the place is not a matter of a person or one group taking the responsibility, all the groups take this responsibility for exploring other possibilities. If on the first of March there is no agreement, we go for 2005.

Hilary (Red Pepper, Transnational Institute): We actually have a consensus, if we're serious about making it work we should get into our working groups.

[claps]

Oscar: There is a lot to be discussed and we don't have …

[Major chaos breaks out. Oscar can't finish his sentences.]

Oscar: The workshops are as follows: room one: enlargement mobilisation; room two: discussion on cultural issues; room three: practicalities discussion; room four: working group about process. Can we now proceed with that? [people start to move] We will start again tomorrow with the report-backs on the WGs.

I include these notes in full because they demonstrate the way misunderstandings of consensus are exhibited and the consequent problems. It also provides (I hope) a sense of what it feels like to be in a meeting that is going nowhere quickly. Many activists refer to this kind of consensus as 'forced consensus' and consider it a violation of the principles of the social forum. To be fair, the ideals of consensus are very hard to prefigure, and there is no section of this movement that I have seen which can employ consensus perfectly in all situations. The ESF, however, struggles more than autonomous networks because the consensus process is being used by actors who are unfamiliar with it, and are instead familiar with hierarchical organising methods. When consensus is practised through the structures of the traditional left, which value long inspirational orations and competitive debating styles, it becomes somewhat unrecognisable. This strange mix of meeting practices exposes the social forum process to Freeman's (1970) famous 'Tyranny of Structurelessness'. Many of the people who are involved in the autonomous sections of the anti-summit mobilisations also have little experience with consensus when they first arrive, but the emphasis placed on 'skill shares' and the explanation that accompanies consensus meetings in these networks compensate for this lack of experience.

What is most interesting about the process debate, however, is not that process became centrally important, but *why* process became so important. The reasons why so many movement actors made process a central concern was because of the way the bid was put together. Because the organising process was initiated by the SWP and was focused on getting the approval of the GLA, the combination of the instrumental attitude of the SWP and the technocratic approach of the GLA and both organisations' lack of interest in consensus meant that process was not a central concern in the bid for a London ESF. Overlooking process, however, was the biggest strategic mistake made by the bid group and process quickly became one of, if not *the* hottest issue in the debate about the location of the next ESF. For this and many other reasons the bid process was perceived by many movement actors to be 'exclusive', 'undemocratic', 'elitist' and 'untransparent':

> The process to bring the ESF to the UK was completely undemocratic, untransparent and many NGOs, unions and social movements were being treated disrespectfully by the bidders ... The Process for organizing the ESF would be deeply undemocratic, given how the process to bring the ESF to the UK was proceeding: secret meetings, exclusion of groups seen as politically undesirable or not 'important' enough, creation of a small committee to take decisions ... The process to organize the ESF in the UK would be dominated by the authoritarian left. (Horizontals 2004)

The connection made here between the bid process, the organising process and the ESF itself, shows the extent to which prefiguration was taken for granted. The means used to 'win' the right to host an

ESF were as important as the end itself. For some, the means were more important than the end, with many arguing that they would rather not have an ESF in the UK at all than see one organised in this way. This assumption of prefiguration was so misunderstood by the bid group that when these concerns were raised they would get frustrated by these off-topic comments and impatiently reply: 'But right now we are just putting together the bid!'

Those excluded from the bid group took the telling step of calling themselves the 'horizontals'. All those at the heart of the UKCC (the SWP, several trade unions and especially the GLA) were, in turn, dubbed the 'verticals'. It is in the allocation of these titles that we get to the heart of the debate about process. The horizontals opposed the way the London ESF was being organised because it was organised in an 'exclusive and centralised' way, which created a strong hierarchy of power between those on the 'inside' and those on the 'outside'. This centralisation and consequent hierarchy and exclusion were felt to undermine consensus decision-making. The horizontals demanded that:

> All bodies of the ESF process should from now on meet in public, be open to observers, advertise their meetings, agenda items and resolutions in advance and provide full minutes on a website for all to see. They should also operate by consensus decision-making processes and have rotating chairs/facilitators. (Horizontals 2003)

However, the word 'consensus' was abstract and many were confused because they felt they were already using consensus. Pierre Khalfa of ATTAC France equated process and consensus, seemingly supporting this position, but he did so in the interest of setting goals beyond process:

> The ESF should become a continuous process, not only an event. We must create a process of collective decision-making and move on to a new level. What goals? What priorities? All of this must be decided by consensus. (18 December 2004, EPA, Montreuil)

The agreement one would assume from the common language used can be deceiving. Even the interpretation of 'open' differs vastly from one corner to the next. Chris Nineham, one of the main organisers within the bid group argued at the London EPA:

> Openness is a principle of the ESF. We need to have a much bigger assembly in January that continues to enlarge the process. It is not just about how we organise, in fact I don't think it is mainly about how we organise. I think it is about making it accessible to all the people who have been mobilised over the past few years. That's not mainly about process. We need to make sure that everyone is clear it is against racism, war and against neoliberalism. The second thing is to actively go out and talk to the trade union and the peace movements, the Muslim community ... Crucially, to go to the trade unions, these organisations have money and we need money. (13 December 2003)

Here we have 'openness' being defined as outreach and enlarging the assembly – as making more people present, it is 'not about process'. Horizontals on the other hand are talking about structures of decision-making that make it possible to have more people be present *and* actively involved, starting with those who are already present, but feel excluded. The result is three different positions towards consensus and process. While the horizontals were pushing for a process-oriented consensus, the key figures in the international ESF mobilisation were desperately trying to implement some form of a decision-oriented consensus and some of the key UK figures were doing their best to circumnavigate consensus all together.

Despite these imperfections, the ESF and WSF are the ultimate examples of the increased importance of process in the alterglobalisation movement. Considering that many of the actors central to the ESF and WSF are members of political parties, trade unions or other ends-oriented mainstream organisations like ATTAC, or all of the above, it is notable that questions of process and prefiguration still define the agenda. Prefigurative politics has been common to anarchist struggles and played a role in the movements of the 1960s and 1970s, but it has not often been a central value of traditional left political parties or trade unions. In the decision process for the location of the ESF 2004, those who spoke most about the importance of process were not the anarchists, but Italian and French (and certain British) communists and NGOs.

At the EPA on 13 December 2003, Luciano Muhlbauer, in his capacity as a representative from the Italian Organising Committee of the 2002 Florence ESF, commented on learning from past ESFs and whether the next ESF should be in the UK:

> The ESF is a process, not event ... If we look to this as a process, methodology is the most important thing. Our experience in Florence, we had no model, we had no experience. The problem we have in a process is not the presentation but is involving and enlarging the network. That means that we need an open process, not closed structures. Open assemblies, open everything. This is not only more democratic, but more efficient.

Anne Shane from the Communist Party of Great Britain echoed Luciano's point about process:

> I agree with Luciano, we need to think about process. I think this is a very important question for us. Not just an event, but a process. In light of the EU constitution, we need to think about what kind of Europe we are for.

Here we have a communist arguing that thinking about an ongoing process is thinking about 'what we are for'. And Luciano tells us that process is about methodology and about being open and inclusive, about creating structures which are not closed. For Luciano, process is essential to being more democratic.

The concern several social forum actors had that there was not enough time spent talking about the 'real issues' because there was too much time spent on process, shows that there are nevertheless actors involved in the social forum for whom the process is not a goal in and of itself. These comments, however, have little to no effect on reducing the amount of discussion that occurs about process. In fact, the power of process is that the more it is opposed, the more process becomes a central issue. Those who advocate process are also understood to have the Charter of Principles behind them. They feel the basic principles of the social forum have been violated whenever the process is undervalued, and when key players argue that process is not important, it proves their point for them.

Anti-summit Mobilisations

The prefiguration of horizontality is nowhere more central than in autonomous sections of the anti-summit mobilisations:

> Our practical response forms part of our political response. Trying to demonstrate in ways that form the way we'd like to see society. That's why Globalise Resistance has marches, because they, like, don't think that people should be actively involved. (South East Assembly meeting, 28 May 2005)

> Until we know what the local groups that want to be a part of this group are actually prioritising, then we can't decide what to take on. Having a process of discussion, well-publicised, fluid discussion that all groups are invited to, a process of consultation about what sort of network we want and what issues. Create some common analysis from that, it will be much more rooted and much more sustainable than the way we have been working. If we conceptualise it as another process of engagement with people more generally, then I think that will create a much stronger process. (Dissent! national gathering, Sheffield, 15 October 2005)

It is within the organising process for the mass mobilisations that prefiguration takes on a level of intention it does not have in the social forum process. This is partly due to the different political backgrounds of the actors involved, and partly due to the overall organising structure. While a social forum is a singular official event, organised centrally through committees and limited by physical spatial boundaries, the anti-summits mobilisations are organised simultaneously by different groups who organise in parallel to each other but only partially with each other. This means that the various strands of political beliefs can function side by side without all of them having to come together or agree on a common methodological approach. Although coalitions and networks are set up which bring many groups together, there is no singular overarching organising committee. The result is that movement actors divide themselves up into various groups along the lines of their own political beliefs. For the Dissent! network prefiguration was a central element, but for the G8 Alternatives network (run by the SWP) and the 'Make Poverty History' coalition of rock stars, NGOs and politicians, horizontal prefiguration was irrelevant. Horizontality is a defining aspect of the collective spaces of the alterglobalisation movement, but as we have seen in the social forum discussion above, horizontality suffers from an inequality of degree and it is far more prevalent in autonomous networks. Horizontality is the subject of the next chapter, but to understand prefiguration, we need to look at some of the precedents to the alterglobalisation movement's practice of horizontal prefiguration.

The Movement's Heart and Soul

Many authors have already made the case that the alter-globalisation movement is strongly anarchic by demonstrating the prevalence of some basic anarchist principles and practices within the movement.[5] In their introduction to the journal *Anarchist Studies*, Welsh and Purkis (2003: 5) write:

> The idea of a special edition addressing the relationship between contemporary anarchist theory and practice – 'anarchist praxis' – seemed timely given the highly visible upsurge in actions bearing the hallmarks of anarchism ... The appearance of the so-called Anti-Globalisation Movement on the world stage, represented several years of hard network building linking displaced indigenous cultures, casualised workforces, environmental campaigners, anti-militarists and hi-tech cyber activists ... given the proactive and prefigurative constituency, we prefer to call [it] the 'Alternative Globalisation Movement'.

Graeber (2002: 62) writes:

> with its rejection of a politics which appeals to governments to modify their behaviour, in favour of physical intervention against state power in a form that itself prefigures an alternative – all of this emerges directly from the libertarian tradition. Anarchism is the heart of the movement, its soul; the source of most of what's new and hopeful about it.

My fieldwork supports this position. Even in spheres of the movement where the traditional left political parties hold power they are often still confined in the use and abuse of that power by a political practice or structure that could be considered anarchic, and are repeatedly caught debating questions that would 'traditionally' be considered anarchist questions – like *process*. It is not my aim here to establish the alterglobalisation movement as an anarchist movement, but it is highly significant that notions of hierarchy and non-hierarchy are at the heart of this movement's shared practices, and are essential to understanding the world they are prefiguring and the democratic praxis they are developing.

Prefigurative politics is closely linked to anarchism and is often considered to be one of the defining characteristics of anarchist praxis (Bakunin 1984, Bowen and Purkis 2004, Epstein 2001, Franks 2003, Graeber 2002, Graeber and Grubacic 2004, Grubacic 2003, May 1994, Morland 2004, Mueller 2001). However, while prefiguration is often acknowledged to be one of the defining principles of anarchism, it is not confined solely to the domain of anarchism. Prefiguration can of course be practised by any sort of movement and is certainly practised by movements across the political spectrum.[6] The ends that are prefigured are essential to determining whether the act of prefiguration is anarchic or not. Even though many right-wing movements have used means that were consistent with their ends, what distinguishes these movements and their prefiguration from anarchic prefiguration is their use of hierarchical structures. Prefiguration is anarchic when the means and ends being used/enacted are self-consciously non-hierarchical (Franks 2003: 26). Or, in practice, when they are attempting to be as non-hierarchical as possible.

This definition of anarchic prefiguration is a second-order interpretation of movement activity and does not imply that actors themselves would understand their practices in this way. Although most self-proclaimed anarchists favour non-hierarchical processes, not everyone who favours these processes is a self-proclaimed anarchist. In fact, even in social movements where the means and ends are intentionally as non-hierarchical as possible, there is not always a self-awareness on the part of the actors that they are engaging in a practice of anarchist prefiguration. And even where the actors do consider themselves anarchist there is not necessarily any consistency between what the various actors consider 'anarchism' to be. When writing about 'anarchism', it seems to be a near universal practice to add the preamble that if such a thing exists, it exists only in the plural form. As Franks (2003: 18) succinctly puts it, 'some ... have contemplated surrender at the prospect of covering such a multitude of incompatible definitions and practices by a single term'.

The idea of social change coming about only through the agent of change him/herself becoming an embodiment of this change is as old as time. So how did the practice of prefiguration come to be considered a basic principle of anarchist praxis today? Looking at the history of anarchist praxis does not provide a very clear answer to this question. Indeed, much of anarchist history could be more accurately characterised by the motto, 'By any means necessary!' rather than, 'Only means which are an embodiment of our ideals!' Certainly the first makes for a far more catchy slogan, but looking at only one of these perspectives would provide a skewed sense of what anarchist praxis has entailed over the years.[7]

Let me begin in classical style by mentioning a famous white man, Bakunin, who, despite being labelled the anarchist thinker who is 'more than anyone else responsible for the violent and menacing shadow of anarchism' (Marshall 1992: 631), considered prefiguration to be the defining distinction between anarchism and orthodox Marxism. "How could one want an equalitarian and free society to issue from authoritarian organisation? It is impossible"' (in Franks 2003: 19). But Bakunin (and Proudhon as well) still saw society as a pyramid and maintained a system of representation. It was only post-Bakunin that 'most anarchists have envisaged the whole social organization as a network' (Marshall 1992: 629). In terms of praxis, however, which is the only place one can really look for prefiguration, there are a number of clear instances of prefigurative praxis within the anarchist tradition. Perhaps the most famous examples derive from the Spanish anarchists, who practised prefigurative politics during the Spanish civil war. But there have been many instances of prefigurative politics since then. Under the influence of actors such as Gandhi and Tolstoy, anarchist praxis placed more emphasis on non-violence, resulting in the rise of an explicitly pacifist anarchism. Although pacifist anarchism did not result in the exclusion of other strands of anarchist praxis, the rise of pacifist anarchism had an influence in practical terms on the centrality of prefigurative politics within the movements of the 1960s, 1970s and 1980s, particularly in the centrality of strategic non-violence to feminist, environmental, anti-nuclear and peace movements, and, as we have already seen, these movements played a crucial role in the formation of the alterglobalisation movement.

Prefiguration as a Strategic Practice

Prefiguration versus Consequentialism

In order to explain prefiguration, Franks (2003: 13) sets prefiguration up in contrast to consequentialist and deontological approaches: 'prefiguration distinguishes direct action from both Leninist consequentialism and the deontological approaches of liberal and anarcho-capitalist traditions'. In Franks' analysis, prefiguration is considered as distinct from consequentialism and deontological approaches because the former declares that only the ends, the consequences of an act, matter,[8] while the latter privileges the means over the ends. Prefiguration, on the other hand, is aimed at the conflation of means and ends. Prefiguration holds the ends to be equally important as the means, and has as its intention (over time, or momentarily) to render them indistinguishable. Prefiguration, therefore, is an approach that neither ignores the consequences of an action, nor does it emphasise the importance of a consequence regardless of the means used. Activists are invariably highly concerned that their actions should have concrete consequences, but this concern does not preclude them from elevating the means to a level of strategic importance.

Marxist approaches to social change have often been understood as consequentialist, and partly for this reason, prefiguration as an anarchist praxis is often set up in contrast to consequentialism.

Franks (2003: 20) compares prefiguration specifically to *Leninist* consequentialism in which 'actions are judged by whether they assist or hinder the revolutionary goal'. People, he writes, are judged along these lines as well:

> Consequentialist methods ... undermine the autonomy of subjugated groups. Paternalistic socialism predetermines the objectives and imposes these ends onto the already subjugated classes. The client class, in Lenin's case, the proletariat, becomes the instrument to reach the desired end.

This type of consequentialism is being rejected by alterglobalisation movement actors because of the central importance of participatory democracy, horizontality and autonomy, as well as the sheer diversity of goals, which makes a purely ends-oriented approach impossible. For many movement actors, the imperative of participation necessitates that the objectives not be predetermined so that actors can participate in the process of *determining* the ends as well as the means. This is the fundamental difference that underscored the conflict about process in the organisation of the London ESF. The bid group was enacting a theory of social change in which the ends justified the means, and the means were small closed meetings intended to simplify the bid process, while others insisted that the ends and means come together, and consequently they felt betrayed and disenfranchised. The small unannounced meetings represented a process that was exclusive and non-participatory and therefore not a prefiguration of the social forum's values.

Here we have a clear example of how a rejection of pure consequentialism (the privileging of the ends to the *complete* exclusion of the means) should not be misunderstood as a rejection of consequences. It is precisely the negative consequences of these small meetings (that they lead to exclusion and undermine forum values of openness and horizontality) that led movement actors to insist on the need for prefiguration. The assumption underlying prefiguration is that means are important *because* they have consequences and because they are consequences. A rejection of consequentialism does not imply that the consequences of an action or practice have no significance. The point is, rather, that prefiguration is a practice that assumes the ends and the means to be inextricably linked, where the means are the result of past ends and result in future ends, and therefore prefiguration rejects a focus on either means or ends to the exclusion of the other.

Tactical versus Strategic Theory

Understanding prefiguration as part of wider movement processes that are neither consequentialist nor deontological, but nevertheless goal-oriented, requires that we reconsider another common dichotomy – that between prefiguration and strategy. Below I argue that, based on different types of movement goals, prefiguration can be understood as a strategic practice. But before embarking on this analysis, it is necessary first to present the argument that prefiguration is not strategic. Epstein (1991: 18) argues that the direct action movement rejects strategy in favour of prefiguring a cultural revolution:

> the direct action movement's rejection of strategy is an expression of a much broader political and intellectual current. The attraction to cultural revolution, and the idea that culture is a substitute for strategy, has been an important current in the movements of the sixties and beyond.

By cultural revolution Epstein (1991: 16) means that societal change would not be confined to the economic and political realm, but it would be 'a broad redefinition of social values'. She is less supportive of this 'a-strategic' approach, however, and concludes:

> the postmodernist spirit, which has become dominant among intellectuals on the left, involves an appreciation of many qualities of the direct action movement … But it reinforces the movement's most crippling weaknesses, it's avoidance of strategy and its disdain for lasting organisational structure. (Epstein 1991: 19)

Here Epstein is conflating lasting organisational structure and strategy in a way that is reminiscent of 1960s and 1970s movements. Polletta (2002: 6) describes this tension between strategy and prefiguration as the main dilemma faced by the

New Left: 'To be "strategic" was to privilege organisation over personhood and political reform over radical change.' Although Polletta ultimately argues that 1960s movements were strategic, she points out that prefiguration could not be considered strategic in a political context where definitions of 'strategic' and 'organised' were still being determined by the traditional left politics of communism and socialism. The challenge that faced movement actors in the 1960s was to transform the definition of 'organised', and consequently of 'strategic', so that prefiguration could be understood as strategic.

It is not clear, however, that they succeeded in transforming these definitions. Indeed, the analysis which posits prefiguration as the opposite of strategic, although often challenged, still remains with us and it re-emerges in the more recent work of Todd May. May's (1994: 10) arguments rest on a distinction between strategic and tactical political philosophy:

> One of the characteristics which binds various strategic political philosophies together, and which distinguishes them from tactical political philosophy is that a strategic political philosophy involves a unitary analysis that aims towards a single goal.

A strategic political philosophy will have a 'core or base problematic'. May (1994: 11) offers the example of Marxism, for which the core problematic is economics. What matters, though, is not the content of the core, but rather:

> the fact that thinking proceeds concentrically. This is what distinguishes it from tactical thinking, which pictures the social and the political world not as a circle but instead as an intersecting network of lines.

This is significant because if there is a core where power is concentrated, May argues, then there is the possibility that there will be people who are 'particularly well placed to analyze and to lead the resistance' (1994: 11). Strategic and tactical philosophies envision power differently. He argues that social anarchists apply a strategic philosophy when their notion of power is such that they understand power to be centralised and the decentralisation thereof to be the strategy through which one turns power exploitation into benign forms of power. If the philosophy of power is such that power is perceived to be multifarious, the result is an anarchist approach much more grounded in praxis and therefore more tactical than strategic.

If we accept this division, then we must place the alterglobalisation movement into the category of tactical rather than strategic, because there is no clear central problematic and, as we shall see in the next chapter, many actors perceive power to be multifarious (although they also understand it to be centralised). However, in my opinion, May does not provide enough of an argument for the elision he makes between the lack of a singular central problematic, the multifarious interpretation of power, and a lack of strategy. Why, for example, does strategy necessarily have to be singular? Why does it have to have a core? What leads him to construct a framework within which strategy has to be a process towards a centralised goal?[9]

Epstein (1991) argues that the movements of the 1960s were prefigurative and therefore a-strategic, setting up an oppositional relationship between prefiguration and strategy. Breines (1989: 49) makes the same distinction by arguing that 'The creation of non-violent social structures within PMOs may be characterised as "prefigurative" politics, as opposed to "strategic" politics' and that '[b]eing realistic was associated with traditional politics, with instrumentality and organisational strategy'. Here Breines equates traditional politics, instrumentality and strategy. Breines (1989: 50) argues that the development of prefigurative politics represented a questioning of instrumental rationality. Although she argues, in contrast to Epstein above, that the movements of the 1960s were not a-strategic, she sees prefiguration and strategic politics as parallel processes:

> alongside the new left's prefigurative impulse was what I have called *strategic politics*, which was committed to building organization in order to achieve major structural changes in the political, economic and social orders. (Breines 1989: 7)

For Breines, strategy involves organisation towards major structural change. For the movements of the 1960s and 1970s, this relationship between organisation and strategy may have been problematic for the prefiguration of non-hierarchical participatory democracy because these movements were entangled in the structures of the 'old' left, for whom organisation *did* mean hierarchy, control and instrumentality. Today this is no longer the case. The traditional left politics is still present, but rather than dictating what constitutes politics, it now tiptoes around the politics of process. The entire debate on process is about getting organised – it is about setting up and using structures of decision-making to organise the other world desired right here, right now. For Breines the 1960s movements were strategic despite being prefigurative, while today the movement is strategic at least partially *because* it is prefigurative. Derrida (1982) argues that 'Strategy orients tactics according to a final goal', and prefiguration is an orientation of the means to the ends, of the tactics to the goals. But this is merely a game with the meaning of a word, which can be filled and refilled to our heart's desire. It does not mean very much to imagine how we *could* define strategy; what does matter is how strategy *is being* defined in the practices of this movement. What constitutes strategy is important for our understanding of movement goals, and this tension between prefiguration and strategy must be resolved.

May argues that decentralised practices are not strategic; Epstein argues prefiguration is not strategic and Breines agrees, but argues that even these prefigurative movements are strategic because prefigurative politics is never used in isolation of other political practices. Finally, Franks (2003: 29), drawing on May (1994), concludes that:

> The rejection of strategy means the refusal of a singular, central problematic whose successful outcome resolves all problems. For tactical politics, there is no central location of power, but different oppressions operate in different forms. These might require longer term, prefigurative methods to overcome.

Perhaps a rejection of strategy means no singular goal, but does a rejection of a singular goal therefore mean no strategy? There is certainly a rejection of a singular, central problematic in the alterglobalisation movement. Still, there seems to be a very clear strategy for social change in place. Fundamentally, strategy in a social movement, however it is defined, is about *how* to create a desired effect. Strategy is a process employed to achieve a certain goal. I have argued throughout this chapter that the prefiguration this movement practices is primarily concerned with questions of *how*. It is not a prefiguration of an ideal society or type of community or abstract political ideology; it is a prefiguration of a *process*, a prefiguration of a horizontal decentralised democracy, which is at once a goal and a current practice of the movement.

Bringing Goals to Life

How movement goals are constituted will of course affect whether practices can be considered strategic. The prefiguration of horizontal democracy is only one among many prefigurations being practised by the alterglobalisation movement and it only represents a small portion of movement activity. While decentralised horizontal democracy is a means and an end in the collective spaces of movement activity, it only represents one of many overlapping unities. In order to understand the role prefiguration plays as a strategic practice, it is necessary to elaborate on the different types of goals that movement actors hold. Social movement goals function on (at least) three different levels. A movement actor may have an ultimate goal (for example, overthrowing capitalism) that is long term and hard to achieve. As part of the struggle towards that goal, she will set up smaller, more immediate goals (like shutting down the WTO). The third type of goal is also a long-term goal, but it is a long-term goal that is realisable to a certain degree in the present (such as the construction of an environmentally sustainable, horizontally organised community).[10] The pursuit of each of these goal types requires different tactics and strategies at various times across contexts. Nevertheless, these three goals are intricately linked; shutting down the WTO is seen as part of overthrowing capitalism, and overthrowing capitalism would have little significance if there were no alternative structures to take its place. Prefiguration exists in some form within the pursuit of all three types of goals, but is a particularly appropriate strategy for the attainment of the third type of goal. Strategies developed towards a short-term goal such as the shutting down of a G8 summit might not be primarily concerned with the prefiguration of horizontality, but there is nevertheless an element of this prefiguration within the structures used to make decisions about which strategy would be best. Short-term goals are linked to long-term goals through the process of prefiguration, where actions taken to achieve an immediate goal incorporate long-term goals. Consequently, prefiguration is a movement practice that exists neither instead of strategy nor alongside strategy as Breines argues above, but depending on which type of goal, can be considered to be strategic in itself because it constitutes a link between different movement goals and allows for the expression and construction of the crucially important movement goal of 'another world'.

Prefiguration cannot function alone, however, because it is not equally suited to all three types of movement goals. Prefiguration cannot replace other movement practices that centre on immediate concrete goals. As Bey (1990) writes about the Temporary Autonomous Zone (TAZ):

> The TAZ is like an uprising which does not engage directly with the State, a guerilla operation which liberates an area (of land, of time, of imagination) and then dissolves itself to re-form elsewhere/elsewhen, *before* the State can crush it.

Prefiguration is the ideal strategy for the construction of an alternative world without engaging with the state or other powers that be, but movement practice must also incorporate a confrontation with these powers, which cannot always be prefigurative. The adivasis in the Narmada valley, for example, are not primarily concerned with prefiguration or process when they are stood knee-deep in flood waters defending what is left of their homes. For many of the adivasis, the most strategic action will not include horizontal prefiguration. The same holds true for autonomous networks who are trying to organise decentralised blockades. In the case of these networks, however, even while planning a confrontation with power through elaborate blockades, movement actors acknowledged the importance of prefiguration and, for many of them, the chance to mobilise around the G8 and have thousands of people live together in a camp in a horizontally democratic way and to experience a society that functions along the lines of their ideals, was more important than shutting down the G8:

> For me, it's not so important what happens at the summit, but more what we create, how we organise. The ecovillage will become a model of how we want to organise our world ourselves, a new way of working together ... This network was about anti-capitalism, anti-state and about taking control of our own lives and creating alternatives. (South East Assembly [SEA] meeting, London, 28 May 2005)

Here prefiguration takes on an instrumental dimension; it is strategic because it is the best means to achieve the end of taking back control and learning to organise the world differently. As one activist put it, 'we do not just prefigure, but we hope that "exemplaric practice" works in the sense of other people being convinced or taking these practices over'. Prefiguration cannot be seen as distinct from or supplementary to strategy because it constitutes a strategy towards certain types of goals. Moreover, this distinction between prefiguration and strategy becomes more abstract once we leave the realm of analysis and return to meetings, streets and discussions of the movement actors themselves, where it becomes very hard to distinguish between 'strategy' and 'tactics', and actors often refer to their 'tactical' and prefigurative practices as 'strategic'.

Nevertheless, raising and challenging this distinction between strategy and prefiguration, and May's distinction between tactical and strategic philosophies (where prefiguration is the methodology belonging to tactical philosophies), remains important because, if we define strategy as necessarily having a singular goal, then there can be no discussion of strategy within the alterglobalisation movement. And yet, when one looks at the movement practices one sees that these discussions are pervasive. The influence of 'strategic' post-structuralist philosophy that May points to cannot be denied, but it can often be overstated. The conclusion he draws about strategy holds important insights, but we cannot conclude that there is therefore no strategy in the alterglobalisation movement (or only a post-structuralist strategy). If one looks for strategy from the point of view of purely consequentialist strategy, then the strategic practices of the movement will be obscured if not obviated. The strategy of this movement is no longer cloaked in the language of consequentialist revolutionary strategy. Instead there is a prefigurative strategy that is more concerned with creating than predicting, practising over theorising. These rejected dreams of revolution belonged to theories of social change that rested on what Nunes (2005: 314) calls 'linear accumulation':

> The difference between networked politics and previous forms of political organisation is that it places *non-linear connection* above *linear accumulation.*

Linear accumulation is based on bringing more and more people to the 'cause' until a moment is reached when 'there are enough of them to storm the Winter Palace'. Nunes (2005: 314) argues that this vision of social change has been abandoned in favour of non-linear connection:

> What was given up with the idea of linear accumulation was the idea that there is a goal. Once you have a goal that can be identified with achieving an action – taking the state apparatus and using it to promote the 'transition to communism' – and this goal is identified as the completion of the entire process, you enter into the realm of linearity: history marches towards an end, and the role of the 'revolutionary' is to speed it up.

The linear view of social change as a march forward towards an end in the future is incompatible with prefigurative politics.[11] It is highly significant how little talk there is in this movement about revolution. Movement actors speak of bringing about major social changes that would certainly constitute a revolution, and they speak of 'revolution' in a general sense, but they do not speak of a revolutionary moment. Perhaps one of the successes of the movements of the 1960s and the 1970s, whether we understand them as strategic or not, was to purge the strategic question in its consequentialist form so that alternatives (to traditional socialist/ communist) movement practices could arise and create a space within which strategy could be reborn in a prefigurative form.

This 'new sort of politics' allows for movement goals to be living, changing entities because they are repeatedly brought to life each time in a different form. Even the imperfection of prefiguration described in this chapter is not a fault; it indicates an ongoing process. Actors find themselves in a problematic, conflictive space that is a part of the process of constructing their values/goals/ideals. I explore these horizontal structures, diversity and the creation of conflictive space further in the next chapter.

3

CREATING CONFLICTIVE SPACES

In a world of diversity, consensus is oppression.

Consensus is Oppression

The above quote was written on the wall of a squatted autonomous social centre in Spain. When I first read it, I was very confused. Consensus is oppression? Everything else I had seen about the alterglobalisation movement said to me that consensus was considered liberating, not oppressive. At first I dismissed it as just another incoherent message written on the walls, but as I started to understand the double meaning consensus had for many movement actors, I realised what an incredibly profound statement this was. I had often heard people say they felt consensus was not always the best decision-making process because it required 'compromise' and 'unanimity', but due to my own familiarity with the consensus process, I had dismissed these comments as examples of movement actors misunderstanding consensus. The only significance I gave these comments was as an indication that the movement still had a lot of work to do in terms of using, improving and disseminating consensus. This conclusion was correct, but not very inquisitive. I did not consider that the way consensus was practised might give it a double meaning that was internally inconsistent. Although in theory consensus does not require unanimity to be achieved, in practice this is often how it is interpreted and sometimes consensus is even forced by the actors themselves to become unanimous. I knew this, I had seen it happen, but still I dismissed these 'incorrect' consensus processes rather than thinking about the consequences they

consensus is forced unanimity.

might have for the way movement actors view both consensus and diversity. Because I presumed to *know* that consensus does not necessarily imply compromise or unanimity, I never stopped to ask myself, why are these people so worried about compromise and unanimity?

It was not until I realised I was repeatedly hearing another word, that the full significance of this question was clear to me. At some point during my fieldwork, the word *conflictive* started popping up everywhere. When people explained what they were doing and why, they said they were creating 'conflictive spaces'. Consensus, it was even said, should be conflictive. Consensus was functioning in two very different forms and one form was heavily preferred over the other. Insistence on conflict was an attempt to create a consensus process that allowed for diversity, a consensus that did not insist on unanimity.

Conflict is welcomed because it represents diversity. Out of diversity comes creativity and creation. This transformation of conflict from adversarial to constructive takes place through horizontality. Horizontality acts as a guiding ethos and practice to actively limit hierarchies to allow diversity to remain constructive. Although many values and goals are expressed by movement actors, 'diversity' is agreed upon by nearly all actors from the anarchists to the political parties and the large NGOs. Having placed creation of diversity at the heart of their decision-making practices, movement actors are constructing democratic structures that radically challenge representative democratic practices geared towards unanimity or homogeneity. These democratic structures are the subject of the next chapter, but before we can discuss these structures, both horizontality and diversity and their relationship to each other, to power and to conflict must be explored.

Diversity is unavoidable, especially in a globalised world, but diversity leads to difference of opinion and sometimes conflict. Democracy has long been about trying to resolve this basic paradox. The alterglobalisation movement actors, rather than denying or suppressing conflict, and rather than assuming that conflict is necessarily competitive and dangerous, assume that one can have constructive conflict without competition. In this chapter

I present some activist definitions of horizontality and explore the assumptions about power that make horizontality both possible and desirable for movement actors. I argue that movement actors have highly fluid and context-specific approaches to power, but that three of these approaches are particularly relevant in relation to horizontality – power as centralised hierarchy, power as decentralised hierarchy and power as decentralised non-hierarchy. I then bring diversity into the equation to examine what happens to unity when diversity is practised horizontally. I begin this exploration by looking at the way conflict is understood and resolved in different movement contexts.

Conflict

> Intense struggles over political vision, tactics and organisational form are not cause for alarm; indeed, they are constitutive of the convergence process that characterises the forums and the broader movement from which they emerged. (Juris 2004)

From diversity comes conflict. This is not a fault, but an opportunity. Through the creation of procedures that resolve conflict in a non-adversarial manner, conflict becomes a source of creative energy and ideas. Advocating a conflictive space transforms the notion of conflict from an impasse between two competing viewpoints to an opportunity to express, accept and create difference. Recasting conflict as constructive rather than adversarial has implications for how conflict is resolved. Differences of opinion are not meant to be resolved by placing them against each other in a may-the-best-man-win scenario:

> We must be able to look at the dissonances and disagreements and see in them not the opportunity to win an argument, but a problem to acknowledge and to take on board, a challenge for imaginative common ways forward. (email, De Angelis 2003a)

One of the main principles of consensus is that no one should win and no one should lose an argument. Instead the aim is to brainstorm until a solution can be found that suits everyone. The movement's conflictive process rests upon the assumption that there are no predetermined 'right' answers to any given problem, but rather that answers and solutions, that knowledge, is constructed, and it is constructed best when constructed collectively. Conflict, however, does not naturally become constructive. Most people are used to treating conflict as undesirable and are used to resorting to competitive means when their opinion, interests, ideas, desires come into conflict. Making conflict constructive is an active and intentional process and is not always a smooth one.

Resolving and Avoiding Conflict

Constructive conflict does not necessarily require that conflict be resolved. Whenever it is possible to resolve a conflict through creative means that do not result in one position winning at the expense of the other, the resolution of conflict is certainly encouraged, but at times this type of resolution is neither possible nor necessary. In practice, conflict is often neither resolved nor unresolved and, at times, the appearance of conflict resolution merely masks the escalation of conflict. This becomes clear when we examine some of the mechanisms in place for resolving conflict in the alterglobalisation movement. At the level of daily movement practices, conflict is often resolved and avoided by placing discussions within frameworks that make agreement more plausible. As we saw in the previous chapter, at the ESF planning meetings and discussions, especially the EPA, there is a great deal of abstract language used without agreement on the particular meanings these abstract words hold. In this way, there can be agreement between political parties, trade unions, anarchists and NGOs because they all desire 'democracy', 'openness' and 'transparency' even though they all mean quite different things when they invoke these words. The unity created around these abstract concepts is very important, but the moment these terms are given concrete meanings divisions arise. This becomes a political problem when combined with unequal power relationships. Under these circumstances, abstract language creates an 'exclusion of conflict' that is resented by many movement actors. Actors who tried to address these differences of interpretation (to bring the conflict back into the process) were often accused of not being 'serious' about the social forum and silenced in favour of a focus on the ends over the means:

> The [ESF] process had been successful in eliminating all conflict under a patina of forced consensus; the result wasn't convergence, but a feeling of back-slapping hollowness. (Nunes 2004: 3)[1]

The ESF organising process was perceived to exclude conflict and this exclusion was experienced by actors as severely negative, even as a violation of fundamental principles of the social forum:

> If Fora will be capable of expressing the diversity of the movement(s) they say to bring together and serve as a public arena, it'll be because of their capacity to incorporate conflict, not to subsume it under a semblance of false consensus. (Nunes 2004: 8)

The Dissent! network also framed discussions to avoid conflict, sometimes even excluding certain types of discussions entirely. However, in contrast to the WSF and ESF, these preparatory meetings were often marked by an avoidance of abstract language and ideological debates. In the Dissent! meetings leading up to the G8 protests in Scotland (and meetings in the US the year before), there was an intentional avoidance of any network-wide discussions on the politics of the G8 and especially any discussion about philosophy or social change beyond the G8.[2] The aim was, as one activist put it, 'consensus about the task at hand, not consensus about everything'.

The way in which the larger political issues came into the meetings during these mobilisations was in discussions on logistical matters. Discussions about how the ecovillage should be organised were discussions about philosophy of social change and shared ideals, but safely disguised behind practicalities so as to avoid ideological conflicts. Unlike the social forum, this mechanism for dealing with conflict did not result in the closing of collective space to difference of opinion and conflict. Instead, this tactic shifted the conflict from the field of ideology and theory into the domain of context-specific practices. In this way, the avoidance of conflict was a technique for resolving conflict made possible by prefiguration. Because the expression of an ideal world was being created in a mini form, it turned out that the differences of opinion about how that world should look could be resolved on a practical level, without the ideological differences underlying these opinions intervening (too often). It was easier to reach agreement and find creative solutions to differences of opinion in a conversation about whether or not there should be security at the Hori-Zone camp than in an ideological debate about what autonomy, authority and self-organisation means. The unintended result of these planning meetings was that ideological differences were overcome piecemeal in a context-specific way and differences of opinion did not escalate into irreconcilable conflict. This makes sense when one considers that it is much easier to admit that you might be wrong in relation to a specific context than it is to admit that your whole worldview and ideological belief system is fundamentally flawed. For example, during one of the Hori-Zone spokescouncil meetings, there was a proposal to allow the media onto the campsite to do outreach around the ecologically sustainable facilities (grey water, compost toilets, etc.). This proposal met with resistance because rejection of mainstream media was taken for granted by most autonomous strands of the movement in the UK. After reasons why the media should be let onto the camp were presented by someone from the practicalities working group, and several of the concerns raised had been incorporated into the proposal (requiring someone to be with the media at all times and that the media not be allowed to film anyone without their explicit permission), there was still one person who was threatening to block the proposal entirely out of an anti-media principle. The meeting seemed to be at an impasse and it looked as though the proposal was going to be blocked even though many amendments had been made to it. Underlying this conflict was a fundamental difference in principles. Some people felt that media attention was essential to getting the message of the camp out to the general public, and others thought the mainstream media had proven that it paints only negative images and must be excluded from the camp at all costs. This conflict was resolved in the end with a small meeting held outside of the spokescouncil meeting tent between the 'blocker' and the 'proposer', facilitated by someone from the facilitation working group. The significant point here is that the conflict was not resolved by convincing the 'blocker' that mainstream media is a good and useful tool, nor by convincing the 'proposer' that mainstream media is evil and should be excluded, but rather by finding a third option that acted as a practical, context-specific solution that took both these positions into account as legitimate positions to hold (in this case that the 'blocker' could accompany the media himself).[3]

Despite the potential of consensus to resolve most conflicts when it is facilitated well, the fear underlying open discussions of ideological differences shows that many movement actors still expect consensus to mean unanimity. This tension imbued in consensus is a crucial challenge to the potential of the democratic system being prefigured by these movement actors. People have a natural (or learned) instinct to look for a singular solution or a singular point of unity as their source of solidarity, and although this type of unity is becoming less and less important from a macro-perspective, it often still matters very much to certain people in particular places and times.

Irreconcilable Differences

This is a dead committee.

No, no, it's uh ... been resting.

Look matey, I know a dead committee when I see one, and I am looking at one right now.

No no it's not dead, it's, it's restin'! Remarkable forum, the London one, wouldn't you say? Beautiful plumage!

/Etc.

Well, the UK Coordinating Committee is an Ex-Commitee.

... let us all be honest and not pretend to represent the UK Organizing Committee, the whole British movement, or other sophistries. Let's turn up to Paris in our own names and/or in the name of our organizations and networks. (email, Reyes 2004b)

The above rendition of the Monty Python 'dead parrot sketch' was sent by one of the main participants in the UKCC almost two months after the London ESF. It was sent in response to an email issued officially on behalf of the UK ESF Office to announce that the UKCC was going to meet again after two months of silence to prepare for the EPA in Paris. The sarcasm of this email strikes at the heart of the conflict between the bid group and the horizontals. The email questions the authority of the ESF Office to decide to have a meeting in the name of the UKCC, as well as the motivations of such a meeting, accusing the 'organisers' of trying to create a veneer of legitimacy around a form of power deemed illegitimate – and doing so by lying and knowingly deceiving others. The accusations implicit in this sarcastically humorous comment demonstrate the deep conflict that pervaded the ESF process and the irreconcilability of certain types of conflict. The theoretically infinite ability to find constructive solutions to conflict, does not always translate into reality. Whether conflict becomes constructive or adversarial depends a great deal on the type of power that is exercised in the process of discussion. As we shall see below, when power is perceived to be exercised hierarchically, movement actors resort to an adversarial form of conflict with each other. These power practices inhibit the constructive potential of conflict, and consequently, conflict is not always resolvable.

At times, irreconcilable differences can only be negotiated through a division of the group and the further decentralisation of decision-making. This can lead to the breaking up of particular networks and unities within the movement, but this decentralisation does not necessarily lead to permanent damage for the movement as a whole. Because the movement is not confined to fixed geographical or spatial boundaries, there is the possibility of perpetually opening up more spaces to accommodate different practices. In the London ESF, when the conflict between the verticals and the horizontals started to lead to exclusion and hierarchy, many horizontals pulled out of the centralised structure of the UKCC and organised 'autonomous' spaces and 'alternative' spaces parallel to the main ESF. After much negotiation these alternative spaces were included in the programme, and were attended by many of the same people who attended the main ESF. The unresolvable conflict between actors added to the overall diversity of the ESF.

The divisions found within the UKCC are not surprising given that these movement actors had such drastically different political beliefs and were tied together by very few overlapping unities that ultimately did not prove to be stronger than their differences. Nevertheless, the UKCC is not equivalent to the movement as a whole, and, despite the loss of certain unities as a result of conflict, these divisions can be understood as neutral, even positive, if we look at the ESF (or the movement as a whole) being constituted not by unity-as-agreement, but by a decentralised network that can have an infinite number of different nodes. Through the conflict between the verticals and the horizontals, many people made alliances on both sides of the divide, resulting in strong working relationships that they otherwise would not have developed; people from NGOs, communist parties and autonomous groups all united under the banner of the 'horizontals'. Due to the network structure, this type of division does not necessarily mean a permanent fissure that disassociates, that cuts the ties and connections between actors and groups, but can mean a realignment of unities and the creation of more and more nodes and clusters and the further decentralisation and diversity of the movement. In this way, even unresolvable or unresolved conflict, is resolved. What counts as resolved, however, changes in that it no longer means everyone is united in one singular form, but that people are still linked to each other through the rhizomatic network structure:

> A rhizome may be broken, shattered at a given spot, but it will start up again on one of its old lines, or on new lines. (Deleuze and Guattari 1987: 10)

That having been said, the nature of the interactions between the nodes of the network can at times be important and it seems that, for these divisions to be productive, the division must not be the result of exclusion. When conflict leads to *forced* division, the flows between groups that are still in the network are reduced.

The increased diversity gained through conflict in the London ESF did not alter the fact that, because of the conflict in the UKCC, there are many movement actors who can no longer work together, and the temporary overlap created by the crossing of these political differences into the unity of the ESF process was irreparably severed (to say nothing of the newcomers who were deterred by these conflicts). This temporary unity has turned into a permanent division that made working together during the anti-G8 mobilisation harder than it might otherwise have been. This is one of the main reasons for asserting the constructive power of conflict through horizontality – to ensure that division, which is essential for diversity, occurs amicably so as to keep the communication between fundamentally different sets of political ideas flowing. I return to this question of inclusion and exclusion in the next chapter, but first we must explore horizontality and the approaches to power that it implies.

Horizontality and Power

What is Horizontality?

Movement approaches to horizontality are fluid and diverse, but all notions of horizontality share in common the aim of limiting hierarchical power relations. Juris (2004) describes horizontalism as 'learning to manage conflict without reintroducing formal centres of command'. Horizontality is about creating equality. As we shall see in the next chapter, the practices of the collective spaces of movement organising show that equality is not assumed to be born into human beings, but rather is created through active construction of non-hierarchical relations by challenging existing inequalities between people (gender, sexuality, language, skills, etc.). Although the whole alterglobalisation movement cannot be characterised by horizontality, the collective spaces of decision-making certainly can be, even when horizontality is not advocated by all the actors involved. Within a diverse community, horizontality is a mechanism for limiting the abuse of power to avoid the exclusion that many actors presume to result from hierarchy. Consequently, it is a method for turning adversarial conflict into constructive conflict. Horizontality is where diversity meets equality; it is the means through which movement actors break the mental link commonly made between equality and sameness, and challenge the political project of homogenisation implicit in liberal democratisation.

Identifying the function horizontality is meant to fulfil, however, does not tell us very much about what horizontality is or about how horizontality achieves these roles of diversity enhancer and constructive conflict facilitator. What does horizontality look like? What kind of power relationship does it express? 'There are many horizontalities', I am told, and from what I have seen this certainly seems to be true. Nunes (2005: 310) writes:

> horizontality is not a model (or a property that can be predicated of things) but a practice. And as a practice, it remains permanently open to the future and to difference. As soon as one says 'this is what it looks like,' one is closing the door to all future and different things that might come under that name. The point here is not that horizontality is problematic, but that democracy as such is problematic. And problematic means just that: permanently open.

The fact that there is no one way horizontality 'looks' does not mean that there are not similarities between all the different looks horizontality has. At its core, horizontality refers to a decentralised network structure that produces non-hierarchical relationships between the various nodes (people, groups, ideas) of a network. The word 'network' is an abstract term devoid of particular content; hierarchical networks of unequal power relations are plentiful, but the term 'horizontality' acts as a qualifier, it provides the meaningful content for the movement's decentralised network structure, indicating that it facilitates the shift from hierarchical power to non-hierarchical power. A horizontal network rejects representation and the delegation of command, allowing actors to reclaim 'control'.

Horizontality, however, does not only refer to a structure of networked relationships. Movement actors often use the term 'horizontality' to describe an attitude, an ethos. Chico Whitaker

(2004: 111–20), one of the founders of the WSF, describes horizontality as a regulative ideal of non-hierarchical relations reflected in the forum itself through the creation of 'open space'. Juris (2004) writes that 'horizontalism means always remaining open and flexible to diversity and difference – within certain limits'.

Horizontalising Dissent!

After the G8 in Scotland, the Dissent! network experienced an 'identity crisis'. The previously strong overlapping unity that the network had shared had fallen away, and a new one was needed. This new focus, it was felt, could not be decided from 'above' by any small group of people, or even by a national Dissent! meeting, because everyone in the network had to have a chance to contribute, and a meeting necessarily always excludes people who cannot be there because of time, money or travel distance. This dilemma was extensively discussed at several national Dissent! gatherings and it was finally agreed to organise a large meeting, or two sets of meetings, called a 'reconvergence' (after much debate about the name). This reconvergence was to be preceded by local-level consultations of all groups involved in the Dissent! network. The rationale behind this organisational structure was described as follows:

> The aim of this consultation is to achieve a more horizontally based network that is representative of the politics and activity of the autonomous groups and individuals who are involved, that will facilitate those groups and individuals to work with others on specific activity/actions and network this with a larger body of people. (email, Dissent! Reconvergence Working Group 2005a)

This reconvergence represents a conscious intent to horizontalise the network and the section on 'how' this would be done demonstrates a potential incarnation of horizontality:

> The agenda of this gathering will be composed of the presentations made by the groups/individuals involved in the initiatives they propose. In order

for this to happen it is important that a consultation period of discussion, self-organisation and preparation takes place. It is also important that the working group organising this gathering can collate and distribute all necessary information to aid others discussion and prepare the agenda for the gathering. For this reason there is a questionnaire below and a time line for the consultation leading up to this gathering. (email, Dissent! Reconvergence Working Group 2005a)

This vision of horizontality that involves the decentralisation of decision-making and discussion to the local level and then back again to the national or international level, mimics the structure of the spokescouncil format in the consensus model. In this case, increased participation as involvement in the discussions about the future of Dissent! is akin to more horizontality. This increased participation is achieved by the limiting of existing power inequalities through decentralisation of discussion and centralisation of the topic for discussion (a centralisation of the *what* and the *how*, and a decentralisation of the *who* and the *where*). However, increased participation and horizontality is not only defined by involvement as physical presence, but also as a 'sense' of belonging:

the consulta[reconvergence] hasnt reached people. So how is any feeling of belonging going to develop? And without that, where is horizontality? (email, Slowcode 2006)

There is no horizontality without a 'feeling of belonging'. Those who are participating should not only be present and involved, but they should feel that they belong and that they have ownership and control over the process and the network as a whole. This increase in involvement, both real and perceived, was necessary because it was felt to be a defining characteristic and prerequisite to considering the network horizontal.[4]

The discussion that led to the decision to hold a consulta/reconvergence was a lengthy and conflictive discussion. There was disagreement about whether or not Dissent! should continue after the G8 and about in what form it should continue. There was disagreement about whether another large gathering would be more successful at addressing horizontality than the previous gatherings, and finally there was disagreement about what form the meeting should take. Despite all these disagreements the discussion went relatively smoothly, until some of the participants started to express their concerns about the gathering in terms of a fear that Dissent! might end up taking on the role of a 'vanguard', by assuming it was the only network through which anti-capitalist activities could be organised. The discussion moved from comments such as:

> In our discussion on the future of Dissent!, we have to bear in mind that dissent isn't the only thing that is happening. We don't need some completely overarching revolutionary strategy, what is more useful is to look at what role Dissent! has had over the last two years. If Dissent! vanished, where would the vacuum be? (Dissent! national gathering, Sheffield, 15 October 2005)

to accusations of the following nature:

> Whatever Dissent! is, it is not THE network of resistance, we shouldn't be trying to involve everyone possible, or we monopolise everything. I don't see Dissent! as some kind of revolutionary council. We should get back to being what we already are, a network. This is a vanguardist position. I don't like where it's going. (Dissent! national gathering, Sheffield, 15 October 2005)

Although this accusation of vanguardism was countered immediately, 'I don't think it's a vanguardist project, we're not asking people to fall in line with us, we don't have a line', it altered the dynamic in the room and the discussion became more adversarial because the meeting had been accused of abusing the power of Dissent! and trying to take control of the anti-capitalist left across the UK. This is no small accusation considering the aversion present in the network towards this kind of power. This accusation was the latest is a series of accusations that had left the Dissent! network highly self-conscious about not being horizontal enough. The point of the reconvergence was to address this problem, so to have the reconvergence itself be accused of being hierarchical and creating a centralisation of power was a stab at the heart of the entire discussion and brought the commitment to horizontality of everyone involved into question.[5] In the end:

> It was agreed that the aim of the reconvergence process was not to arrive at 'a' or 'the' 'strategy' for anticapitalism – just to renew the Dissent! network and have more space for strategic discussion. (email, Dissent! Reconvergence Working Group 2005b)

Although agreement was finally reached, this discussion about the fear of the vanguard gets to the heart of horizontality and the theories of power that horizontality assumes.

Power

Most social movement actors are not political theorists and do not employ perfectly coherent or consistent theories of power. Nevertheless, for our purpose here – that of exploring horizontality – movement actors' approaches to power can be roughly grouped into three categories: centralised hierarchical power, decentralised hierarchical power and decentralised non-hierarchical power. The first type of power is most commonly associated with the power of 'institutions' (multilateral organisations, the state, corporations), but, as we shall see, movement actors employ this meaning of power fluently to include any group of people exercising power-as-domination through a centralised structure.[6] 'Institution' refers, then, to the fact of centralisation and hierarchy itself, and the relative rigidity of this power compared to the second, and especially the third, way power is envisioned by horizontal movement actors. This first type of power is experienced by movement actors (those resisting this power) as the ability of a 'of a man or a number of men to realise their own will even against the resistance of others who are participating in the action' (Weber 1978: 926). This power is, therefore, viewed as oppressive, vested in identifiable localities of fixed and sanctioned 'authority'. This power is understood to function through a command-obedience framework (Arendt 1970), where 'authority' is legitimated by those subjected to it, and for movement actors it must therefore be confronted through acts of conflict and 'disobedience' – protest, abstention, destruction. Movement actors attribute a great deal of intent to this first type of power, holding the people who exercise (or have the potential to exercise) it, the 'system' that perpetuates it, and the people who they believe perpetuate the system, responsible for the negative effects of this power. When confronted with the reality of centralised power, this approach to power leads movement actors not to the belief that power is naturally or inevitably centralised, but rather to the assumption that power takes this form because it serves someone's purpose, that people (especially, but not only, those who benefit from this power) actively maintain this centralisation. It therefore becomes the responsibility of movement actors to actively resist this centralisation.[7]

The second way movement actors use the word 'power' is to refer to a decentralised hierarchical power that results from perceived inequalities between people, such as sexism, racism and many other isms, as well as structural inequalities like access to resources and education. This power is understood as relational and is viewed in a more Foucauldian way as something that circulates. This power is diffuse and found in the dynamic between two people or groups of people, but is linked to structural discriminations. This power is also power-as-domination, but it is power exercised in a more decentralised manner and can therefore be difficult to identify or isolate. The exercise of this second power can be intentional or unintentional, and is understood to be an inevitable, but negative, manifestation of power that needs to be acknowledged so that it can be actively limited. Because the second type of power is considered harder to identify, and is often exercised unintentionally, intent plays a more important role in determining how those exercising this power ought to be treated. Although the exercise of this type of power is nowhere acceptable in horizontal spaces of movement activity, movement actors do 'make distinctions between those who dominate knowingly and those who dominate without realising they do so' (Dowding 2006: 136). When this power is exercised intentionally it is dealt with in the same way as centralised power, through confrontation. When it is exercised unintentionally, it is considered a problem with the group dynamic and more horizontality becomes the mechanism through which it is limited.

Finally, movement actors also speak of power not as domination, but as something positive and constructive.[8] This type of power I dub *prefigurative power*. Prefigurative power is a decentralised, non-hierarchical, *collective* power of a group of people to take control of their lives, work, neighbourhood, community, 'when you take control of your education, work, and relationships like us, that's creating power – not state power, but popular power' (Compañera 2, quoted in Sitrin 2006: 160). This type of power is prefigurative because it is about creating something new; it is a practice of constructing new power relationships (in the means of movement organising) so that the old ones may become obsolete and the new power relationships might replace them (becoming an end). Prefigurative power is not merely the decentralisation of existing power. Decentralising power is often cited as an anarchist strategy for dealing with power (see Dolgoff 1970, Kropotkin 1927, Proudhon 1923), but a confusion arises between decentralisation of power and the redistribution of power. In the latter, power is considered to be the property of individuals (rather than a relation), 'a kind of stuff that can be possessed by individuals in greater or lesser amounts' (Young 1990: 31), and the redistribution thereof to be the key to equality. But movement actors are aware that decentralised hierarchy exists, and this type of decentralisation would not be horizontality, which requires that the decentralisation of power be combined with the de-hierarchisation and de-individuation of power through the construction of collective processes. Alterglobalisation movement actors seem to believe something closer to Irigaray (1985: 81), who argues that if feminists attempt 'the distribution of power, leaving intact the power structure itself, then they are resubjecting themselves, deliberately or not, to a phallocentric order'. Prefigurative power, therefore, is a qualitatively different power, a collective power based on horizontality: 'social movements are thinking of a different kind of power that's distinct from the power of dominance, the power of transforming daily relations' (Paula quoted in Sitrin 2006: 162).

For horizontal movement actors, the first and second types of power are to be actively confronted and/or limited, and prefigurative power is to be expanded to take their place. For this reason the power of centralisation and vanguardism within the movement is of particular concern to movement actors. A vanguard involves a centralisation of power into the hands of identifiable, locatable and therefore separable 'authority'. For movement actors, if one can identify those with power as distinct from oneself, or as distinct from the group as a whole, then the collective aspect central to prefigurative power is undermined and the power (exercised or potential) is deemed illegitimate. Here the centralisation of power is linked to the hierarchisation of power, where hierarchy is akin to domination. Consequently, within the horizontal framework of the alterglobalisation movement, an abuse of power occurs the moment the ability to identify *who* rules exists.[9] This rejection of centralised, hierarchical power underlies the movement's rejection of representative structures and any service conceptions of power. This rejection of representation will be discussed in the next chapter, but I mention it here because it helps to explain horizontality. Horizontal movement actors reject representation because it stands in direct contradiction to prefigurative power. They perceive representation to be the few acting on behalf of the many, while prefigurative power is everyone (where 'everyone' refers to those involved in any given decision or project) taking collective control of themselves. Horizontality is primarily the decentralisation and de-individuation, or de-localisation of power (in the sense of it being localised in a select few places/people). Horizontality rests on movement actors' assumption that certain power inequalities are inevitable and that they need to be countered through a particular practice. These assumptions about the nature of power, however, only represent a small portion of the various movement approaches to power.

Despite the clear theoretical distinction that one can draw between types of power, in practice, these visions of power are not opposites or mutually exclusive. Although the agents of centralised power are quite identifiable and fixed at the extreme end of this power framework, who falls into which power category is continuously in flux. During the London ESF, the SWP felt that the autonomous groups were abusing their power and 'hijacking the process' to pursue 'non-goals' that were 'not radical' and had no hopes of speeding up the onset of the revolution. The autonomous groups, on the other hand, felt that they were 'reclaiming' the ESF process from the SWP who had 'taken over the process' and were acting as a 'vanguard', 'dominating' the ESF. For the autonomous groups the openness of the process *was* the revolutionary aspect and therefore could not be sacrificed for a future revolutionary dream. These mutual accusations of abuse of power, demonstrate different movement actors' under-standings of power, but it is the form these accusations take that is perhaps of greatest interest. When a movement actor is accused of abusing power, the accusations often equate the power practices of the movement actor(s) with those of the government or corporations. Noel Douglas, an active member of Globalise Resistance, attempted to discredit the horizontals within the LSF by equating a meeting with the leadership of ATTAC France to a meeting with the 'right-wing':

> some of the more 'right-wing' forces in the movement such as the leadership of ATTAC, people like Bernard Cassen ... seem to have a vision of the movement which is limited to being a kind of lobby group of social democratic practices. (email, Douglas 2003)

Here Noel, not a 'horizontal', is equating the leadership of ATTAC France, one of the main political forces behind both the WSF and the ESF, with a lobby group and uses the term 'right-wing' to describe them (and all social democrats). Noel is not alone; this email was quickly followed with one from Alex Callinicos (2003) of the SWP in which he accused the LSF of 'providing a vehicle for some of the most right-wing forces associated with the anti-globalisation movement'. These are examples of how movement actors, who were themselves often accused of 'dominating the process', use the centralisation of power within ATTAC and the acceptance of representative structures (implicit in lobbying), as proof that ATTAC leadership is not true to movement values and should not be cooperated with, but confronted.

The SWP were not even the ones who most commonly made these types of accusations. The 'horizontals' regularly referred to any political party or organisation that centralised power as the 'authoritarian left' with the intonation of a swear word. This type of derision often takes the form of sarcastic humour with jokes that conflate movement actors with institutional power, such as referring to the eight founding organisations of the WSF as the 'G8'. Any centralisation of power (which includes traditional left politics) is considered to be similar to the power of 'institutions':

> it would be better to try to do it [the planning of the reconvergence] a bit more properly this time, do the online form as part of some sort of outreach strategy to be thought about and implemented with us all (we are not sounding too corporate here are we? ... mind you there is a difference tween not wanting to behave like a corporation and talking your project dead seriously ... la-la, la-la, lala) anyway! we, z,k,t aka 'le polit bureau' aka 'the sockretiarat' came up with a text for the website. possibly some of us wont like that, but we have to warn everyone, that we dont accept any critic, unless its not followed by action from your side. (email, Z, K and T 2006)

In this highly sarcastic comment, Z, K and T are equating the fact that they wrote a text for the website (without the rest of the group) with communist practices, dubbing themselves 'le polit bureau'. The suggestion that they develop an 'outreach strategy' they worry jokingly, resembles corporatism. This humour highlights the awareness of the 'horizontals' that they need structures and task allocation, but that they run the risk of centralisation, and therefore of creating hierarchical power. They realise the need to stay aware of this dynamic fluidity to avoid the easy flow from prefigurative power to hierarchical power.

Sometimes these sarcastic remarks are directed at others. Anita Bressan of the LSF replied to Alex Callinicos' email (above) with hostility:

> Apparently you have your own little truth you stick to which does not allow you to see very far. In my opinion this mirrors nothing more than the same

old world you claim you want to change, where everyone is tightly attached to their own believes, and are not prepared or even able to understand that there is people who think differently (and maybe they have some interesting ideas). (email, Bressan 2003)

Accusations of abusing power directed at other movement actors demonstrate the fluidity with which the different approaches to power are applied, with movement actors themselves often getting placed into the category of hierarchical power. This recategorisation is significant because if movement actors are considered to be exercising power-as-domination, it follows that they can be treated similarly to the state, corporations, etc. and therefore be approached with a confrontational attitude leading to adversarial, often unresolvable, conflict. Fabian (quoted in Sitrin 2006: 165) argues that this is the reason there are no leaders who assume power within the movement: 'There's no lack of leaders in the movement who could assume power, but to the extent that a leader assumes power, he is violating his own principles.' A movement actor's right to the respect of horizontality, to be included in the collective construction of prefigurative power, is revoked the moment that they partake in the centralisation of power, either by centralising power or by benefiting from power that is already centralised. The 'horizontals', when confronted with the UKCC as a centralised form of power, first tried to decentralise and de-hierarchicise it, then, failing that, confronted it, and finally rejected it and all the movement actors involved in it, as illegitimate because they were maintaining this centralised/ hierarchical locus of power. For horizontal movement actors, one cannot be treated 'horizontally' if one is not actively involved in the process of decentralising power. Horizontality is not just a theory of ideal power or social relations through which everyone should be treated; it is a practice that is limited to a particular context – to all those that accept it and believe in it – and anyone who does not adhere can be treated differently.[10]

In this way the movement resolves the problem of needing to at once create alternative power structures and overcome existing power structures. The creation of new power structures can proceed along lines of very strict rules about the inclusion of everyone in the networks and decision-making processes of the movement and horizontality as an 'ethos' and a 'process' can be developed and practised, while at the same time the power of the state, corporations, governmental and inter-governmental institutions can be aggressively challenged. The movement actors have no delusion that all types of power can be overcome through horizontality. Horizontality can create processes that limit the decentralised power in human relationships, indeed, the inevitability of this decentralised power is horizontality's *raison d'être*, but the centralised power of institutions is another matter. This latter type of power represents a site of conflict that should not be resolved, but fought and won.

Partly due to the multiple ways in which power is understood and practised from one context and moment to another, the alterglobalisation movement can 'experiment with a variety of innovative connections and combinations between autonomous self-organised power and initiatives to transform, as well as confront, the state' which challenges the 'old dichotomy between on the one hand changing the world through autonomous self-organised sources of power or, on the other, seizing/taking state power' (Wainwright 2004). Within this framework, the alterglobalisation movement as a whole, as well as each set of actors, is potentially capable of prefiguring an alternative world at the same time as combating, in whatever way necessary, the power of the state and capitalism:

> The Zapatistas believe that force in any instance whether carried out by the left or the right is an imposition. This, however, does not preclude armed struggle as self-defense. However, self-defense needs to be looked at in terms of place and time. Would armed self-defense cost them momentum and support? So far, the Zapatistas have not fired a shot since 8 January, 1994, only eight days into the fighting. Although the government has not detained themselves from the extensive forms of violence, the Zapatistas have refused to respond with armed self-defense. (Flores, in Flores and Tanka 2001)

This flexibility in approaches to power allows movement actors to apply different strategies in different situations with varying degrees of centralisation and horizontality. The preceding description, it should be stressed, refers to power in relation to horizontality, where horizontality represents only one movement practice, albeit a 'central' one.

Autogestion and Prefigurative Power

At the heart of the movement's own power, its prefigurative power, lies the notion of *autogestion*. Literally translated, *autogestion* means simply 'self-management', but it is used in a more holistic way to mean a process of repossession of the power to collectively determine every aspect of our lives. *Autogestion* helps us to understand what it means to say that prefigurative power is a constructive and collective power that cannot be held by any individual. What would it mean to have self-determination if it was only determination over yourself, but not the actions of any others or the structural constraints around you? It would, some have commented, mean liberal democracy:

> What [horizontality] does not mean either is the fetishisation of diversity and differences. In fact, the whole attitude that constrains debates because 'diversity must be left alone' ... smacks of liberalism. Not only because it takes differences as given, but also because it reduces them to individual property, be it of a person or of a group ... This accepts two of the tenets of liberalism: first, an irresolvable distinction between individual and collective good; and second, the liberal concept of individuality. (Nunes 2005: 311)

In contrast to this liberal formulation of diversity, *autogestion* is not based on an individualistic notion of the self; the 'auto' refers to the group as a whole. The practices of horizontality and *autogestion*, movement actors argue, make prefigurative power possible and they facilitate a process in which people liberate themselves from many of the oppressive structures of daily life and recreate their communities anew. Holloway (2004) says of Subcomandante Marcos that:

> he dreams that one day we can all live in a cinema programme ... where we could choose to live a different film each day – the Zapatistas rebelled because they have been forced to watch the same film for the last five hundred years ... I think that is a lovely answer because it points towards absolute self-determination. Self-determination (that is social self-determination because there can be no other) means liberation from the past, liberation from history, the capacity to recreate ourselves completely each day.

Although this ideal is far from realised, the alterglobalisation movement has many different structures and rules through which to facilitate this potential to do what one could otherwise not do, to recreate oneself and one's world continuously. The *structures* associated with horizontality make the expression of this collective, prefigurative power possible. As we have already seen, these structures are not fixed structures, but flexible ones that are transformed from one context to another by the movement actors themselves. Not, however, by individual actors; as we shall see in Chapter 5, structures are shaped through communication, which is necessarily always a collective endeavour whether it be communication between two people or thousands of people.

In the collective spaces of movement activity, horizontal structures rest on various forms of consensus, where consensus is the means through which power-as-domination (when exercised by movement actors) is transformed into prefigurative power:

> If individual people or groups ... seem to act in ways that contradict these principles ... then we challenge them and hold them accountable. Who is the 'we' who does this challenging? Anybody who feels an abuse of power has occurred, or a 'betrayal' – intentional or not – of the principle of inclusiveness, horizontality and participation. But we do not do so through fixed bureaucratic procedures, rather through a democratic decision-making based on consensus that empowers us all to have a sense of responsibility towards the other. (email, De Angelis 2003b)

Consensus as a procedure wields power over the collective spaces of movement activity because it is deemed to be the only legitimate decision-making method for limiting hierarchy and increasing horizontality. Although there is no desire that all participants should be bound to obey the outcomes of a decision reached, even by consensus (there is always the option to stand aside, or to leave the group), there is a 'duty to obey' the process of how decisions are made. Collectively, movement actors are perpetually changing consensus and inventing new aspects to it, but it is hard to imagine the outright rejection of consensus. Through consensus and horizontality, the locus of power shifts from the question of 'Who rules?' to a focus on 'How do we rule?' If we have an answer to the second question (whatever that answer may be) we no longer need an answer to the first question – providing the *how* functions successfully. Horizontal organisation, with strict but diverse and flexible rules, replaces the need for a rigid structure of hierarchical power.

While the first two types of power inspire agency in the form of resistance (outright confrontation and rejection) as a reaction to the power of domination, this third type of power is a form of agency as action not reaction. Ahern (2001: 115) argues that 'oppositional agency is only one of many forms of agency', and Sherry Ortner (2006: 139) draws a distinction between two types of agency: 'as (the pursuit of) "projects" or as (the exercise of or against) "power"'. She describes the difference between these two agencies in a way that resonates with movement actors' rationale for prefiguration:

> the point of making the distinction between agency-in-the-sense-of-power and an agency-in-the-sense-of-(the pursuit of) projects is that the first is organised around the axis of domination and resistance, and thus defined to a great extent by the terms of the dominant party, while the second is defined by local logics [in which] people seek to accomplish valued things within a framework of their own terms, their own categories of value. (Ortner 2006: 145)

The creation of space to pursue their own aims based on their own values is one of the main reasons for creating *les espaces autogérés* (self-organised spaces). In the case of the alterglobalisation movement this 'agency of projects' is intricately linked to the 'agency of power' in that these *espaces autogérés* are usually set up in and around acts of resistance to the power of institutions. Prefigurative power is built up and learned in the process of confronting power-as-domination. This link is essential for movement actors because prefiguration alone has little potential to bring about (an)other world(s) if it is not within the framework of resistance to and confrontation with centralised hierarchy. As Ortner concludes, 'the agency of project intrinsically hinges on the agency of power' (2006: 148).

Power of Knowledge

> Autonomy is asset based and builds off the strengths of the community. In the video *Zapatista* produced by Benjamin Eichert, one of the Zapatista women says it best, as she asserts that Zapatista autonomy is, 'the profound conviction that the answers are in us'. (Flores, in Flores and Tanka 2001)

To say that the answers are already in us is a defiant act. It reclaims the right to know from those who have the power to sanctify knowledge. One of the most damaging ways power has been exercised over the past 500 years is by centralising the right to legitimate knowledge. This power, a power which is implicit in claiming to *know better*, is a power that is deemed oppressive by most movement actors. Many movement actors feel that this power has been exercised over 'them' for centuries, first by the colonial powers and now through discourses of 'development' and 'help':

> Neoliberal globalisation is presided over by techno-scientific knowledge, and owes its hegemony to the credible way in which it discredits all rival knowledge, by suggesting that they are not comparable, as to efficiency and coherence, to the scientific nature of market laws. (Santos 2004: 237)

Redefining the way legitimate knowledge can be constructed is therefore part of a political struggle for the right to self-determination. Escobar (2004: 350) writes of the WSF:

> At play is a micro-politics for the production of local knowledge ... This micro-politics consists of practices of mixing, re-using, and re-combining of knowledge and information.

Challenging what counts as legitimate knowledge has been at the heart of many movements over the past 40 years, from feminist movements to indigenous movements. Le mouvement du 22 mars of France 1968 even included an 'outright rejection ... of so-called neutral knowledge' in their manifesto (Eley 2002: 343). Santos (2004: 237–38) calls the paradigm of legitimate knowledge a 'monoculture of knowledge' that rests on the production of non-existence. He argues that 'It turns modern science and high culture into the sole criteria of truth and aesthetic quality, respectively. All that is not recognised or legitimated by the cannon is declared non-existent.' Therefore the act of redefinition is not only about reclaiming knowledge, it is fundamentally 'about what it means to be human'. It is asserting the right to exist.

The alterglobalisation movement, rather than accept these legitimated knowledges, chooses to write and create its own knowledge. But the knowledge created by this movement is not a universal knowledge that, once written, cannot be unwritten or rewritten. Knowledge is created through a collective process and is therefore held by everyone, there is no privileged actor who knows. There are, of course, actors with certain skills, with more information, who are more connected than others, but the emphasis placed on the diffusion and transferring of these skills and information demonstrates the belief that even these practical knowledges, held by a particular someone, ought to be circulated and spread across the network. The type of knowledge that is most resisted by this movement is the type that claims to *know better*, to know what *should* be done, to know what will happen next – the knowledge of prediction. The Zapatistas capture this movement practice of unknowing poetically when they say, 'walking we ask questions'. Holloway (2004):

> we have to start by admitting that we don't have the answers. The fact that we think that state power is the wrong way does not mean that we know the right way ... To think of moving forward through questions rather than answers means a different sort of politics, a different sort of organisation. If nobody has the answers, then we have to think not of

hierarchical structures of leadership, but horizontal structures that involve everyone as much as possible.

In this way movement actors detach 'the power of truth from forms of hegemony, social, economic, and cultural, within which it operates at the present time' (Foucault 1980: 133).

Activists need some sort of truth to be able to act; they need a belief in something to motivate their actions, but they do not need to believe that their ideal is the only one worth fighting for or that it represents the only acceptable method through which to fight. The alterglobalisation movement plays itself out in so many different contexts that there are few who would claim to *know better* for all contexts at all times. One must understand the movement as a 'transitory knowledge building community' (Wood 1998) and recognise that this refusal to *know better* demonstrates a commitment to diversity. There is no need for one movement actor or set of actors to convince the others that they have the right answer, because the common struggle does not rest on a shared worldview. There is no single right answer in this movement, for which knowledge is a context-specific construction. For this movement, 'there is no ignorance or knowledge in general. All ignorance is ignorance of something, and all knowledge is the overcoming of a particular ignorance' (Santos 2004: 239).

On the level of meetings and daily practice, this attitude towards knowledge is expressed through a caution about telling others what to do, realising that no matter how much knowledge or skill you may have, there is no legitimate basis for claiming to know better. This was very clear in the Facilitation Working Group at the Hori-Zone camp during the mobilisation against the G8 in 2005. Even in this group of 'experienced' facilitators, there was not a fixed idea about how the meetings *should* be facilitated. In the discussions about the options, the language used was contextualised, 'The way we usually do it is ...' When one travels from one location to another, it is hard to assume to know what is best in that unfamiliar context. To make an assumption of knowledge would reproduce the structures of dominance inherent in the development and colonial paradigms.

In this case, the open approach resulted in the adjustment of the ideal model of consensus decision-making to the specificities of the Hori-Zone camp, where for example, it was felt that a slightly more ad hoc construction of the small groups (for small group to large group, spokescouncil consensus) was needed because so many of the people turning up at the camp were 'unorganised' and had no pre-existing group to which they belonged.

The Reality of Power

Describing horizontality requires a discussion of the ideal with the necessary deviations from this ideal. Of course, there are certain kinds of power that one cannot easily escape. These powers were especially present in social forum processes. One such power is the power of money. Oscar Reyes writes of the ESF 2004 organising process:

> Those of us who seek alternatives have to be realistic about the fact that 'vertical' control has been bought rather than gained on the intellectual battlefield. 'Another world is possible, but it is very expensive' is its slogan, money = power its rationale ... If we fail to do this, we'll keep winning symbolic victories and finding that these can easily be ignored. (email, Reyes 2004a)

The price-tag placed on inclusion is a common problem facing the poorer organisations wanting to get involved in social forum processes. Although there is room within the official structures of the social forum to include organisations without money, this is often nothing more than a token gesture. Even in social fora less dominated by funding bodies than the London ESF, money is power, and access not only to meetings, but to decisions, often has to be bought. Within the decision-making spaces outlined above, those that have the relative power to turn decisions in their favour will be the possessors of one or two essential ingredients (preferably both): they will either represent an organisation which has already donated (or might donate) a substantial amount to the social forum process or they represent a large number of people.

While consensus is designed to equalise power and to avoid fixed representative structures, it is primarily through unofficial (or even official) representation that one gains relative power within the social forum process. The social forum anywhere in the world inevitably falls victim to power structures created by the need for funding and the presence of an official social forum office where certain people are empowered to take decisions and others are not. In theory, a social forum office is only an implementation body and the people running the office do not take any major decisions, but no social forum office where I worked actually functioned in this way. It becomes hard to convene Organising Committee meetings as the date of the social forum approaches and when decisions have to be made quickly, they are made in the office. This tension is important because it rests on a distinction that is not primarily about who decides, but about how to decide. In most cases those working in the office will be members of the Organising Committee, so the distinction between office staff and committee is not that significant in terms of who, but it is a substantial difference in terms of how. A social forum process is meant to be as inclusive as possible, and decisions should therefore be taken by as many people as possible through discussion and brainstorming, not unilaterally by an ad hoc group of people, or, worse, a single person, who happens to be in the office at the right time.

The WSF in India was better than the ESF in London or Paris in this respect. The line was drawn and continually reinforced between the legitimate decision-making procedures and the carrying out of those decisions. Part of the reason for this was the First World/Third World power dynamic that is present in the organising of a WSF. Many of the office volunteers were from Europe and North America, while the official national Organising Committee was largely Indian. In the WSF India office there was a sense (often unspoken, but also sometimes shouted!) that the WSF was not a space for Europeans to come and tell Indians what to do and how. Although I did not work in the Brazilian WSF office, this feeling was similar there:

> When we arrived at Porto Alegre, we quickly realised that the WSF was organised on the ground almost exclusively by members of the Workers' Party (PT) who had no desire to share their work and their power with anyone, much less with foreigners (especially Europeans). (email, 'Nouvelles d'Amerique Latine' 2005)

This statement exposes another problem present in both the ESF and WSF – the question of ownership. This ownership of the social forum process often renders horizontality impossible. Due to the fact that the social forum organising process has an identifiable centre, a centralisation of power occurs and groups that are less committed to the active decentralisation of power often stake a claim of ownership, guarding the spaces of power in a highly exclusive way. This leads to an organising practice that is in reality far more hierarchical than the expressed ideal.

This discrepancy, however, is not necessarily a cause for alarm. Oscar Reyes reminds us to view power horizontally when he writes:

> It is clear that there are several people and organisations involved in the ESF process – let us call them 'verticals' – who think that they can control the space of the Forum by controlling the organising processes ... But if we assume that they have actually [w]rested control of the Forum processes by these maneuvers then we are using exactly the same conception of power as them ... power is domination, the 'verticals' are dominating, therefore we should disengage. But what if power is thought of as a relation as a shifting terrain of practice? Our conclusion looks somewhat different then. We are left to affirm the importance of democratic process and an ethics of practice – which is exactly what the horizontals seek to do ... the ESF (like the WSF) is a format that is very difficult to control because self-organised events lie at its heart ... When 30,000 people get together in 300 spaces and countless more informal ones, how can any one organisation control that? (email, Reyes 2004a)

Despite the incongruity between the reality and the ideal, we can see that even when movement actors intentionally try to centralise power, the decentralised network structure of the movement undermines this power by refusing to acknowledge it as legitimate.

This is a key reason why division is central to fostering diversity in the movement. Actors must have the option to leave the group, to set up their own group, or to pursue entirely different actions or ideas, otherwise consensus becomes oppression. If divisions are allowed, but communication is maintained, the network simply decentralises itself, making the centralisation of power more and more difficult. In this case, the attempt to centralise led to decentralisation. The importance of Oscar's point is that even intentional hierarchies of power within movement practices do little to threaten the overall diversity of the movement. Santos (2004: 245) makes a similar point when he writes, 'the cleavages end up neutralising or disempowering one another. Herein lies the WSF's aggregating power.'

Diversity

Unity as Subordination

Underlying horizontality is the desire for diversity. To say that there can be no centre of power that dictates or controls, even no centre that can determine what is true and not true, does not mean having no power; for the alterglobalisation movement it means having many such loci of power. Horizontality refers to a radical decentralisation of power, and to the creation of new types of power that allow people to 'take control' not of others, but collectively of themselves. Horizontality becomes a mode through which diversity lives. I have witnessed no space of this movement where diversity was not valued, at least in principle. The implications of diversity are deep and pervade most aspects of movement practice, indeed, diversity redefines the very meaning of struggle:

> The issue is no longer to express a common way of struggle, nor a unified picture or one-dimensional solidarity, neither an ostentatious unity nor a secretly unifying sub-culture, but the profound understanding and the absolute will, to recognise the internal differences and create flexible groups, where different approaches connect with each other reasonably and for mutual benefit. (Lang and Schneider 2003)

This diversity stands in defiance of discourses of unity. For many movement actors, the idea of imposing unity onto a diverse movement and a diverse world is equal to subordination:

> The party, the people's army, the modern guerrilla force all appear bankrupt from their perspective because of the tendency of these structures to impose unity, to deny their differences and subordinate them to the interests of others. If there is no democratic form of political aggregation possible that allows us to retain our autonomy and affirm our differences, they announce, then we will remain separate, on our own. (Hardt and Negri 2004: 86)

Diversity becomes a prerequisite to engagement with the movement. Each movement will only join this 'movement of movements' if they are not forced to change as a result. Joining together with other groups and movements inevitably changes them, but this change must occur willingly. This is a distinction made possible by concrete movement practices that enhance respect for diversity.

One good example of diversity in practice is the action planning meetings at the Lausanne campsite during the 2003 anti-G8 mobilisation. There were many different groups planning a variety of actions to blockade the delegates from gaining access to the port (the port was the access point to the summit taking place across the lake in Evian). Some of the initiatives and strategies present were: the pink and silver bloc, who wanted to use their large size to do a series of 'flying blockades' throughout the 'yellow zone' (the no-protest zone); the aqua bloc, a pacifist bloc that wanted to do a fixed blockade as part of a non-violent civil disobedience strategy; the black bloc who wanted to take a confrontational attitude towards the police and damage property; and, finally, several independent affinity groups that were planning their own blockades at important points of access to the port. The main focus of the meeting was to ensure that all these different groups could do what they were planning to do. This meant ensuring that the actions of one group did not interfere with the actions of any other group. This principle was succinctly expressed by an activist at a Dissent! België meeting three years later: 'Everyone has to find their own way to express themselves, but without getting in the way of the others.'[11] This process of negotiating various action strategies is always a delicate matter because each group needs to protect the details of their actions to ensure successful blockades. Anyone can attend these meetings (including undercover police and journalists), so there is a tendency to share as little specific information as possible at public meetings. In the case of Lausanne, although specifics were kept secret, the general tactics used by the different groups were discussed and, after much deliberation, it was agreed that the black bloc would tone down their actions because it was deemed safer for the other blocs. Consequently, on the day of blockades, they 'ran' as a dark grey bloc instead of a black bloc. The shift to grey was a symbolic indication that they would take less of a black/white stance in terms of tactics and adjust their own tactics according to the position and actions of the other groups on a case-by-case basis.

In the social forum movement there is also an active attempt to foster diversity. The WSF Charter of Principles takes a very clear and strong stance on the question of diversity, and especially on the question of diversity of outcomes. Whatever actions, conclusions, positions result from the WSF, they cannot be assumed to represent the opinions of everyone involved in the WSF and certainly cannot be applied/enforced upon everyone. The WSF as a body cannot hold a singular position on any matter; it can only hold non-binding multiple positions:

> c) ... the WSF 'does not constitute a locus of power to be disputed by the participants in its meetings' and no one will be 'authorized, on behalf of (...) the Forum, to express positions claiming to be those of all its participants' ...
>
> d) 'The WSF will always be a forum open to pluralism and to diversity of activities and ways of engaging' (point 9), which is a source of wealth and strength in the movement for another world. The Forum will coexist with contradictions and will always be marked by conflicting opinions among the organizations and movements whose positions lie within the bounds of its Charter of Principles. (WSF BOC and IC 2002)

This description of the WSF as an open forum that takes no singular position claiming to be that of all its participants, fostering instead the 'wealth and strength' of diversity is a very strong statement about how different politics can be from what we have been told it is. The movement creates a space for democratic decision-making that assumes 'the people' to hold very different, even *conflicting* interests, yet does not conclude that the nature of human relationships is necessarily competitive nor that democracy's task should be to homogenise this conflict into submission. The 'conflicting opinions' are considered a positive element of the process. The WSF and ESF also disseminate these values to sections of the movement that have not placed the importance of diversity above unity within their own organisations. Even Alex Callinicos of the SWP, a political party that very much adheres to a unitary socialist analysis, writes of the WSF:

> One of the great beauties of our movement – and the forums that have emerged from and helped to sustain it – is the way in which people from all sorts of backgrounds and with the most diverse preoccupations come and mix together, participating in a process of mutual contamination in which we learn and gain confidence from one another. (email, Callinicos 2005)

The Limits to Diversity

Despite the success stories, diversity is a work in progress. At the heart of diversity is the issue of inclusivity and exclusivity. To say that a movement is diverse is one thing, but obviously it does not include everyone. Not all diversities are acceptable; the diversity that is given expression in this movement is a diversity that expresses many viewpoints, but largely from the same side of the political spectrum. Diversity is fostered by a *process*, but this process is limited by a set of concrete principles and guidelines. In a 'call-out' for a planning meeting issued by Dissent! België the invitation proclaimed 'everyone welcome' and was followed by:

> By everyone we mean of course people who want to work together on the basis of grassroots democracy (according to the PGA hallmarks). (email, StopG8 2006; see also PGA n.d.)

Even within this side of the political spectrum, not everyone is included in this diversity. Julie Boéri and Stuart Hodkinson (2005) of the Babels network point out that diversity has had only limited success in prefiguring itself:

> the nice sounding rhetoric of diversity and inclusion within the WSF Charter of Principles still remains largely unrealised in many social forums, especially the ESF. Just as at Florence and Paris, the large majority of the 20,000 participants (and interpreters) in London were mainly white able-bodied western Europeans. This failure over three years to significantly include those either living in or originating from central and eastern Europe and the global south, not to mention from the disabled and deaf communities, cannot simply be explained away by the systematic refusal of visas, problems of disability access or the gargantuan cost of international travel from outside the EU.

Boéri and Hodkinson remind us that even the diversity of the alterglobalisation movement is a significantly limited diversity. It is a diversity of ideas and practices and 'answers', and in some ways a diversity of people, but that diversity applies only to those who are already in some way included. Once included in the movement spaces, one can be divergent and diverse, but there are many intended and unintended exclusions. Some of the implications of this will be raised in the next chapter, but for now it is important to emphasise that, even in these highly diverse spaces, some differences matter more than others, and the result is often exclusion.

Letting Diversity Flow

One form of oppression this movement resists is unity. Although there is no contradiction being expressed between unity and diversity – in that one of the elements that unites this movement is the desire to reinvent democracy on the basis of diversity – the imposition of a unity is resisted by most movement actors. It would not necessarily be inaccurate to describe the relationship between unity and diversity as a type of unity in diversity, but such an explanation would emphasise the unity while the element of diversity (often as a rejection of unity) is the crucial factor to understanding this movement. At a Dissent! meeting in Sheffield, one of the participants argued the following about the role of unity within the Dissent! network:

> The G8 is over and we're having an identity crisis. Two years ago we had this crisis, only then the answer was clearer, we were going to mobilise against the G8. Now it is a bit less clear, mobilise against capital in general? Part of the reason it worked well, we let people take initiative and autonomy based on affinity groups. How do we prevent unofficial hierarchies? How do we prevent some people like myself from talking all the time? Then there is another position that says we need one framework through which to organise. Historically this comes from anarchist groups that have failed and are thinking about why. I think this is a bad analysis, the reason dissent works is because it doesn't force one particular line, it has a diversity of options, there is no unifying programme. We don't have a Das Kapital to sell people. Some groups have that and want that and that is fine, but I don't think dissent should go down that line. (Dissent! national gathering, Sheffield, 15 October 2005)

In the autonomous spaces of the ESF, diversity is also valued not as a source of unity but *instead* of unity. Unity serves the function of public relations, but difference is the basis of internal relations:

> We developed our working collaboration in a decentralized manner through online wiki pads, email lists, phone calls and regular meetings … the attempt to agree on a common call out was a highlight …! This involved trying to explain and understand our own 'differences' as a source of strength whilst finding ways to transmit this to audiences traditionally looking for 'unity' and 'sameness'. (Bodie 2004)

Here the only significance of unity is its value as communication between the movement and the world beyond it. We must address unity because unity is what the spectator looks for to be able to attach labels (meaning) and singularity. This unity, although it satisfies the spectator, is not of central importance to the movement or its participants. It is no longer the case that 'Likeness is prized because it appears as the prime ingredient to unity. Unity in turn, is thought to be the sine qua non of collective power' (Wolin 1996: 32). Quite the contrary, this imposed unity threatens the practice of horizontality and its ability to allow diversity to function.

Deleuze and Guattari (1987: 9) argue that unity is an act of hierarchical power:

> The notion of unity (*unité*) appears only where there is a power takeover in the multiplicity ... Unity always operates in an empty dimension supplementary to that of the system considered (overcoding). The point is that a rhizome or multiplicity never allows itself to be overcoded, never has available a supplementary dimension over and above its number of lines ... All multiplicities are flat.

Unity is also rejected by the alterglobalisation movement because of its inextricable link to the 'western imperial programme' (Inden 2001). We see from many colonial writings that this notion of unity has led to strong hierarchies of power where the 'Indians' are deemed to have no values merely because their values are 'different' from those of the colonialists (Pagden 1982, Todorov 1985). This 'othering' leads to an erasure in a system that insists on unity and similarity (de Certeau 1988, Fabian 1983, Hernandez 2002, McGrane 1989, Stoler 1995, Taussig 1993). As Hogden (1973: 26) argues, colonialism was based on a Judeo-Christian assumption of homogeneity that brought with it the idea that civilisation necessitates the homogenisation and centralisation of diversity. The shift towards valuing diversity rather than unity is an act of resistance to the homogenisation of 500 years of colonial history, contemporary democracy, the mass media and consumerism. It is this invisibility and homogeneity that the Zapatistas and many other movements across the world are resisting. The alterglobalisation movement's re-articulation of knowledge as a constructed and context-specific phenomenon is a part of this rebellion against unitary historical narratives.

Once we understand this deep-rooted rejection of unity, we can acknowledge that even unity is given space in diversity. Although it is partially necessary in movement discourses to understand unity and diversity as opposites, most movement actors do not interpret them this way. The alterglobalisation movement displays a great deal of unity. There is unity in the concrete aspects of movement processes. The very act of making decisions together is a type of unity. The act of presence is an act of allegiance, whether it be presence at a meeting or on an email list or at a protest. The concrete aspects of movement practice are exchanged and shared through a horizontal network structure. The flows that travel across this network unite. These flows can be ideologies, stories, symbols, information, people, skills, even material resources. Although these flows are not equal or congruent with each other and disjunctures exist between them (see Appadurai 1996), the flows unite. The complex web of unity and diversity being woven here is a series of overlapping and intertwined unities that, when traced, all lead to each other and therefore to a type of unity unrecognisable to the 'traditional' eye. Even as movement actors find different solutions to similar situations, and therefore appear to go in opposite directions, they remain linked through the network of overlapping unities. Subcomandante Marcos of the Zapatistas expresses this relationship between diversity and unity more concretely when he says: 'The question everywhere is the same, but the answers may be different' (quoted by Flores, in Flores and Tanka 2001).

This separation of the question and the answer is one way that conflict is mediated by this movement. Diversity leads to conflict, it is true, but adversarial conflict is not caused by this flow of diversity, instead it arises when these flows are blocked. Conflict can be productive if it is given space for expression. Nurturing the constructive power and limiting the adversarial power of conflict requires continuous work:

> We must be vigilant that our collective powers to do things (the decision-making aspect of democracy) is preserved in such a way that we do not reproduce rigidified structures of power ... if we believe in a world of difference and dignity, democracy cannot be postponed until 'after the revolution,' but must be constituted here and now through concrete practices. Democracy must be learned by ourselves. There is no teacher out there who can give us the model that satisfies all the needs and aspirations of our pluralities, so democracy must be self-taught. We learn by reflecting and acting on the ways we relate to each other. (email, De Angelis 2003a)

These 'collective powers', the 'world of difference', the prefiguration of this world being 'constituted here and now through concrete practices', that there is 'no teacher' and knowledge must be constructed by each of us – all of these we have explored in this chapter and the previous chapters. But what does it mean to say 'democracy must be learned by ourselves'? And how does the movement do this learning? What have we learned so far? These questions are the subject of the next chapter.

4

REINVENTING DEMOCRACY

Globalization is in essence a crisis of representative democracy ... what is the solution? To articulate an alternative participatory democracy. (Klein 2005: 225)

This is a movement about reinventing democracy. It is not opposed to organization. It is about creating new forms of organization. It is not lacking in ideology. Those new forms of organization *are* its ideology. It is about creating and enacting horizontal networks instead of top-down structures like states, parties, or corporations; networks based on principles of decentralized, non-hierarchical consensus democracy. Ultimately, it ... aspires to reinvent daily life as a whole. (Graeber 2002: 70)

The Democratic Context

Today, liberal democracy is being declared triumphant as a universal truth and simultaneously proving itself to be riddled with problems, continuously undermining its own values. The twentieth century has been dubbed the century of democracy, most famously by Francis Fukuyama (1992) with his claim that liberal democracy represents the uncontested future of world history in his famous phrase 'the end of history'. Amartya Sen (1999: 3) declares that, 'among the great variety of developments that have occurred in the twentieth century, I did not, ultimately, have any difficulty in choosing one as the preeminent development of the period: the rise of democracy'. However, others have claimed that democracy is in crisis (Crozier et al. 1975) and that democracy in the early twenty-first century is 'at a highly paradoxical moment' (Crouch 2004: 1, cf. Dahl 2000, Eisenstadt 1999, Held 1994: 313, Mouffe 2000). On the one hand, democracy continues to spread across the globe, but on the other, the legitimacy of democracy in western Europe, the US and Japan is being undermined by deep levels of distrust (see Pharr and Putnam 2000). Democracy has become a trademark of nation-states that use this brand to produce legitimacy. This branded democracy, however, has become a symbol dislocated from its original referent and is losing its meaning for citizens across the world. Perhaps activist and author Antonio Negri summed up the perception of the state of democracy most appropriately when he wrote:

> Rarely has the corruption of political and administrative life been so deeply corrosive; rarely has there been such a crisis of representation; rarely has disillusionment with democracy been so radical. When people talk about a 'crisis of politics', they are effectively saying that the democratic State no longer functions – and that in fact it has become irreversibly corrupt in all its principles and organs. (1996: 214)

The perceived inadequacy of representation on both the international and national levels creates a distrust of the state apparatus which is considered to limit freedom, rights, justice and, especially, diversity. Two analytical categories, the individual and the state, are at the centre of all liberal solutions to this paradox, but neither category is especially relevant to the alterglobalisation movement's democratic praxis. The democracy of the alterglobalisation movement is a non-state democracy, for some actors an anti-state democracy, and therefore the solution offered by this movement is not a solution that either asserts more state or less state, but one that develops a decentralised network practice(s) which 'no longer needs to operate with the notion of a social whole centred in the state and imagined as a goal oriented subject writ large' (Habermas 1996: 26).[1] The alterglobalisation movement's democratic practice stands in opposition to the global trend in which power is becoming more and more centralised and the range of autonomous decisions that nation-states can take is diminishing.

Subverting Individualism

The category of the state is not the only one being displaced by the alterglobalisation movement; it is also enacting a shift in the unit of analysis away from the 'free and equal' individual. This shift is essential for understanding the democratic praxis of the alterglobalisation movement and the different visions it presents from liberalism, even as it invokes the language of liberal democracy.[2] This difference comes down to a shift in the way the movement negotiates the relationship between diversity and unity. Discourses of pluralism have been central to liberal democratic theory since Locke and Hobbes. While neither Locke nor Hobbes can be considered to be a 'liberal democrat', their political theory is of central importance to liberal democracy (see Dunn 1980: 53–77). For Montesquieu (*The Spirit of Laws*, 1748) the concern with creating 'in institutional means a way to take account of the interests of different groups in public life while not sacrificing the liberty of the community overall' (in Held 1996: 84) becomes a central focus. Madison (*The Federalist Papers*, 1788), heavily influenced by Montesquieu, translates this need to account for different interests 'into a coherent political theory and strategy' (in Held 1996: 89).[3] Madison was also influenced by Hobbes and adopted the Hobbesian belief that the human condition is defined by conflict and the struggle for power. This conflict, for Hobbes (1968 [1660]: 220), can only be resolved when 'A multitude of men, are made *One* Person, when they are by one man, or one Person, Represented.' For Madison this conflict and rivalry between competing factions is inevitable because it is 'sown in the nature of man' (*The Federalist Papers*, no. 10: 18, in Held 1996: 90). However, while Hobbes felt this conflict could be resolved through unity under one singular power, Madison believed that the best one could hope for was that the worst aspects of this conflict could be limited through a political system of representation. This inevitable causal relationship from plurality to detrimental conflict is deeply ingrained in liberal democratic theory and practice.

As we have seen, the alterglobalisation movement also places conflict at the centre of the democratic structures they are developing, assuming conflict to be inevitable if not 'natural'. However, because the individual is not the analytical category through which interests are formed, conflict assumes a dual nature; it becomes both potentially destructive and constructive.

The alterglobalisation movement actors tend to approach interests as something that can be constructed and changed through a collective process and, as such, conflict can lead to the opening up of possibilities and result in creative new solutions to problems because different ideas and opinions are being merged into new shared interests. In strong contrast to Hobbes, the alterglobalisation movement's democratic praxis uses not unity but diversity as the resolution to conflict by creating space (both physical and metaphorical) for differences to coexist without any forced unity. In this way, the movement breaks with most democratic theories and practices. Even deliberative democratic models, which are presented as alternatives to liberal democracy set agreement and unity as the ultimate aim:

> all voices are free to enter into the discourse and no expression of interest is excluded. But the telos of the discourse, what characterizes its aim and method, is agreement. Difference is something to be gotten past ... Diversity may be the original condition of a polyvocal discourse, but univocity is its normative principle. (Gould 1996: 172)

It is precisely this normative principle of univocity that is being challenged by the alterglobalisation movement. Mouffe (1996: 246) argues that 'pluralism is not merely a *fact* ... but an axiomatic principle. It is taken to be constitutive *at the conceptual level* of the very nature of modern democracy and considered as something that we should celebrate and enhance.' In his discussion on conflict in liberal democracy, Barber (1984: 6) outlines three types of liberal democracy – anarchic, realist and minimalist – and argues that 'anarchism is *conflict-denying*, realism is *conflict-repressing* and minimalism is *conflict-tolerating*. The first approach tries to wish conflict away, the second to extirpate it and the third to live with it.' It could be argued that the alterglobalisation movement is closer to Mouffe's position than any of these three liberal approaches and is conflict-embracing, welcoming conflict as a sign of diversity, resolving it by rejecting the normative principle of singular unity and expanding the constructive potential of conflict.[4]

The prevalence in the liberal democratic model of an adversarial notion of conflict is not surprising when one considers that competition is one of the core components of liberal democracy. Held (1996: 74) writes of the different 'variants' of liberalism that 'they were all united around the advocacy of constitutional state, private property and the competitive market economy'. It is no coincidence that the alterglobalisation movement promotes non-competitive notions of democracy and diversity when one considers that the rejection of this competitive market (and the competitive rationale that underlies it) is a central unity in the overlapping unities that constitute the movement. Two core democratic values of democracy – liberty and equality – re-emerge as important values in the alterglobalisation movement, but these values are perceived to be hindered and not complemented by the competitive capitalist market. In this way the democratic praxis of the alterglobalisation movement encourages the observer to make a distinction between democratic systems and democratic values. They reject the liberal democratic system, but it is the existence and widespread acceptance of these liberal democratic values that makes it possible for the movement to criticise multilateral organisations like the WTO, the IMF and the World Bank. The ambiguity of meaning that the words 'participation', 'liberty' and 'equality' have works in favour of the movement actors as they simultaneously redefine these concepts and appeal to their existing importance established by liberal democratic systems.

A Democratic Disclaimer

The centrality of democracy in the practices of the alterglobalisation movement ironically reinforces Amartya Sen's statement quoted above. Today, the only alternative to democracy is democracy. Not more democracy but different democracy. Even in the process of re-envisioning all of global society, democracy lies at the centre of the project for another world and presumably this is the historical legacy of democracy to which Amartya Sen refers. Considering this association between democracy and the hegemonic world order, it seems appropriate to ask: what are the implications of using the term 'democracy' to describe the alterglobalisation movement's practices and how widespread is the use of this term?

The use of the term 'democracy' is pervasive in the alterglobalisation movement. Many movement actors use the term 'democracy' to refer to their own practices, and the Charter of Principles of the WSF clearly cites democracy as an aim (WSF BOC and IC 2001). The Zapatistas have even equated democracy with being human in their desire for a 'more just, more free, more democratic, that is, more human' world (quoted in Lorenzano 1998: 129). Nevertheless, there are movement actors who prefer not to use the term. Some of the more anarchist movement actors feel the word cannot be dislodged from 'authoritarian connotations'. Other movement actors have pointed to the inherent 'western bias' of the concept and still others have argued that democracy has always rested on the exclusion of 'minorities', women, children, etc. These actors point out that the term has been used over hundreds of years, and is used today, to enforce particular norms and practices in the 'third world', particularly secularism and individualism. These critical voices are useful to temper the risk of what Warren (1996: 243) calls 'romantic dogma', arguing that 'radical democrats almost without exception hold that democratic participation is an attractive activity, one that people would naturally choose'.

There is good reason to be careful when using the term 'democracy' and the values with which it is related. Even the seemingly most benign democratic value, 'participation', one at the centre of the alterglobalisation movement's democratic ideal, has been shown to lead to 'neo-orientalist delegitimising' in the context of development projects (Mosse 2002: 33, cf. Cooke and Kothari 2001, Nelson and Wright 1995, Paley 2001: 140–81). The other democratic values – liberty, equality, representation – do not escape critique either: 'Celia Amoros and others say these values have been laden with patriarchal and colonial assumptions, so why should they be the beacons for building another world?' (Ponniah and Fisher 2004: 179). Perhaps the most important has been the feminist and 'southern' critiques of 'western' rationalism. Democracy today is deeply connected to the project of modernity, which rests upon the rational subject, rational argument and the formulation of universal principles (Touraine 1997). This assumption of a rational subject is challenged by feminist critiques that argue that 'ideals of reason have incorporated an exclusion of the feminine' (Lloyd 1982: 8) and excludes the communicative styles of all 'socially marginalized' groups (Coombe 1998: 278) as well as postmodern critiques of Enlightenment rationalism, essentialism and universalism (Benhabib 1996: 5). This rationalism is still very present in the alterglobalisation movement, which maintains as part of the rules of engagement a severely logical and emotion-less style of discussion.[5]

Despite these concerns, movement actors employ both the term and the values of democracy with an astounding frequency. Still, defining this democracy remains difficult. It is a democracy that is intentionally fluid, changing from one context to the next. Nevertheless, this fluidity and malleability circles around certain commonalities and shared aversions. We can say for sure that this is not the democracy of ancient Athens or the democracy of the French Revolution, and it is often set up in direct contrast to contemporary liberal representative democracies. There is no mention of the state or an official government, no fixed structure of representation and no electoral system. Nevertheless, the activists often refer to horizontality and diversity as 'democratic' and when they call for more democracy these are the values they are invoking. This movement is certainly not the first movement to have taken on democracy as a central issue, but it is in the combination of these values, the fact that they are already being put into practice, and the global scale at which they are applied that the novelty arises. This is democracy as we have never seen it before, at least not with the term 'democracy' attached to it. Prefiguration, horizontality, diversity, decentralisation and the network structure all challenge certain aspects of liberal representative democracy and, when combined, offer an interesting if not yet realistic alternative. In order to draw out this fluid, changing democratic praxis, I present some examples of decision-making in the alterglobalisation movement, offering analysis in terms of limits and potentials organised around implicit and explicit interpretations of the classic democratic principles of liberty, equality, participation and representation with the added category of 'diversity'. Despite the significant implications of these democratic practices, it is not my intention to develop a comprehensive and consistent theory of this democracy or to propose a method by which this movement's democratic praxis could become a democracy practised by everyone the world over. What I offer here is an ethnography of a set of democratic practices within the alterglobalisation movement. In order to highlight the significant elements of this emerging democratic praxis, I bring ethnographic fieldwork into dialogue with existing democratic theory and raise questions about democratic practice and theory in a global age.

Locating the Power to Decide

Edinburgh Spokescouncil

It was early evening and Kevin and I were packing up our flipcharts and magic markers after a two-hour training session in decision-making in large groups. Bill, one of the people helping to coordinate the week of activities in the Edinburgh convergence space, was waiting for us at the door. His was a face I had seen many times over the past six years and, although we barely knew each other, we were both usual suspects at these meetings and had many common friends. A few days earlier he had asked Kevin and me if we could take on facilitating the first spokescouncil meeting at the Edinburgh convergence space, to which we both readily agreed. Kevin and I were part of the Action Trainers Collective and the facilitation working group that was set up during the 2005 anti-G8 mobilisation. The latter was set up specifically to ensure that the large spokescouncil meetings would get off to a good start and that there would be a clear point of access for anyone who wanted to help in the difficult task of facilitating large consensus meetings.

As we walked from the training space to the meeting hall, Bill was running through the most important agenda items. He told us that the train chartered from London carrying hundreds of activists was going to arrive at the station that evening and there were already reports of heavy police presence at the station. Two decisions had to be made: we had to decide whether or not we should all go to the station to greet the train in case the police tried to stop them, and where to take those who were arriving since there were still major problems with surveillance and police control at the designated campsite. In addition to this, we had to decide whether or not the Dissent! network would call for people to take part in the Make Poverty History (MPH) march that was planned for the next day. There were a couple of other logistical matters on the agenda, but these were the two items that could potentially have been points of contention.

While Bill and the others from the convergence working group were the first to add items to the agenda, it was Kevin and I who decided in what order the agenda items would appear on the large white sheet of paper to which we gave the title 'proposed agenda'. We hung it up on the wall next to the poster that said 'proposed group agreement'. We chose to put the discussion about the train at the bottom of the agenda because we thought it would be the most contentious and we wanted to have all the other matters out of the way before starting that discussion. So once the room was full and everyone was sitting down in a very large circle, Kevin began by introducing the group agreement and gave a very short description of what consensus is, why we use it and how it works. Kevin read out the five items he had put on the group agreement and asked people if they wanted to add anything or if they had concerns about any of the existing items. A couple of people asked for clarification, but there were no concerns and the meeting moved on quickly to the agenda. We ran through the items we already had on the agenda and asked for any additions. Several suggestions were made and we added them to the agenda in an order that seemed logical to us, to the person who made the addition and to everyone else in the room. This involved a lot of asking, 'Is it all right if we put the item right before the MPH discussion?' and 'Is that okay with everyone?' The meeting then dealt with informational points and practicalities before moving onto the discussion about the MPH demonstration.

This discussion was organised in a small group to large group spokescouncil format and proceeded as follows: first, the agenda item was introduced and explained by the facilitators (Kevin in this case). Then we, the facilitators, asked if there were any questions or need for clarification about the topic for discussion. A couple of people asked specifics about when and where the demonstration was going to take place and who was organising it and what kind of contact 'we' (the Dissent! network) had with the organisers. Then one person started to say, 'I don't think we should take part in the demonstration if it's being organised by those NGOs ...' but he was quickly interrupted by myself and Kevin who told him that we were still just asking for questions and clarifications, not yet starting the discussion. There were no more questions and so Kevin and I split the large meeting into smaller groups so that everyone would be able to take part in the discussion and share their opinion. The groups were based on where people were sitting, not on previously existing friendships or connections. The groups were told that they should voice and collect (write down on a big flipchart poster sheet) initial reactions, personal interests and/or needs, gather ideas and then discuss the ideas, record questions, possible suggestions or proposals and especially any major objections to proposals raised. Then, after ten minutes of discussion, the groups were asked to choose one person to act as a 'spoke' to come into the middle of the circle and present the feedback from their group.

These 'spokes' then formed a small circle inside the larger circle. They were first asked to present all the ideas, reactions and concerns or objections that were raised in their group. Kevin made it clear that this should just be presenting of ideas, not a discussion about those ideas. This step was done in five minutes, and the next step of discussing these many ideas began. First the discussion was only between the spokes, with all the others watching and listening. The spokes were given ten minutes to highlight points where all the groups had agreement, and the concerns that were raised several times, and to put together a proposal based on the common ideas that addressed all the concerns. The meeting then split up again into the same small groups for ten minutes and the spokes discussed the proposal they had made with everyone in their group, checking for agreement and collecting any objections and amendments to the proposal.

Kevin and I then asked the small groups to pick another person to come into the centre of the circle to act as spoke and to present the feedback their group had given to the proposal. It was immediately clear that there was a lot of disagreement and many objections and amendments were raised in these smaller groups. Kevin and I recorded all of these, grouping them into categories, and presented a two-minute summary of the main concerns to focus the discussion. We then checked with everyone if they felt our condensed version was an accurate representation of the concerns – 'Is there anything we are forgetting? Does everyone agree this is a good description of where we are? Are there any questions or points of clarification?' The spokes then discussed for another ten minutes until they had a proposal that addressed all of the concerns raised and incorporated some of the amendments. The group then split up one last time into the smaller groups to discuss the new proposal and check for agreement, or at least to make sure there was no longer strong opposition. This last round of small groups approved the proposal because it had abandoned trying to get everyone involved in one course of action. The first proposal had been to go to the MPH demonstration, but to make our difference from MPH clear by wearing bright colours (instead of the requested white) and by handing out flyers called 'make capitalism history'. This first proposal had incorporated most of the concerns raised, especially the fact that some people didn't want to support a section of the movement that was reinforcing the legitimacy of the G8. When the proposal was sent back to the small groups, it was clear that dressing differently was not enough for many people who felt that they could not go to the march, and that the Dissent! network should not put out a call asking everyone to go to the march. In making the second proposal therefore, it was decided that the entire network did not need to go to the march, that everyone should have the option to either go to the march or to take part in an alternative action. The proposal, therefore, included two possibilities for action. The group would send out a call for people to meet at one location, but then they would split up and one group would go to the MPH march (critically, with an intent to challenge it) and the other group would do an action that happened simultaneously but in clear opposition. This proposal received approval from all the small groups and the meeting moved on to the next agenda item.

By organising the meeting in this way, it became possible to discuss a highly contentious item that reflected quite strong political divides in a way that included everyone. The discussion gave everyone present a chance to have input in the process at several stages of decision-making. And it did so without everyone having to listen to everyone else, one after another, for hours on end. This discussion also prevented the network from putting out a call that would have received little support from the rest of the network and might have alienated many people within the network. Points of agreement were quickly identified and summarised, and the points of contention were also raised and addressed rather than ignored, denied or out-voted. Incorporating these concerns made for a much better proposal, one for engagement with MPH, but for critical engagement that expressed difference through clothes colour and a leaflet with a distinct political message. Even though this first proposal seemed to respond to the concerns raised in the small groups, this was not the case. But it was only once the proposal was sent back for consultation that the inadequacy of the proposal became apparent. The final proposal, on the other hand, made it possible for those who did not want to go to the MPH march to still be included in the day of actions by setting up an alternate action. Choosing to have a common meeting space made it possible for people who were not at the meeting to be briefed about the decision taken and to decide for themselves what course of action they wanted to take the next day. At no point were the different opinions about MPH and whether their march was politically useful or not pitted against each other. All of the concerns raised were framed as concerns about a common proposal which everyone was building together, and which would incorporate all of the conflicting opinions even if it meant making a proposal that actually advocated two different, but connected, courses of action. The meeting was consciously set up to allow for this possibility. The structure used, of large group to small group spokescouncil consensus was meant to allow for everyone to have a say and be heard. When this type of inclusion is achieved, it often leads to highly creative proposals that involve multiple courses of action.

Locating the Power to Decide

Allowing everyone to have a say and be heard in the context of movement meetings is about challenging the centralisation of power. It requires that movement actors think clearly about where the power to decide is located and set up structures that allow it to be located elsewhere, that intentionally spread it out across the network. Where, how and by whom decisions are made is of central political importance in a movement that is prefiguring a democracy based on horizontality. As we have seen in the previous chapter, horizontality as a practice presupposes the presence of power inequalities. Horizontality, it is argued, is necessary because even within movement structures power centralises and therefore continuous decentralisation is required. In the alterglobalisation movement, there are two ways power is centralised (localised) and exercised: there are official, intentional loci of power, and unofficial (sometimes) unintentional loci of power.[6] As we saw in Chapter 3, there is a consistently more centralised and hierarchical power structure in the social fora than in the autonomous strands of the anti-summit mobilisations. This is partially due to the more rigid structure of the decision-making process and the presence of people and organisations from the 'traditional left', and partially due to a centralisation inherent in the social forum that one does not find in anti-summit mobilisations. There is only one 'official' European or World Social Forum at any time in any one location, but there are always many simultaneous mobilisations against any one summit. This power of 'officiality' is the first kind of power exercised in the social forum process that is not present in anti-summit mobilisations. This officiality influences the types of powers that emerge and highlights the main difference between the loci of power in a social forum versus an anti-summit mobilisation: a social forum will always have fewer loci of power of which most are official, while an anti-summit mobilisation has considerably more loci of power of which most are unofficial.[7]

The Anti-G8 Mobilisation 2005: The Dissent! Network

The most important aspect to highlight about decision-making in the Dissent! network, is that decisions are taken at meetings. As such, the kind of decision that is most valued is the collective decision. Sometimes these are small working group meetings, sometimes local or regional meetings, and sometimes national and international Dissent! gatherings. Within the Dissent! network there is a direct relationship between the importance of a decision and the number of people needed to make a decision. For any decisions affecting the entire network in a fundamental way, as many people as possible need to be involved from as many different subgroups and strands of the network as possible. This importance placed on quantity stems from two assumptions held by the actors. The first is the assumption that the quality of the decision reached is better when more people are involved in reaching it. There is no need for a philosopher king if only many minds can think together. The fallibility or incompetence of any one imperfect actor will be compensated for by the other actors. The 'perfect ruler', or in this case, decision-maker, is constructed collectively. The process of consensus has this value built into it. In consensus, a particular problem or topic is raised, followed by brainstorming on the subject until there is a proposal put forward. That proposal is then improved upon by anyone or everyone through the addition of amendments until the proposal is satisfactory to all. Reaching decisions by consensus is a cumulative process that assumes knowledge to be something collectively constructed through interaction (rather than something possessed by an individual) and therefore more participation in decision-making is necessarily always better. This approach should not be confused with aggregative democracy, however, which despite being 'skeptical about conceptions of the common good' (Cohen 1996: 105) and despite resting upon the equal consideration of interests and a 'presumption of personal autonomy' (Dahl 1989), has 'bequeathed a view of democracy in which competing for the majority's vote is the essence of the exercise' (Shapiro 2003: 3). Rather, the movement enacts the construction of a cumulative process in which diverse ideas are merged into single, if complex, proposals as one of the mechanisms through which decision-making is transformed from adversarial debate between competing ideas towards constructive cooperation, even when those proposing the ideas perceive themselves to be at odds.

The second aspect underlying the importance of quantity in making decisions is illustrated by one of the most common concerns raised when decisions are being taken – the question of representation. Although it is rarely phrased in terms of representation, the concern raised as 'I don't think we have enough people at this meeting to make this decision' is ultimately a concern about representation. Because diversity is essential, and the representation of diversity through singularity or even by the few is considered impossible, there is a strongly felt need to have a certain number of people from enough different groups in order for a decision to be considered legitimate. Although the exact numbers are not fixed, and depend on the decision being made, the representation of highly diverse interests by the few is presumed impossible and an increase in the number of people present is considered more likely to result in a decision satisfactory to all.

The Hori-Zone 'Ecovillage'

The intention of the Hori-Zone campsite (and the many other campsites that have been organised at anti-summit mobilisations and alongside the social forum) was to create a living example of an alternative society while at the same time fulfilling the practical function of housing activists coming from all over the world. The campsite housed several thousand people organised into geographically delineated neighbourhoods, called 'barrios'.[8] Camp-wide decisions were taken at two spokescouncil meetings, one in the morning for practical matters and one in the evening for discussing action plans. These were fed into by the barrio and working group meetings. In the Hori-Zone camp, as more and more people arrived and the evening meetings began to grow in size, one of the evening meetings decided that a facilitation working group was needed and some of us from the Action Trainers Collective, together with other interested people, set up a working group to coordinate the facilitation of these meetings. Shortly after the G8, this facilitation working group sent out a questionnaire that described the decision-making structure of the Hori-Zone space as follows:

The Hori-Zone was split into three meeting-types:

BARRIO (NEIGHBOURHOOD) MEETINGS
To organise life within the barrio and make decisions on policies/actions. Meetings once or more a day, time set by the individual barrios, attended by people from the barrio. Barrio meetings send one or two spokespeople each to the site co-ordination and action spokescouncils.

SITE CO-ORDINATION MEETINGS
To co-ordinate the practical aspects of the overall camps, such as food, compost, greywater, site security. Usually 9am attended by spokespeople from site working groups (such as grey water, kitchens) and from each neighbourhood.

ACTION SPOKESCOUNCILS
To co-ordinate actions. Attended by spokespeople from each barrio/affinity group/action working group as well as individuals.

Site co-ordination meeting and action spokescouncils tried to use consensus decision-making as did many barrios.

(Facilitation/Process Group 2005, email)

These three sites of decision-making were the closest the Hori-Zone campsite came to an 'official' decision-making structure. There were also many other sites of decision-making in the camp, but none were camp-wide. The convergence working group (which was quickly given the insulting nickname of 'the bureaucracy bloc'), together with highly skilled people (plumbers, electricians) had a camp overview in their heads, giving them a decision-making power outside of the meetings, albeit a power largely limited to the technical realm. And there were many individual affinity groups and task-oriented groups (medics, trainers, Indymedia) and ad hoc groups of people who made decisions affecting the outcome of the actions, but not the running of the camp as a whole. The overall structure of decision-making was highly decentralised, with central coordination through spokescouncils.

The Social Forum Organising Process

In contrast to the autonomous sections of the anti-summit mobilisations, the decision-making processes within social forum organising are not fully constructed by those taking part in organising the forum. Those who organised the first WSF and ESF helped construct the decision-making processes, but today those processes are partially cemented into place. When the decision is taken as to the location of the next social forum, the city of choice not only inherits the social forum, it also inherits the decision-making structures.

In the WSF organising process, there are five official loci of decision-making power. The first two are the International Council and the national Organising Committee. There are also local committees or councils in the city where the forum is to be held and working groups on specific tasks. Finally, there is the office space, which becomes the main site for the implementation of decisions. Because the office is meant to be a practical tool for implementation, it is not officially thought of as a decision-making space. Nevertheless, as we have seen, important decisions are taken by office staff, especially in the last weeks before the forum. The regional fora that grew out of the WSF inherited this general structure and adapted it only slightly. In the organising structures of the ESF there is no IC. There is instead the European Preparatory Assembly (EPA), open to anyone, which is officially the highest decision-making body of the ESF.[9]

There are also several unofficial sites of decision-making power. In the London ESF 2004, these unofficial sites held far more decision-making power than the official ones did (although the official sites of power were used for the legitimation of the unofficial power). In the organising process of the ESF 2004, there were the above-mentioned five official sites of decision-making power: the EPA, the UK Organising Committee (UKOC), the UK Coordinating Committee (UKCC), various working groups and two office spaces. The UKCC was the London-based group that met once a week at City Hall, which was meant to be a space where all practical matters and problems involved in organising the ESF could be discussed on a regular basis. The working groups worked in conjunction with the UKCC but often took decisions about their own projects independently. Within these official decision-making structures, decisions are usually taken through a negotiation process between a variety of groups and people at the local, national and international level. The London ESF, however, witnessed a stark shift in decision-making power, where ESF structures were not only being adjusted for the day-to-day reality of organising requirements (as they have always been to varying degrees), but also because alternative structures were being created.

In London a dual system of decision-making emerged. The first system was very simple, the Greater London Authority (GLA) decided single-handedly. The second system was more complicated and decentralised, but far less influential. In the second system the 'administrators' of the forum, the staff and volunteers doing the day-to-day practical work of organising the forum, could make decisions about the logistical and technical side of the social forum without the GLA (if these decisions did not cost more than £50). Because the GLA was the only major funding body, they had a near absolute (but unofficial) decision-making power. A GLA representative made this power very clear to me when I spoke to her about implementing a decision taken by the UKCC. She was against the decision and told me point blank that she wasn't going to release the funds because 'the coordinating committee doesn't decide these things, I do'.[10]

While money talks in the world of social fora, this power is not absolute. The GLA could not control all decisions (although to most 'horizontals' it felt as though they could); there were some spaces of technical decision-making that the GLA was not interested in controlling. For example, Babels had the power to make decisions about interpreter selection and booth *planification* without explicit GLA permission, even though Babels was directly overseen by a GLA staff member. This highlights the non-congruous relationship between power and control. Although having absolute power never guarantees complete control, in the social forum process there is great distance between having power and having control. The GLA approached the ESF in the same way they would have approached the organisers of any other such large event. They looked at where the power was centralised and they tried to control that space. They were very successful, almost unconditionally successful, in controlling that space (the UKCC and the offices), but what they did not understand about the social forum process is that it is not centralised, it 'does not constitute a locus of power to be disputed'. So while the GLA managed to achieve control over the organising structures by being the only major source of money, they could never achieve complete control over the ESF itself. When the participants arrived from all over Europe, the ESF took on a life of its own, and there was nothing anyone could do to control which interactions took place between whom and with what result. The network structure that is inherited from one year to the next of an 'open space' of plenaries and seminars and workshops whose content is filled by various groups from all over Europe, creates an uncontrollable diversity of interactions and outcomes. The power over decisions taken in the organising process of the social forum is to a large degree located in the Organising Committee, but even complete control over these decisions will never render complete control over the social forum as a whole.

The Power of Money

This attempt at control by the GLA, highlights one of the most influential factors in the creation of centralised power – money.

Movement actors' attitudes towards money determine to a large extent the eventual centralisation of power. In the London ESF, money represented one of the central sites of conflict. In the Dissent! network, however, money was almost insignificant. The budget working group of the Dissent! network was even an exception to the above-mentioned quantity rule in decision-making. While in the London ESF the fact that the budget group was made up of only a few people was one of the main conflicts, in Dissent!, even though the budget group was also made up of only a few people, I heard almost no complaints about this. Several factors went into making the budget group in Dissent! an acceptable exception to the general quantity rule. Firstly, the Dissent! budget group, like all working groups, had to run their decisions past the national gatherings (this was not the case in the London ESF), so their decisions were in the end actually sanctioned by, if not determined by, as many people as possible. Second, there was a lot of trust within the network that the budget working group would make the best decisions for the allocation of funds (a trust that, due to the 'bid' process, was not present in the London ESF). Third, many groups within Dissent! were self-funded and therefore had little stake in the decisions taken by the central budget group. However, these factors do not provide a sufficient explanation. To understand this phenomenon we need to examine the relationship to money that exists among many of the people involved in the Dissent! network.

For many within the Dissent! network, money seems to grow on trees. Whenever questions of how to fund something came up in larger meetings people would shrug off the concern by saying they would have a benefit concert or a party. Whether or not the money finally did come from a concert, the message of this statement was clear: do not let money stand in your way – just plan, think and act. But rather than concluding from this that money does in fact grow on trees, it is more useful to understand this attitude as exposing a cultural practice that often involves getting things for free, and being creative and innovative rather than just relying on money to make things possible. It is a political practice that entails a rejection of what the Zapatistas have called the 'cultural practice of throwing money at problems, buying solutions' (Flores, in Flores and Tanka 2001). Many people within the network hate money and feel the world would be a better place without it. They are not resigned to its inevitable necessity. At a training session organised as part of the mobilisation against the G8, one activist was asked what she would change if she could go back in time and change any one thing. She replied that she would 'stop the invention of money'. This range of feelings, from disdain to dislike, underlies the lack of importance attributed to money matters in the Dissent! network. While discussions of money dominate entirely the social forum planning context, here money is considered almost insignificant, and money therefore loses its centralising and governing power.

Being There Gives You Power – Maybe

There is one type of power common to all movement spaces that needs to be stated explicitly. To have power in the collective decision-making processes of the alterglobalisation movement, presence is required. Both social forum and anti-summit mobilisation processes have in common the emphasis on collective decision-making at meetings, with a greater importance placed on meetings at which more people are present, preferably from as many different places and groups as possible. Meetings are used as the main site for decision-making so that everyone will feel included in the decisions, but of course, you have to be at the meeting to feel included.[11] Inclusion here is defined as participation, and participation is defined as presence. Presence is the necessary prerequisite for inclusion and power, but it is not sufficient. To have a say you have to be present, but being present is not a guarantee to having a say.

Being present for the implementation of decisions can also be crucial. In the Hori-Zone camp, this is the type of power the 'bureaucracy bloc' was being accused of wielding. Once a decision is made, someone has to implement it and there is not always perfect congruency between decisions made and decisions implemented. The demonstration held at the end of the ESF 2004 is a good example of this incongruity. The EPA decided that the slogans for the demonstration should not focus exclusively on George Bush and America, but also address wider issues of racism, privatisation and precarity. However, those organising the logistics of the demonstration did not consider these latter issues very popular among the British public and, although they ultimately lost the debate in the EPA, they did not make any particular effort to include other topics in the demonstration. This situation is not unique to the ESF 2004; it is a structural problem inherent in the official ESF decision-making process. Without any way of ensuring that the decisions taken at the EPA are carried out, the local organisers end up with power over most decisions simply because they are there.[12]

Transforming Democratic Values

Within movement decision-making processes there is a common democratic praxis emerging that is central to understanding what constitutes the aims and methods of this movement. Below I develop an outline of the central elements of this praxis through the use of conflictive ethnography that presents these elements not as perfectly functioning democratic ideals, but as real practices complete with contradictions. The democratic praxis being developed by the alterglobalisation movement is in perpetual negotiation. Even as it takes form, it is changing again into several variations on that form. It is very much a case of Derrida's 'iteration', where every repetition results in the creation of a slightly different form; these forms, however, leave 'traces' that share commonalities (Dillon 1993: 199). My aim is to draw out some of these commonalities and their implications.

Democracy as a Decision-making Process

Democracy is most commonly understood to be a system of 'rule by the people' (Held 1996: 1) or rather 'of the people, by the people and for the people ... a system within which the people rule: collective self-rule' (Wolff 1996: 68). But of course such a definition does not tell us very much about how a democratic system would work. How exactly it is that 'the people' should 'rule' is unclear. What decision-making structure or process is required to ensure this sovereignty of the people and even what constitutes 'the people' varies from theory to theory. However, if we shift the emphasis from the static entity, 'the people', who enact democracy, to the *process* of democracy, we reach another common definition of democracy which defines democracy instead as a system of decision-making (Knowles 2001: 300).[13] Defining democracy in this way requires us to construct a different and broader history of democracy. Graeber (2001: 87), implicitly accepting this definition of democracy, places the origins of democratic practice in an original light when he asks:

> We are usually told that democracy originated in ancient Athens – like science, or philosophy, it was a Greek invention. It's never quite clear what this is supposed to mean. Are we supposed to believe that before the Athenians, it never really occurred to anyone, anywhere, to gather all the members of their community in order to make joint decisions in a way that gave everyone equal say?

Or as the Zapatistas so eloquently put it:

> Our path was always that the will of the many be in the hearts of the men and women who command ... Another word came from afar ... [and] gave the name of 'democracy' to our way that was before words travelled. (quoted in Nash 1997: 264).

The alterglobalisation movement reclaims the word 'democracy' not only to liberate it from the restrictive definition of political theory, but also to free themselves from a liberal representative democracy that monopolises the meaning of democratic values which they consider to be collectively theirs and which precede the oppressive democratic systems they have known (especially in Latin America). As we shall see below, defining democracy in terms of decision-making rather than in terms of who rules (even if it be 'the people'), is essential to the methods of decision-making being developed by movement actors.

Equality

Movement actors assume that equality must be continuously created and constructed. It is not a natural state of affairs that needs merely to be acknowledged or declared by some authority. This assumption about equality leads to the active construction of procedures for fostering equality. Consensus is one of the ways movement actors try to continuously create equality. In most collective spaces of this movement voting is considered an automatic violation of equality. Voting violates equality because it silences minority voices. As one activist put it in an email with the subject line 'Democracy', 'Historical experience and current political reality have precisely shown that voting reproduces injustices' (email, De Angelis 2003b). Even in the social forum processes voting is not an acceptable practice. When the UK mobilising committee to the 2003 ESF in Paris voted to decide who the UK representatives would be, and especially when they voted to decide which plenary speakers to send to Paris, there was outrage and chaos at the meetings. Accusatory cries were flung across the room that 'social forums do not vote' and the SWP was criticised for 'packing the room' to get their speakers chosen. This outrage did not stay in the meeting room; word of the vote travelled across Europe and infused the decision-making process with strong tensions. And when the decision was finally taken to send the next ESF to London despite concerns about democracy, Sophie Zafari gave the UK delegation a stern warning that 'we do not vote in the social forum' (10 November 2003, Bobigny, Paris).

Underlying this outrage was a history of experience that led activists to feel that voting necessarily leads to stark inequality, exclusion and consequently less diversity. These experiences were not only linked to alienation within nation-state democratic systems, but also to democracy within the movement. In an email critiquing the above-mentioned vote within the social forum, one activist cited his experience inside the UK Stop the War Coalition:

the Stop the War Coalition is a good example to use. When we examine, for example, the 'delegate assembly' that Alex points to as a triumph of the SWP-style process, it becomes quickly apparent that such a process goes utterly against the principles and spirit of the ESF and the social forum phenomenon. 800 people delegated from local groups, who then spend their time listening to 'big-name' speakers and voting on slogans to take to the masses is NOT participatory, is NOT empowering and is, in the end, utterly self-defeating. I say this as one of those 800 delegates. (Sellwood 2003)

When voting was used within the ESF organising process, groups that had more members present at the meeting would get their speakers chosen and the groups who had only a few people would be scrapped from the list regardless of their abilities as public speakers. Voting was being objected to because it led to a numerical equality based on majority and not merit (a criticism Aristotle makes of Athenian democracy). This type of equality is not deemed to be equality by most movement actors because it means that only the relatively more powerful and homogeneous opinions are heard. The conflict at this meeting was not so much about voting as it was about what constitutes equality. For these movement actors, voting is an exercise of de Tocqueville's (2000 [1835–40]) 'tyranny of the majority' that rests on 'the "either/or" binary thinking approach' (Polletta 2002: 193), which many movement actors repudiate. This vote went against a notion of equality that is common in the alterglobalisation movement, but which is not fully accepted by the traditional left sections of the movement. This concept of equality insists that if equality is deemed to exist in the alterglobalisation movement's democratic framework, it must exist in the process and the outcomes of decisions, not only in terms of individual input.[14] It is not enough that each individual can contribute equally with one vote, if the outcome of those votes collectively favours one group over another.

This conceptualisation of equality stems from an assumption held in most collective movement spaces, namely that complete equality cannot exist among 'the people' as such because power inequalities of all kinds are assumed to be inevitable (see

Chapter 3). Equality is always intrinsically desirable, but never fully achievable. Therefore, if there is to be equality, or if the inevitable inequalities are to be limited, they must be limited through the construction of decision-making processes that take these inequalities into consideration and create practices which compensate for, rather than ignore, these inequalities. This is why many meetings are introduced with comments about anti-sexist or anti-racist behaviour and agreements that encourage everyone to limit how much they speak and to actively listen to each other. At some meetings a leaflet was handed out called 'Tools for White Men and Other People Socialized in a Society Based on Domination' that included advice like 'practise noticing who's in the room at meetings – how many men, how many women, how many white people, how many people of colour, is it majority heterosexual, are there out queers, what are people's class backgrounds. Don't assume to know people, but work at being more aware' and 'you will be needed in the movement when you realize that you are not needed in the movement', among many other helpful tips. Tools like these are part of a collective process of helping each other limit power inequalities that inevitably arise, and to limit the degree to which these inequalities can influence the decisions reached. For many movement actors, the decision-making system needs to allow for equal outcomes even where there are unequal inputs (or in other words when the actors have unequal power) because there are always assumed to be unequal inputs. What is meant by the 'result' of a decision is not merely the content of the decision reached; it refers also to the effect the decision *process* has on the dynamic between participants. When movement actors feel excluded or ignored, there is a problem with the process that ought to be addressed. Movement actors are concerned with whether or not the method used to reach a decision resulted in more or less inclusion, more or less power inequalities. This was the main concern underlying complaints about the exclusive nature of the 'bid' process for the London ESF. Although there is an assumption that inequality is inevitable, there is also the assumption that decision-making structures can be set up to limit inequalities, and a good outcome is when a decision is made with the least possible exercise or creation of power inequalities.

The presence of inequality in voting as a decision-making system is especially important in the case of this movement because 'the people' is not a fixed group determined by time and space. There is no way to allow everyone within a network to have a vote. There is no beginning or end to a network, so universal suffrage is impossible.[15] Instead, a further inequality arises where only those who are present are included in the 'equality'. And once this is the case, it is a very simple matter of getting enough people of one opinion to come to a meeting to automatically place more power in one kind of vote than in another. This was the accusation being made when the SWP was accused of 'packing the room'. They were disproportionately represented in the meeting and therefore each of their votes held more power than the votes of every other person. This competitive bargaining is in quite strong contrast to the democratic praxis otherwise characteristic of the alterglobalisation movement.

Still, these moments of exception are telling. When a practice reveals itself as an aberration to the acceptable or normal behaviour of the group, the values held by the group are exposed. The consensus process, it is argued, allows for the inequality of 'the people' (assumed to be inherent in voting) to be compensated for by simultaneously requiring participants in meetings to hold the interests of the group above their own, and by giving absolute power to each individual to block decisions that violate their most fundamental interests. In consensus the relationship built between group interests and individual interests (or in Rousseau's terminology the general will and the particular will) is not one of opposition. There are two reasons for this. First, the individual actor is expected to put the interests of the group above their own, except when her basic values or principles would be violated by the decision being reached. In such a case, the group is expected to respect the individual, not the other way around. It is a two-way street that allows for an individual to hold the group's interests above their own without any threat to the most important of her own interests. When a block is used (in large groups), it requires that the whole group take seriously the individual's concern and try to understand it in order to either rework the proposal to resolve the concern (which is what usually happens) or to find a satisfactory way out for the person blocking. In movement lingo this latter option involves a shift from a block to a 'stand aside', which means that the person who does not like the proposal does not have to be involved in or linked to the proposed course of action. This respect for individual interests is possible because the assumption underlying the 'block' mechanism in consensus seems to be that if a decision genuinely violates the most fundamental principles of even just one member of the group, then the decision is not in the best interest of the group as a whole.

The second reason for this lack of tension comes from neither the group interest nor the individual interest being a fixed, reified essence. The group interest is the constructed product of various interests shared by different people and the negotiation between these interests in particular contexts. Interests that are negotiated become highly context specific, allowing for the multiple identities of individuals to be expressed at different times depending on which identity is most relevant to the interests being pursued at any given moment. The insistence on putting the interests of the group first does not require that the individual put their own interests aside. Instead it requires that the individual put their own interests into the group for feedback and negotiation with other people's interests. The aim is to create collective interests. This shift in the way interests are understood challenges the 'assumption of narrowly self-interested individuals [that] has evidently appeared to be "natural" to many modern economists' (Sen 2006: 21). The process assumes that we never create our interests in a vacuum and therefore interests are always collective, at least partially:

> Climate change, G8 and all are about what is the end point, I think we should discuss and outline the process of how we get there. What I think is a good thing to work on depends on what everyone else thinks is worth working on (Dissent! national gathering, Sheffield, 15 October 2005)

This shift to collective interests changes the way equality must be understood. Equality cannot be an essence, nor can it be a fixed state of affairs established by some authority or some common agreement between all those involved as in a 'one man, one vote'. Rather than being attributed to 'the people', it becomes a product, an outcome, of a decision-making *process* that negotiates the interests of all those present in and with the continuously changing contexts of the movement. Equality is continuously made, not declared.

If there is a fixed type of equality built into the structure of decision-making in movement processes, then it is an equality of participation in influencing decisions (outcomes). Consensus creates equality by allowing for each person participating in making a decision to have equal influence on the outcome. This kind of equality is rarely assumed to exist, and literature on consensus decision-making as well as practices like the 'group agreement' demonstrate that movement actors do not take this kind of equality for granted. Rather, it exists only if the actors make a conscious effort to behave in a way that maximises this equality, or rather minimises the inevitable inequalities. The implied belief is that consensus decision-making makes equal participation more possible than other systems, but only if the participants self-regulate their behaviour accordingly and take an active role in constructing that equality. The structures for this type of equality have to be set up from the start of a process or a meeting. As can be seen in the example of the first Edinburgh spokescouncil meeting described above, the agenda items were partially determined ahead of time by people from the convergence working group, then they were discussed with me and someone else from the facilitation working group and we prioritised them in a way that we thought would make the most efficient meeting and finally, we presented the agenda to the large convergence-wide meeting as a 'proposed agenda'. The first step (after the group agreement) was to ask for additions to the agenda, to ask for alterations and points of clarification. This three-step agenda process includes everyone who is present not only in the decisions being reached, but also the process of determining what gets to be decided and what not.

This practice of self-awareness and collective construction of relative equality, however, is far more prevalent in the autonomous strands of anti-summit mobilisations than social forum processes. Most of the actors in the autonomous sections of the anti-summit mobilisations were more familiar with consensus and more ideologically committed to it than those in the social forum organising processes. In the social forum spaces there was often an assumption built into the process that there was already equality between all those present at meetings. To be present was to be equal; an equality akin to that of one man, one vote. In the social forum processes, the place where inequality is acknowledged is in the difference between those who are able to be present at meetings and those that are not. The enlargement working group of the ESF, for example, has as its sole purpose to try and equalise the inequality of access for actors from eastern European countries, and Babels repeatedly highlights the inequality of access by insisting on having marginalised languages represented in the interpretation of the planning meetings, plenaries and seminars. In social forum processes, it is assumed that equality can be created by removing structural obstacles that stand in the way of participation. Once inclusion, like presence, is achieved, equality is assumed to follow. The irony of this, however, is that often this assumption that equality can be achieved simply by removing the obstacles to participation actually worsens the inequality among those present at social forum planning meetings. Most of the inequalities that are perpetuated in the social forum processes are perpetuated, and often exaggerated, through this denial of inequality.

Liberty

Consensus decision-making can only work when strict guidelines are adhered to, and these rules of engagement have implications for liberty in the democratic praxis of the alterglobalisation movement. Despite the standard (although inaccurate) characterisation of anarchism and anarchists as the epitome of limitless liberty, where 'there is no acceptable limit to the liberty of the individual' (Wolff 1996: 116), this movement seems to have very

clear ideas about how liberty should be limited and why, largely
due to the anarchist influence. When Wolff wrote the above he
was specifically contrasting the position of anarchists and limitless
liberty to Hobbes and his belief that the state may 'enforce
whatever rules and restrictions it wishes' (Wolff 1996: 116). If
we were to accept this opposition between liberty and rules, then
it would be surprising to see that it is in the anarchist-dominated
spaces of this movement that we tend to find the most rules and
restrictions. The decision-making processes of this movement
indicate that the actors involved assume a very different notion of
how liberty is achieved. These rules and restrictions on behaviour
are believed to enable not disable people to be free and equal.

The movement's relationship to rules and restrictions and
consequently to liberty can be illustrated through the example
of a common practice in the anti-G8 summit mobilisation in
2005. At many of the meetings, especially the large spokescouncil
meetings held during the G8 summit, a consensus facilitation tool
called the 'group agreement' was used. When groups of people
come together to meet for the first time, the group agreement
is sometimes used to ensure that everyone shares at least some
principles and has the basic understanding required for successful
use of consensus. Most importantly, it functions to ensure that
everyone is involved from the very beginning in determining how
the meeting will be run. The ideal group agreement would start
as a blank slate and people in the group would fill it with what
they want to have as their guidelines. However, I have never
actually seen the group agreement process occur in this way. More
commonly, the facilitator will propose a group agreement at the
beginning of the meeting. The agreement itself is usually a very
basic set of guidelines which are largely unobjectionable within
the context of the anti-summit mobilisation meetings. The group
agreement we introduced at the first spokescouncil meeting in
the Edinburgh convergence space contained the following five
points: (1) make sure everyone is heard, (2) respect each other's
opinions, (3) practice active agreement, (4) use hand signals and
(5) help keep to time. The same group agreement was proposed
at other meetings with various additions being made, especially

the common addition requiring those present to 'practise anti-oppressive behaviour' (anti-racist, anti-sexist, etc.). At a Dissent! meeting in Belgium the proposed agreement included practising anti-oppressive behaviour, and the additions that were made by the participants included respecting the house rules of the squat where the meeting was being held, actively helping in the practicalities like cooking and cleaning (it was a weekend-long gathering) and one about non-communication with the police or media.

The group agreement functions to create a collective process from the very beginning of the meeting and involves everyone in determining how they choose to relate to one another. At the level of the group it works as a mechanism through which the group collectively decides to use the consensus process, and on the individual level it is a type of initiation. Even for those who have never heard of consensus before, after they have taken part in constructing a group agreement they have the basic information and skills required to participate in a consensus meeting productively. Because the people in the group can remove or add any items to or from the agreement, it helps to build up a certain level of individual commitment to the group. The group agreement functions as a set of parameters through which behaviour is controlled, but importantly, self-controlled. For example, when there is a point about anti-oppressive behaviour in a group agreement, that is a restriction to what one can and cannot do or say during the meeting, but it is one meant to enhance the liberty of all. All the points in the group agreement require active commitment from the actors not just to refrain from doing something but to make an effort to participate in particular practices, everything from actively listening to helping with the logistics of running the meeting. Liberty in the alterglobalisation movement is not a passive liberty to be consumed by the individual, but just like equality, it needs to be built and actively worked on by the actors. Although there are many rules (usually euphemistically called 'guidelines') and restrictions defining acceptable behaviour in the movement's democratic praxis, these rules and restrictions are fluid, they can be brought into question, discussed and confirmed or rejected by the actors whenever necessary. These basic rules and restrictions are one way in which the activists attempt to create an environment that is as inclusive, equal and free as possible – but within limits.

Exploring how this movement understands liberty leads to a conclusion that would confuse many political theorists. We have a social movement heavily influenced by anarchism, some of the movement spaces made up almost entirely of people who would identify as anarchist, and yet still this 'absolute liberty' is missing. Rather than a liberty based on a 'live as you like' policy, we have a liberty that allows for people to collectively live as they like, based on a set of 'guidelines' that not only say what should not be done, but also what should be done. Yet, this is only a contradiction from the point of view of certain strands of political theory. On occasion I did meet movement actors who were made uneasy by the guidelines for behaviour in certain contexts, and I have seen these guidelines go very far, but generally speaking no one seems to feel their liberty is threatened.[16] Instead they offer the comfort that one can be involved and *heard* in making a decision; a liberty they have long been denied in liberal representative democracy. This involvement is the liberty valued most by movement actors. One need not insist on one's individual liberty if one has a voice in the group and if the group can be trusted to recognise and respect that voice whenever it becomes threatened.

Diversity

The French revolutionary movement added a third concept to the heart of democratic theory to create the democratic trinity known as '*liberté, égalité, fraternité*'. Today's movement offers an alternative third category – that of diversity. Where liberty and equality reign as the fundamental values of traditional democratic theory, here diversity joins their ranks. As we have already seen, consensus creates a social environment within which diverse and even conflicting groups, people, ideologies, actions, can coexist. Many democratic theories acknowledged the plurality of 'the people', recognising that 'the people' will never all share one opinion and often even have conflicting interests, but the democratic practice being developed by this movement addresses this dilemma by shifting the focus away from what constitutes 'the people' to looking at what kinds of outcomes are sought through which kind of decision-making processes. The significance of this movement's focus on diversity is not that it understands 'the people' to be diverse and complex, although it does, but that it allows this diversity in 'the people' to be translated into a diversity of outcomes. In this way, 'diversity' becomes more than the acceptance of Rawls' 'fact of reasonable pluralism' (see Cohen 1993) because, by stressing the outcomes and acknowledging the inequalities of input, movement actors bring the political back into a 'pluralism that misses the dimension of the *political*' (Mouffe 1996: 247). This also reflects an understanding of 'power relative to outcome', where the importance of an issue can be determined by looking at how the people are affected by the outcomes (Lukes 2005). With this view of power in mind, creating plural outcomes is part of decentralising power. Allowing outcomes to be diverse is therefore a prerequisite to achieving the kind of equality outlined above. If equality partially lies in the outcomes of decisions, and if it requires that people should feel they can play an active role in reaching these decisions, then often those decisions cannot be singular. Equal outcomes are often diverse outcomes.

Diverse outcomes are only possible where diverse inputs are encouraged. This desire for diversity of opinion is part of the reason why conflict is welcomed. As we saw in the previous chapter, valuing diversity requires a shift in the way conflict is viewed, emphasising its constructive potential rather than its adversarial nature. This constructive conflict is only possible once the divisive approach to difference of many identity-based movements is overcome. Differences need to be understood as strands of a network that can be woven together to create new structures, not as oppositions of which the 'best' one need be determined to the elimination of all others. While 'the fundamental project of … the modern nation-state … is to elaborate and resolve the contradiction of differentiation and unity' (Kearney 1991: 55) through a 'modernist imperative for uniformity' (Katsiaficas 2006: 211) resulting in exclusion (Eisenstein 1988, Pateman 1988), the

alterglobalisation movement has an understanding of difference
that acknowledges the inextricability of sameness and difference
and allows the two to coexist, indeed even acknowledges the
necessity of the one for the other. Difference here is, therefore,
closer to Derrida's notion of *différence*, where difference is not
just defined by contrasts, divisions, oppositions, but by deferral.
Difference is no longer the oppositional relationship of division
that it became in the era of identity politics, but becomes also an
expression of commonality through an overlapping with other
differences to which each difference defers for its own meaning.
As Harvey (1998) argues: '[w]hereas the affirmation of universal
values excludes dissident voices, the assertion of pure difference
denies the relational character of all identities'. Difference in the
alterglobalisation movement is not an assertion of pure difference,
but a development of relational difference. Rather than seek to
'obliterate the fuzziness of communities' with 'mechanisms of
normalization' (Chatterjee 1993: 227), this fuzziness becomes
essential for the functioning of the decision-making system
being developed, which relies on an assumption of differences
overlapping with similarities in order to view conflict as creative
and to limit the adversarial habits of those who find themselves
in such conflicts:

> Creativeness requires we are humble enough to admit that we do not have
> all the answers, honest enough to recognize that among ourselves there
> are many different views, and firm enough to stick on a difficult inclusive
> and participatory process that does not alienate minority positions among
> ourselves with voting defeats. (De Angelis 2003a)

The alterglobalisation movement actors, thus, simultaneously challenge the two most common approaches for dealing
with diversity in contemporary nation-state based representative democracies – homogenisation and isolation. These two
approaches are by no means independent. Due to the fundamental
irreducibility of diversity, homogeneous communities require
separation and active isolation from difference. When integration
of differences in the nation-state based model of democracy fails,
then often division and isolation is the solution. This can be seen

in the contemporary surge towards the reinforcing of boundaries and borders through the literal construction of walls. The walls between Israel and Palestine and the US and Mexico are good examples, but even more insidious, perhaps, are the walls that infuse urban architecture that attempt to resolve the lack of homogeneity in urban environments through the construction of gated communities and active policing of internal boundaries (see Calderia 1996, Davis 1990) to say nothing of the literal walls erected every year between the G8 and the public. Somewhat unintentionally, identity politics, although challenging homogen-isation, played into this practice of dealing with difference through isolation and the reinforcing of boundaries (see Schöpflin 2003, Wolin 1996). In welcoming diversity and conflict by understanding difference to be relational, the movement challenges both the divisive tendencies of identity-based movements and the adversarial nature of contemporary democracy.[17] Consequently, it questions the existence of 'the people' or a 'common good'. Although there are movement spaces where a type of common good is expressed, the significant development is the space created which is available to be governed democratically without any presumption that such a common good can be achieved or is even desirable.[18]

Solidarity as *Acopañamiento*

Replacing the French *fraternité* with diversity, however, is not a privileging of diversity over solidarity, although it does represent a shift away from solidarity as it has been practised in the past. Despite the importance of diversity, there is a strong sense of common struggle in the alterglobalisation movement and this common struggle leads to relationships of support and solidarity, but what constitutes 'support' is changing. When foreigners turn up in Chiapas, Mexico, wanting to help the Zapatistas, they are told, '[y]ou can help by helping yourself by struggling from your own foxhole' (quoted by Flores, in Flores and Tanka 2001). On the one hand this statement is a rejection of the entire neoliberal development paradigm that chooses who to define as needy and who not, but on the other hand it is an act of creation by establishing a common purpose between two otherwise seemingly disparate processes. I struggle in my neighbourhood and you struggle in yours, and whether we ever meet or speak or hear of one another, we are struggling together. The Zapatistas call this *acopañamiento* or accompaniment:

> Accompaniment is recognizing that people in the U.S. are differently oppressed. They are suggesting that we in the U.S. relook and rethink of support as part of an overall attitude projecting attitudes of superiority and arrogance. That we consider 'support' as part of the colonial thinking that considers the poor and the different incapable of determining their own destiny, as helpless victims that can't solve their problems. (Flores, in Flores and Tanka 2001)

You struggle there and we struggle here against the specific problems that affect our respective locations, but we fight together, in accompaniment. We are 'separate, yet connected'. The emphasis on connection through simultaneous but separate activity, rather than direct support or solidarity is a significant change in the approach compared to the movements of the 1960s and 1970s, in which links were created through 'help' provided by the more privileged to the less so. Starhawk (2001: 132) argues that:

> solidarity means supporting each other's intentions and goals, even when we only partially agree with them. Not just my saying, 'you do your thing and I'll do mine' but by actually taking responsibility for our actions and for the impact they have on others beyond ourselves or our immediate group.

Hardt and Negri (2004: 223) use their concept of the 'Multitude' to explain the nature of this connection, asserting that the multitude, although a singular noun, is not a unity but an expression of a 'common social and political capacity' that 'must be able to make decisions and act in common'. This ability to act in common, although important, must be understood as one among many unities, and can only be understood as unifying if we interpret 'common' to include acting simultaneously but separately. Communication (of ideas, information, decisions), then, becomes essential for the constitution of this unity through separateness. Accompaniment is a form of solidarity that fosters diversity and decentralisation without creating or reinforcing hierarchical relationships between those helping and those-to-be-helped.

Representation and Participation

The relationship struck between representation and participation in any democracy seems always to be a point of avid discussion and adding the ingredient of diversity does not simplify the matter. The range of positions as to the normative relationship of representation to participation covers all possible views from those in which the two notions are complementary to those in which the terms are deemed to be antagonistic to each other. The idea that there is a contradiction between representation and participation, a belief implicit in this movement's practice, is foreign to most advocates of representative democracy. Indeed, representation was originally intended as a means through which to increase democratic participation at the scale of the nation-state. Hardt and Negri (2004: 238) point out that the task of the French revolutionaries was:

> aimed in part at addressing the question of scale ... to reinvent the concept [of democracy] and create new institutional forms and practices. Representation ... was central to the modern attempt to address the crisis of democracy.

In an ironic twist, today it is precisely the problem of scale that underlies this movement's aversion to representative structures. Many movement actors feel that most of today's governmental and especially intergovernmental institutions are not representative of anyone's interests but their own or those of corporations (see Hoedeman 2005, Leys 2005, Miller 2005). The past decades have also witnessed a disillusionment with the hope that communism might offer an alternative representative system based in equality. In the organising process of the ESF, whenever someone suggests electing a committee or setting up a representative structure, there is much more than mere disillusionment underlying the resistance and distress released by such a suggestion. The ESF has created a space within which people can express their political ambitions and dreams directly, and play an active role in determining not only the shape of the ESF but also, many people believe, the shape of 'another world'. They are not ready to give up this newly found power. Furthermore, the sheer diversity of the ESF process makes it nearly impossible to compile a committee of people that could realistically represent the interests of all the participants.[19] And once one accepts that the aim of a meeting or an assembly is not to reach unanimity, but rather to create a space within which a diversity of perspectives can be expressed, then representation is no longer an ideal structure because representation functions on the assumption that a certain portion of the group will have identical interests and creates a circumstance in which only these *shared* interests get expressed.

This deep-felt distrust for representative structures, however, does not preclude certain types of representation in the WSF and ESF. One form of implied representation in the ESF can be seen in the ritualistic practice of mentioning one's organi-sational affiliation when intervening in discussions. Even if it is generally understood that no one is present at the assembly in the capacity of an official representative, these references are made in part to show that the speaker is representative of more than just themselves (even though technically they are not, affiliation is often interpreted as representation). The examples of this practice are plentiful, but one of the best examples was at the Berlin EPA in June of 2004 when one woman claimed to 'represent one million students' because she was on the steering committee of the National Union of Students (NUS) and even said that she was 'in daily contact with all of them'. What is interesting about this statement is not the impossibility of this claim, but the relationship this claim bears to the level of conflict in the room and the process as a whole. The more contentious the discussion item is and the more defensive the speaker is, the more important it becomes to mention how many people one represents. This is related to a sense of decreasing control and power. When the meeting mechanism of being given a chance to speak, for example, does not offer the desired power of influence, other mechanisms are employed to establish authority, and claimed representation is one of these authority-establishing mechanisms. This act of reverting to familiar practices of representation, however, cannot create a formal structure of representation, or even a de facto structure, because such a structure would require legitimation to exert power, and this legitimation is lacking.

Consequently, I would hesitate to interpret these practices as jeopardising the democratic praxis of this movement. It would be unrealistic to expect political practices to change as fast as rhetoric. These are the moments within which we see the negotiation process that goes into the reinventing of democracy. There is a clear rejection of fixed representation on the level of rhetoric and official collective structures, but the participants come from many different types of movement organisations and they each have their own political style. This transition between styles has proven to be more difficult in the social forum processes than the autonomous sections of the anti-summit mobilisations because there is a much larger presence of traditional left political parties, trade unionists and NGOs, many of whom are still very comfortable with representative structures and have not shed these structures in their own organisations.[20] These actors feel more comfortable in the familiar safety of representation than in the diverse and unpredictable circumstance of the EPA where 'any one person can mess up the whole process'. The official structure of the meeting is a transition that appeases those who want to do away with representative structures, and the unofficial structure satisfies those who cannot yet do without. Nevertheless, the movement's democratic practice has the capacity to simultaneously incorporate and undermine some of these representation habits. Built into large-scale consensus decision-making, through the use of 'spokes' in spokescouncils, is a type of representation that is fluid and temporary. Although the transition has thus far not been wholly successful, the perceived need for representation could be channelled into these more fluid structures and consequently the negative effect of power imbalance through disproportionate representation would be at least partially undermined. This transition would, however, require a much stronger structure in the ESF organising process, and attempts at creating such a decision-making structure have thus far failed.

The decline in movement actors' trust in representation also has to do with internal movement practices. Over the past 30 years, as identity began to play a more central role in defining movement actors' politics, representation slowly became undesirable and even impossible. The idea that a single person in the form of a representative could accurately understand, much less represent, multiple experience-specific, subjective identities slowly grew more and more implausible (Young 2000: 126). Eschle (2001: 118) comments on feminism in the UK:

> A radical suspicion of representation as alienating and elitist was given a specifically feminist spin with the argument that it had functioned historically to delegate women's voice to men acting on their behalf in the public sphere.

The assertion of particular and exclusive 'identities' that often went unrepresented resulted in a strong shift towards consensus decision-making and participatory democracy, but one that was fundamentally based on division and opposition between various identities. Difference was perceived to necessarily lead to relations of subordination and exclusion. The relationship between representation and participation was severed and representation was purged from the repertoire of movement democratic ideals. Representation in the French revolutionary ideal was a way to achieve presence in the polity without having to be present, but in the 1960s and 1970s the idea of representation as presence in absence was increasingly being undermined both by the state-level democratic practices and by the movements' own practices. Presence began to look more and more like absence, and it quickly became political suicide to question or challenge the claims of exclusion made by oppressed identities within the movement. The idea of participatory democracy as a democracy without representation dug in and grew roots.

Participation in the Alterglobalisation Movement

> Our alternative to the top-down globalization of huge multinational corporations and their militarized nation-states is an internationalism founded upon autonomous nuclei of popular participation. (Katsiaficas 2001: 32)

The internal movement politics of 1960s and 1970s movements brought consensus and participatory democracy into the mainstream of movement activity, and after an incubation period in the 1980s and 1990s, it has resurfaced in a highly structured less divisive form in the alterglobalisation movement. When consensus is used by this movement it is still a work in process, but there is no lack of concrete ideas about how to structure and organise consensus decision-making, even on a mass scale among people who have never met before. The camps against the G8 summits and the autonomous spaces during the ESF and WSF organised year after year are a testament to this. An excellent illustration of this highly structured decision-making process is the description from the website of the Climate Camp (n.d.):[21]

How We Work
We work through collective decision-making, where everyone gets an equal say in an open and transparent way. No one is paid and we reject all forms and systems of domination and discrimination. The way we are building towards the camp is made up of three basic parts:
The monthly meeting:
   These meetings generally last two days with the purpose of getting working groups together and making decisions that require the input of everyone. The meetings use consensus decision-making and will have facilitators whose role is to help the process rather than taking on a leadership role.
Working groups:
   This is a large undertaking and the process is divided into sections to make it more manageable. Working groups are trusted to make autonomous decisions which fit with the camp's overall aims, or to bring decisions that affect the wider process to the monthly meeting. The camp will largely be

organised by these working groups. They cover everything from plumbing, toilets, legal and welfare to workshops and entertainment.

Local groups and neighbourhoods:

While the main priority of the meetings and the working groups is to organise aspects of the camp that require some kind of collective process, it is equally important that the process supports and encourages the formation of local groups and groups committed to taking on neighbourhoods. The camp itself will be a combined effort of working groups, neighbourhoods and local groups. We hope that all these various groups will help the formation of networks that take action on climate change long after the camp is over.

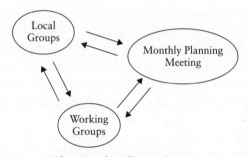

Planning the Climate Camp

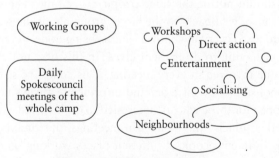

Climate Camp Aug. 26–Sept. 4

There is plenty to do and believe it or not, you don't have to go to endless meetings to get involved.

What will a social movement for climate justice and against the fossil fuel economy look like? We don't know, but if we get together with the people who've made a start, if we can take experience and mix it with the ingenuity and energy of the new, if together we can engage with the issue in both word and deed then we can be a powerful moment, a pulse, in what has to be a growing local, national and international movement.

This Climate Camp statement captures perfectly the relationship between the *how* and the *what* of organising in the alterglobalisation movement, especially the more autonomous sections. There is a very clear definition and agreement as to the *process* that will be used to organise the campaigns against climate change, but *what* the result of that process will be is left entirely open, 'We don't know' and would not dare to claim such knowledge.

This model of organisation is common in the autonomous sections of the anti-summit mobilisations. The structure of small meeting to large meeting exchange comes from the spokescouncil model for consensus in large groups developed (in part) by anti-nuclear movements and refined over the past 20 years into this large-scale structure. There are local-level groups and working groups that work on their campaigns or a particular logistical task all year round, some people from these groups come once a month to the national meeting to report and discuss, and then they 'feed back' to their local groups or working groups. In principle these should not be the same people every time. The working groups also 'feed back' to the larger group about the work they have done, so everyone knows what is being done and by whom without having to do it themselves. In this way not everyone has to be involved in every meeting. This collective structuring of responsibility is not fixed and in principle always leaves the door open for those who are interested to get involved. Although, altogether, much time is spent in meetings, this time is divided among different people in different places working on different tasks. The meetings and responsibilities are decentralised so that they do not require too much from any one person or group. These decentralised groups are then networked with each other so that the necessary communication is still possible, and so that those who do not have time or the interest to work on a particular issue can still follow the developments.

Inclusion and Exclusion

This democratic praxis shows promise, but certain central questions remain unaddressed. The aim of horizontality is the continuous limiting of power inequalities, and it is more successful to this end than systems that assume equality to be something declared and then forgotten, or something inherent in the human species irrespective of political realities. But many problems persist. An equality of outcomes often requires a diversity of outcomes, which sometimes requires separate outcomes, and this, we have already seen, sometimes requires that groups split to allow different beliefs and projects to be pursued. Often, this division remains at the level of tasks and particular projects, and is therefore inconsequential, but sometimes it stems from, or results in, a much more fundamental break in the network. Under such circumstances several important questions arise. First, when a group splits, who stays and who leaves? Do those who leave end up constituting a new node to the network, as I am suggesting they do, or do they leave the network entirely? When people decentralise the network through splitting, do resources stay centralised? Does splitting exacerbate or relieve inequalities? Given the general perception that centralisation is equivalent to organisation, how does this decentralisation affect the way the movement is perceived by non-movement actors? And if these were people who had to live together on a daily basis, making more important daily life decisions, would this tactic of splitting be possible, and if so with what negative consequences?

I cannot answer all of these questions in depth here, but will attempt to use my ethnography to allude to potential answers. In the London ESF 2004, the division between the verticals and the horizontals had both positive and negative consequences. Certainly, it led to a far more dynamic ESF because the horizontals were able to organise not only one alternative ESF, but at least four. These spaces were well attended and were included in the official ESF programme. This link between the alternative spaces and the official ESF, and the overlapping of people, programme and resources made it so that the divisions in the UKCC and the exclusion of many horizontals from the organising process created diversity. On the other hand, this division and the near dictatorial power of the GLA also resulted in a decidedly monotone official ESF, heavily dominated by groups from traditional left backgrounds. What is perhaps most important here is that the irreconcilable conflict in the UKCC never led to a discussion about who should stay in the UKCC and who should leave. It was clear from the start that a split would result in the exclusion of the horizontals from the official ESF. Significantly, this exclusion of the horizontals was experienced as a forced exclusion. Many of them stayed in the process as long as possible, hoping to have at least some effect on the shape of the ESF, but as their input was received with more and more hostility, they slowly withdrew. This distinction between eviction or forced exclusion and voluntary non-involvement is crucial. Many of those who withdrew wanted to stay in the process but realised it was pointless. Although the result was decentralisation and increased diversity, this was not an increased diversity based in equality. Due to the power inequality between the verticals and the horizontals, when the group split, it was the horizontals, not the verticals, who were forced to leave the official ESF process and, worse, they had to leave the ESF process in the hands of those they disagreed with. Significantly, the verticals also kept all the money, offices, website, email listservs and so on.

The decision-making processes of the London ESF, although based only in theory on consensus, demonstrate the exploitation to which consensus decision-making is susceptible. Those with less power, less money or fewer people have to leave the group, creating a new version of the 'tyranny of the majority' that consensus decision-making is meant to resolve.[22] Consequently a struggle ensues between the actors that comes across to outsiders as decidedly absurd and many newcomers leave after just one meeting, never to return. The element of ownership in the ESF, although not technically a locality, reflects the reality that not all decisions can be deterritorialised, and therefore some decisions will always be linked to certain geographic spaces, will be necessarily centralised and, consequently, decentralisation as conflict resolution is not always possible. The democratic praxis of the alterglobalisation movement relies on this potential for splitting, for separateness, to foster diversity, but at times this diversity is the result of inequalities that were not resolved but exaggerated. This relationship between diversity and inequality is acknowledged, and that is where horizontality comes in – to limit these inequalities – but the structure of decision-making in the alterglobalisation movement relies heavily on the people within the structure to implement it. In the autonomous sections of the movement where this is done diligently, horizontal decentralised network democracy shows remarkable potential, resolving many of the problems outlined here, but in spaces where the actors are less careful, the consequences can be unequal exclusion. Although most movement actors I spoke to were adamant that they do not assume that human nature is benevolent and that horizontality is necessary precisely for this reason, there seems nevertheless to be an assumption of this sort within horizontality. Perhaps only the facilitator or the majority of people involved have to be benevolent, and horizontality takes care of those who are not, but it is not yet clear how this dynamic would function in a group of people who had only a mixed commitment to horizontality. Indeed, horizontality seems to be an all-or-nothing proposition, which only works well when everyone adheres to the principle and works poorly when only a portion of the group actively values horizontality. The spaces of movement activity where horizontality works are the spaces where there is a preceding self-exclusion – spaces where only those who believe in horizontality get involved.

The question of exclusion is confounded by the fact that in the social forum process, participation is defined *solely* by presence. If you were present, by definition, you participated. In the consensus method used by autonomous groups at anti-summit mobilisations, by contrast, being present is only the first step, one has to take an active part in the meeting as well – it means being a part of the process to determine not only what is decided but also *how* it will be decided. This conflation of presence and participation in the social forum process often led to confusion and miscommunication. People present at meetings would express their sense of exclusion, their feelings of irrelevance, and others would dismiss them immediately because to be there was to be included by definition, so how can they dare claim exclusion? These different understandings of exclusion, combined with the lack of political motivation to understand this difference, led many to drop out of the ESF organising process. One such person stated at a meeting of the UKCC:

> There seems to be a process of excluding African people from the process. It's in everything you are doing. Even in your language. The question is how we will mobilise people ... people have come to these meetings. Exclusion is not just when you say 'go away from meeting', it is also refusing to accept that there are different perspectives and issues that need to be included. (Kofi, UKCC, 1 July 2004)

Kofi is perhaps an example of the reality that even under diversity some differences matter more than others. Many participants in the ESF organising process felt that, despite the emphasis on participation, the result was never inclusion. Although the London ESF is an extreme example when it comes to inclusion and exclusion, it is common that in the ESF organising process the opinions of those who participate more, who come to more meetings and say more at meetings, often have more weight in decision-making processes. In both the ESF and WSF the opinions of those who represent larger and richer organisations have relative power. The equality outlined above, which is ideally being 'created' by these actors, is often simultaneously being undermined.

Putting Limitations into Perspective

Acknowledging the limitations of the decision-making practices of the alterglobalisation movement is essential to understand its implications and to highlight that it is a work in progress and will likely always be so. Nevertheless, we need not exaggerate these problems either, and should avoid throwing out the proverbial baby with the bath water. To this end it is important to make a distinction between ideal and actual democracy. No democratic system functions as perfectly as its ideal, and so far none have been free of the problems described here, all having been permeated with inequalities, exclusions and conflicts. As Dahl (1998: 29) writes, 'None of us, I imagine, believes that we could actually obtain a perfectly democratic system, given the many limits imposed on us in the real world.' The question, rather, is one of degree; how can we create a democratic system (now on a global scale) that is the *least* exclusive and creates the *least* power inequalities? The practices outlined here offer some interesting ideas for a democracy based on decentralisation. But movement actors go further in that they are not just developing these ideas, they are *practising* them. The common argument that participatory democracy, democracy without representation, requires 'small, decentralized, self-sufficient units' (Young 2000: 124), and that even these smaller units tend to have a form of de facto representation built into them (Dahl 1989) is being challenged by the alterglobalisation movement, which declares the possibility for and sets about creating structures for making decisions in a participatory way on a global scale. Dahl assumes the inevitability of representation because he assumes that voting will be the decision-making tool. The alterglobalisation movement shows that, even when certain spaces of movement activity can be dominated at certain times, complete domination is an impossibility due to the decentralised network structure that is intentionally and unintentionally created on the level of collective mobilisation. This movement turns the relationship between scale and representation on its head, showing that it is exactly due to scale that representation is not only impossible, but also unnecessary. Exercising the above vision of democracy across a network structure requires the ability to say of the outcomes, 'We don't know'. These network structures and the systemic vision they imply are the subject of the next chapter.

5

RESISTING UNITY THROUGH NETWORKS

The point is finding the contexts in which horizontal practices can enter or open new spaces, meet new situations, establish different relations by identifying in the present lines of conflict, points of leverage and conjunctural possibilities that link different struggles and create commonalities between what is different. If horizontality means putting connectivity above accumulation, there is one answer to the age-old 'what is to be done': connect. (Nunes 2005: 317)

Social Change Through Connectivity

Communication, and especially *connectivity*, is crucial to how movement actors envision the shift from representative democracy to decentralised network democracy to be possible. A single approach to social change is a near impossibility for a global movement based above all else on diversity. However, there are strategies for social change that many movement actors share in common, and one of the most important of these is *connectivity*. A decentralised network has no start, no end and certainly no geographical boundaries fixed over time. This lack of defined boundaries is of great significance in the democratic praxis of the alterglobalisation movement. The nation-state based system of representative democracy can only work when there is a clearly defined 'the people' who are governing and governed over. As we have already seen, such a constituency does not exist in the alterglobalisation movement. What defines the constituency of the alterglobalisation movement instead are networks across time and space. Consequently, 'the people' in a decentralised democratic praxis are constituted by the links they make with each other, literal and virtual, and the resulting communication between actors.

In this chapter I tie together loose ends left by the discussions in previous chapters by exploring some of the implications of these movements practices in relation to the concept of connectivity. I start with a brief discussion of what connectivity means in the context of the alterglobalisation movement, examining the role of feedback and reciprocity in the process of communication and link formation within decentralised networks. I then bring in complexity theory, which has been used by commentators and movement actors alike to understand the alterglobalisation movement as an emergent system.[1] I argue that a modified version of complexity theory is an apt framework for understanding the alterglobalisation movement because of the emphasis it places on communication as feedback between actors. Particularly, the principles of 'more is different' and 'ignorance is useful' (Johnson 2001: 78–79) which lie at the centre of complex emergent systems, can aid our understanding of the relationship between connectivity and social change in the context of the alterglobalisation movement. In the final section, I examine the role of 'local rules' which govern behaviour in complex emergent systems, and draw on the work of Anthony Giddens and Pierre Bourdieu in an attempt to bring human agency into the complexity framework. In complexity theory, agency vis-à-vis the system is attributed to the communication between local actors, based on a set of local rules. I argue that the idea of communication as an agent of social change resonates with the alterglobalisation movement practices and introduce the work of Ronald Inden to develop an understanding of agency that does not take the indivisible individual as the basic unit of analysis.

Connectivity as Reciprocal Contamination

In the above quote, Rodgrigo Nunes, an activist involved in the ESF, WSF and anti-summit mobilisations, asks: what is to be done? and answers his own question with one word – connect. The agenda of the alterglobalisation movement ought to be, according to Nunes, to continuously make links to create the new spaces and relations deemed necessary for horizontality and diversity to thrive. Connection is the glue that holds the alterglobalisation movement together in the absence of a nation-state, unitary ideology or other political structure, but what does it mean to connect? How does connectivity help to make diversity possible? What can connectivity tell us about the way the alterglobalisation movement practices social change?

Connectivity is the difference between linear approaches to social change and networked approaches. Rather than setting out a single goal in the future towards which all movement actors must strive, a goal determined by a 'vanguard' that presumes to know how history will unfold, a process of connecting and communicating is the means through which change occurs:

> Instead of the linear march of the faithful to the tune of the vanguard the alter-globalisation movement is traceable in those rhythms of thought and action that prefer to privilege encounters and transgressions, communication and reflection. These traces are multiple and non-linear. (Chesters 2004a)

Connectivity is decentralised, horizontal and non-linear (or multi-linear) because connections are made in many different directions at once. Connectivity, however, is more than connections and communication; it is a particular form of communication characterised by what De Angelis (2003a) has dubbed 'reciprocal contamination', where contamination means:

> not only that we interchange ideas and actions, but that in the process of doing so we begin to look at the world with each other [sic] eyes and begin to develop corresponding ideas and actions.[2]

Connectivity represents an ideal relationship that is constructed in the network links between movement actors. The importance placed on making links becomes clear only once we understand the transformative role connectivity is believed to have. Movement actors rarely speak directly about connectivity, but nearly every movement activity has 'making links' and 'expanding the network' as central goals. After major mobilisations, or in the preparatory process, I repeatedly heard movement actors reflecting on the new links made as either the most important aspect of the mobilisation or as a worthy consolation prize. Luciano Muhlbauer on the Florence ESF: 'the most important thing was not the 60,000 delegates, but building for the first time in the last years a European network of movements. Before there was no relationship like this between networks' (EPA, London, 13 December 2003). Building these connections, exchanges, communication channels, is often the sole rationale given for the WSF and ESF.

The most famous examples of movement activity aimed at connectivity are the Zapatista's *encuentros*. Chesters and Welsh (2005a: 195) argue that the *encuentros*, based on 'the concept of creating a global "mirror and lens" (collective recognition and focus) for antagonistic movements', are a strong influence on the central place the notion of encounter holds in the alterglobalisation movement as a whole. They argue that '[t]his process enabled activists to "bridge worlds" through the deliberate construction of spaces wherein links between diverse movements could be made'. However, it is not merely that links are made, it is equally or more important what *kind* of links are made. The links must enter 'new spaces, meet new situations, establish different relations' (Nunes 2005) and ideally, they should have a transforming capacity to help each actor to see with the eyes of others (De Angelis 2003a). Encounter, Chesters (2004a) argues:

> also implies a degree of friction and confrontation. Which can energise or debilitate depending upon how it proceeds. Such friction is often a necessary part of movements traversing problems and oppositions and provoking intensities that leap the gap separating the potential from the actual.

Here, Chesters alludes to the role of conflict as constructive in the alterglobalisation movement, but he also points to the debilitating potential of conflict. Connectivity is the key to understanding how conflict becomes either constructive or destructive – it depends on the nature of the links between those who come into conflict. Conflict remains constructive when the communication built between movement actors is reciprocal, when there is two-way feedback between the actors. This is not to say that the interaction should necessarily be amicable, but that the interaction should alter the behaviour of each actor without severing the link between them. Destructive conflict occurs when the flow of communication between actors is broken and the collective learning process is consequently limited. This ideal interaction shifts the way movement actors understand the matter at hand, but at the same time it should not force the movement actors to reach unanimity or to adopt a shared political ideology.[3] In a meeting of the South East Assembly in London, one activist was praising the success so far by pointing out that 'The South East Assembly has brought people together who otherwise never work together. Not a group forced under one banner. Groups keep their political autonomy, but still work together.' The openness achieved through the lack of a singular political 'banner' aids the further dissemination of movement practices and values because there is no particular ideology one must adhere to in order to join the movement, making many different kinds and degrees of involvement possible.

Creating Pedagogical Spaces

Connectivity is about developing this new way of working together in which the different actors and the different groups of the network are not required to adhere to the same beliefs. In fact, connectivity works best when those communicating do not have the same beliefs because this creates 'new spaces and relations' and the potential for 'reciprocal contamination' described by De Angelis. This type of outreach – outreach through connecting – represents a shift from how movements have dealt with politics in the past. Rather than determining right and wrong and mapping out a political platform to attract an ever-increasing audience, this movement envisions the inclusion of more people through a practice of reciprocal contamination in which all those who connect teach each other and learn from each other, whether they are over-educated Europeans or illiterate adivasis. This type of communication necessitates a non-reified approach to knowledge and a continuous limiting of existing power inequalities as described in Chapter 3.

Connectivity becomes a means through which horizontality can be expressed, dispersed and developed. It is through the treading of new terrain that horizontality remains horizontal because these unfamiliar spaces remind the movement actors that they do not know better and that much knowledge is context specific. Creating diversity of circumstance and continually establishing 'different relations' is necessary to keep movement actors humble and to ensure that they are learning from each other. The focus placed on mutual learning, on the creation of pedagogical space, is a defining characteristic of the communication desired by movement actors. Chesters and Welsh (2005a: 197–200) describe this process with their idea of *reflexive framing*, arguing that when social movement actors are reflexive in interaction with one another, every act of reflexivity takes on a slightly different form, creating a dynamic process of learning and emergence.

Part of this learning process includes connectivity between people, but also between ideas. Movement actors speak about the need to 'make the links' between different issues and between abstract concepts like the G8, neoliberalism, the IMF and people's daily lives. The issues being addressed by alterglobalisation movement actors are often complicated and seemingly removed from the chain of cause and effect. As George (2004: x) writes:

> in the late 1960s, you could say (or shout) 'US get out of Vietnam' and everyone knew what you were talking about. Thirty-five years later, if you say – little point in shouting – 'Impose a moratorium on the GATS' or 'abolish structural adjustment', you're likely to get a blank stare. Getting to another possible world now requires particularly well informed citizens.

Under these circumstances, 'making the links' between the G8, neoliberalism, precarity, unemployment, poor social services, immigration and many other issues becomes essential to the 'success' of the movement.

Connectivity, like most movement values, is an ideal put into practice. Despite considerable obstacles, consensus decision-making functions as a method for turning communication into connectivity. The strict rules of engagement that (in principle) accompany consensus decision-making are aimed at creating an environment conducive to building constructive links. In a voting system each person could pass their verdict individually, without ever communicating. In consensus, by contrast, a decision *cannot* be reached without discussion and communication. When discussion takes place in the form of decentralised networks, with discussion first at the local level and then the regional, national, global level, discussion by discussion, until a decision can be reached, whatever decision is reached, the result is hyper-connectivity. Expanding connectivity between movement actors not only helps movement actors to build skills and structures by learning from each other, but it also creates an ever-larger decentralised network.

Connectivity and Social Change

Connectivity is the means through which prefiguration is transformed into a strategy for social change. Connectivity represents an increase in particular types of communication that take place through network structures. It is how the movement spreads and learns. Instead of preaching ideology in an attempt to convince the masses, mutual relationships of reciprocal contamination constitute the growth of the movement. At the turn of the twenty-first century, it has become commonplace to argue that movements (if not everything) are organised in a network structure (Castells 1997), and this is certainly true of the alter-globalisation movement. In the 1960s, activists would set up an organisation to start a new campaign, but today, activists set up networks. The G8 decides where and when they are going to meet. That information gets spread over email and even before the exact location or date is decided, groups all over the world are doing outreach and planning their actions. In the UK, small meetings among friends and acquaintances started in several cities almost two years before the 2005 G8 summit. National gatherings like the Earth First! gathering were used to hold meetings where activists from all over the country could exchange ideas and start to plan their resistance in communication with each other. The Dissent! network was set up with the intention that it would function through decentralised interconnected groups, with national and international meetings as needed. E-listservs mushroomed and soon information and ideas were flowing all over the country. In the beginning communication was slow and meetings were few and far between, but by the summer of 2004 there were regular national meetings and many e-lists. Slowly activists in other countries started to prepare as well, especially in Germany where the G8 summit in 2007 was already on activists' agendas. In February 2005 the first international mobilising meeting was held in Tübingen, Germany, and it was attended by activists from all over western Europe (including Scandinavia and the UK) as well as Russia, Israel, Lebanon, Chile, the US, Canada, Greece and Belarus. Many of those present from abroad were living temporarily in western Europe, and they acted as conduits for information between their friends at home and the mobilisation in Europe. This basic sequence of events was repeated for the G8 in 2007 in Germany, where the process started much earlier and the existing networks set up for previous G8 summits were used to increase the speed of dissemination of ideas and information and improve the infrastructure of organisation. The activists mobilising against the G8 in Japan in 2008, in turn, built upon the connections made in Germany for the 2007 G8 summit and they used German networks and structures throughout the mobilisation to help organise and support their own actions. What we see over time is that, even as specific networks disappear, the links made between groups are lasting and becoming more frequent and much stronger.

What is most interesting about these networks, however, is not their size or their internationality, but the *type* of networks forged. To say that the alterglobalisation movement is a network structure is to say that communication between different actors and the construction of meaning takes place through links between people, through nodes, hubs, clusters and degrees of separation in a decentralised flow. The idea of a network as an abstract descriptive framework explains how links are organised, but it does not describe the qualitative nature of the links made. This is where the concept of connectivity is helpful. For Watts (2003: 55), networks are dynamic in two different ways. The first he dubs the *dynamics of the network* which 'refers to the evolving structure of the network itself, the making and breaking of network ties'. The second type of dynamic is the *dynamics on the network*, where the network itself is relatively fixed, but the 'individuals are doing something – searching for information, spreading a rumour, or making decisions – the outcome of which is influenced by what their neighbours are doing'.

The functioning of the democratic praxis of the alterglobalisation movement requires that connectivity be a defining characteristic of the 'dynamics on the network'; the existing movement actors have to come into frequent contact (not per se in person, although this is necessary to some degree) and this contact must involve a two-way (at least) flow of communication. The concerns repeatedly expressed that the large plenaries of the WSF and ESF are 'not interactive enough' or too 'top-down' represent movement actors' attempts to maximise the flow of multidirectional communication. As do movement spaces such as the 'Hub' during the ESF in Italy in 2002, which the flyer proclaimed was set up 'as a connector. It is not a space already marked by pre-established content' (in Juris 2008b: 257). When we think in terms of the 'dynamics of the network', on the other hand, movement actors' perception of connectivity as a force for social change becomes visible. For the movement to be 'successful' it must manage to make more ties than it breaks; in other words, it has to expand in terms of numbers. However, the alterglobalisation movement actors also claim to have abandoned the traditional left politics of 'linear accumulation' (Nunes 2005) and do not believe that more people will in itself result in change. De Angelis (2003a) calls this principle the 'pig principle of mobilization, that is that more (mobilization) is always better'. For the alterglobalisation movement, expansion in terms of numbers is not enough; the links must result in productive communication:

From inside the dominant culture we create not only alternative subcultures but, more important, new collective networks of expression. Communication is *productive*, not only of economic values but also of subjectivity, and thus communication is central to biopolitical production. (Hardt and Negri 2004: 263)

This productive communication also has to reach outside of the existing networks for connectivity to serve as a mechanism for social change. This is an area where movement actors often criticise themselves. Trott (2005: 215) writing about the J18 day of actions, argues that activists 'made much of the importance of "making connections"; the problem was, however, that these connections were almost entirely connections between "activists". The same, it must be said, was the case with the Gleneagles mobilization [G8 2005].' Trott mentions the flyer handed out at the J18 protests entitled 'Give Up Activism' which 'argued this sort of link-making is "an essential prerequisite for further action"', but the flyer proceeds to warn that:

It is not enough merely to seek to link together all the activists in the world, neither is it enough to seek to transform more people into activists. Contrary to what some people may think, we will not be any closer to a revolution if lots and lots of people become activists. Some people seem to have the strange idea that what is needed is for everyone to be somehow persuaded into becoming activists like us and then we'll have a revolution. ('Give Up Activism' n.d.)

If links are to have potential for creating change, they have to reach outside existing networks while simultaneously strengthening them. The movement must 'bridge unconnected shores and consolidate existing bridges' (De Angelis 2003a). However, these links are not enough; if they consist of everyone becoming 'an activist' or any other singular category, they are not reciprocal, demarcating the space for resistance in a highly limited manner, and they cease to be productive.[4] Hannerz (1992: 44, citing Hannerz 1980), draws a 'basic distinction' in types of networks:

between a tendency to keep ... cultural sets apart, engaging with them in different relationships but segregating them, and a tendency to integrate them, to bring the cultural content of one sector of one's network more directly and perhaps overtly to bear on the management of meaning in another sector.

Change through connectivity requires the integration of networks. It is not enough to make links, but the networks, ideas, practices being linked must overlap and partially fuse with each other (cf. Marriott and Cohn 1958), so that they are creating meaning together, all the while maintaining the autonomy essential for an open network.[5]

Constructing Collective Interests

This balance between integration and autonomy is what makes the relationship between individual and group interests in the democratic praxis of the alterglobalisation movement possible. As we saw in previous chapters, there is an assumption among many movement actors that interests are not the property of the individual, but rather they are created within social interaction. The final ingredient necessary to understand how this works is, again, connectivity. Through consensus decision-making, decentralisation and networks, movement actors attempt to create circumstances conducive to understanding different perspectives and to letting those understandings influence one's own interests. Some movement actors even explicitly state this desire:

> Part of our commitment to people is so that they themselves can say that what they are for. And what they are for is important to us and to what we are for. (Dissent! national gathering, Sheffield, 15 October 2005)

Connectivity is a connection made with this attitude. Once communication of this kind is achieved, the dichotomy between individual and collective interests dissolves. The assumption is that interests are highly subjective and once an individual sees something from another person's point of view, their own interests will shift. As another person at the same meeting phrased it:

> I will do something that 10,000 people are willing to work on, even if it isn't what I would focus on, if there is an emerging consensus for that.

This attitude, however, is hard to achieve, especially for movement actors who tend to be quite attached to their beliefs. Nevertheless, in the collective spaces of the alterglobalisation movement, despite many problems, the success of this approach is astounding.

One way in which this openness is furthered is through action. Due to the fact that in social movements most action is collective action, action often helps people to make this leap from individual to collective interests. Many interests held by movement actors cannot be pursued individually. The idea of competition prevalent in liberal democracy and capitalism trains us to believe that we can and should act on our interests as individuals, but by the time someone has joined a social movement they have probably come up against the impossibility of this fiction at least once. This point helps to explain the role consensus decision-making plays in facilitating the shift from viewing interests as fixed, individual possessions to collectively determined potentials. What the actors are learning is not that interests are constructed by a lifetime of inputs and interactions (they probably have a sense of this already), but that this construction is *always* an unfinished process. Connectivity serves to repeatedly remind movement actors that once an interest is constructed, rather than possessing it in an immutable way (especially by turning it into an identity), the actor has the agency and the responsibility to change their own interests through dynamic interaction. By emphasising dynamic interaction, alterglobalisation movement actors displace the centrality of identity as determinant of politics (see Fuss 1989: 99) and privilege 'the capabilities of relationships and not the attributes of things' (Strathern 1988: 173) where connections are *partially* and *provisionally* determinant of politics.[6]

Resisting Unity Through Networks

This approach is made possible through the decentralised network structure based on the overlapping of networks rather than the unifying of networks. A unity is constituted through the links between individuals, groups, ideas and networks around common action, but this unity is never threatening to any of its constituent parts, because the links between groups and people are partial, provisional and perpetually shifting. People and groups move in and out of particular networks; they change the way their networks overlap in order to accommodate disagreement or to foster diversity (or to satisfy multiple, even conflicting interests one person may have). The overlap between the horizontals and the verticals which was being forged in the ESF 2004 process, for example, shifted to less overlap to make more room for diversity. The links were not severed (well, not all of them), but the relationship between the two networks realigned itself according to the political situation and the overlap between the two networks decreased. The South East Assembly (SEA) was also continuously increasing and decreasing the degree to which it overlapped with the Dissent! network during the anti-G8 2005 mobilisation. Sometimes the overlap was so deep that movement actors did not even perceive there to be a distinction; at other times the SEA intentionally distanced itself to be able to protect its autonomy. Many of the people coming to the SEA meetings actually believed it to be a Dissent! group, as suddenly became apparent at a meeting in May 2005 when a very active member was told to his surprise (and to many people's surprise) that the SEA was not in fact affiliated to Dissent! and had not adopted the PGA hallmarks (see PGA n.d.). This distinction between the SEA and Dissent!, however, was a flexible one. At a Dissent! budget working group meeting a few months later is was decided that Dissent! would help to pay off the debt incurred by the SEA for the train they had organised because 'it was by and for the entire network'. This potential that actors and networks have to continuously determine their own degree of involvement (together with the respect shown to individual interests discussed in the previous chapter) is what allows people to engage without threat to their autonomy.

Connectivity, therefore, is one way horizontality and diversity resist the force of unity – both in terms of internal dynamics and as imposed from outside. When Peter McLaren asks Roberto Flores (Flores and Tanka 2001), 'But isn't the system too powerful, and wouldn't an isolated autonomous community be so vulnerable that it would inevitably fall under the ideological, and cultural, and sometimes military blitz of neoliberalism?' Flores answers that local communities need an 'incubation' period, time to develop their alternative through prefiguration:

> from the beginning, the autonomous method and efforts need to be insulated. This insulation or incubation is the central strategic method to the sustainability and development of that autonomy. The Zapatista strategy includes not only internal structures that help to protect it, but, national and international structures that extend the possibility of survival.

The Zapatistas survive not only because of their local efforts, but also because of the connections they have established with other communities and movement actors all over the world. This is one of the ways that even 'weak ties' (Granovetter 1973, 1983) are a crucial form of connectivity and essential to the functioning of the network. Connectivity acts as security, protecting them from the worst potential oppression by the 'system'. It is a weapon of self-defence for resisting the unity forced onto 'citizens' by the nation-state. It allows for the use of 'global' connections of diversity to resist 'local' connections of conformity.

Connectivity is also useful to help prevent the seizure of power within the movement. As we saw in Chapters 3 and 4, even in movement spaces where some groups have considerably more power over the organising process, this power does not translate into power over the whole movement or even over the particular event being organised. Connectivity is what makes this centralisation of power impossible, because on the one hand it insists that connections should not be based on conformity but mutual exchange, and on the other hand it is a productive process of link formation that no one group or coalition of groups can stop.[7] These links are productive vis-à-vis the network, continuously making the whole more decentralised even as certain hubs and clusters develop. As Hardt and Negri (2004: 82) point out, 'Network organization ... is based on the *continuing* plurality of its elements and its networks of communication in such a way that reduction to a centralized and unified command structure is impossible.' Having a mechanism in place to avoid developing a central command within the movement is equally important to having a strategy for resistance against forces outside of the movement. As Juris (2008b: 15) argues:

> expanding and diversifying networks is more than a concrete organizational objective; it is also a highly valued political goal. The self-produced, self-developed, and self-managed network becomes a widespread cultural ideal, providing not only an effective model of political organizing but also a model for reorganizing society as a whole.

Internal centralisation is perceived to be in contradiction to the fundamental principles and goals of the movement, and in contrast to the 1960s, it is believed to be counter-productive to social change:

> Imposition from the top is the opposite of autonomy and participatory democracy. The Zapatistas say that the autonomous communities and organizations are the ante-sala (lobby) to an alternative democratic system. One of the long-term goals of the autonomous approach is the development of the experience in bottom-up democratic governance that this type of civic arrangement will provide. With the experience in questions of rebuilding the cultural foundations of a community, making decisions in its education, discussions and decisions on its overall effort to be come [sic] economically self-sufficient (autonomous), and all these matters and democracy questions that the autonomous community will deal with, will give it the experience in participatory democracy and will prompt the community to organize structures of governance. This experience in inclusive participation will, in turn, allow it to participate in the overall development of a new type of nation state. Having a preconception of what that state will be and what it will look like is anxiety carried over from the vanguard days. (Flores, in Flores and Tanka 2001)

These slow learning processes, in which an alternative democracy is learned through prefiguration and not via a preconception of what the state will be, are the building blocks for an alternative democracy. This prefiguration, however, is not enough; it is merely the ante-sala. Learning these lessons is indeed necessary, but it is not sufficient. It is when these lessons enter into the larger network – when the communication of these practices, ideas and skills meet similar ideas across the globe or in the next village, and in so meeting are transformed – that the process of connectivity can begin. And it is only once this connectivity reaches a large enough number of people, places and ideas, that 'the development of a new type of nation state', or an alternative democracy without a state, enters the realm of possibility.

Ant Democracy

When I first read about complexity theory it appealed to the activist in me, not the anthropologist. It seemed to provide a potential explanation of how systems could function without centralised authority. It claims that some systems are organised in a decentralised structure of network relationships based on the principles of 'emergence' and self-organisation. The activist in me was immediately interested, and the idea of having a theory that reflected so many of the values held by activists themselves, in turn, appealed to the anthropologist in me. So I began to look into a very diverse body of theory called 'complexity theory'.

Complexity theory originally stems from the mathematical and physical sciences and as such it should not be incorporated uncritically into the social sciences. Manson (2001) divides complexity theory into three main categories: 'algorithmic complexity', 'deterministic complexity' and 'aggregate complexity' (cf. Stewart 2001: 325). I will be limiting the discussion of complexity theory in this chapter to aggregate complexity, or biological complexity, which 'attempts to access the holism and synergy resulting from the interaction of system components' (Manson 2001: 409). I start with the basic metaphor offered by complexity theory and combine this with an anthropologically informed notion of agency to explain the role connectivity plays in the prefiguration of democratic praxis.

Beginning with the Metaphor

The main concepts at the centre of biological complexity theory are 'complex adaptive system' and 'emergence':

> Such a system would describe the most elemental form of *complex* behavior: a system with multiple agents dynamically interacting in multiple ways, following local rules and oblivious to any higher-level instructions. But it wouldn't truly be considered *emergent* until those local interactions resulted in some kind of discernible macrobehavior ... a higher-level pattern arising out of parallel complex interactions between local agents. (Johnson 2001: 19)

A common example used to explain emergence in the biological sciences is the ant colony:

> We see emergent behaviour in systems like ant colonies when the individual agents in the system pay attention to their immediate neighbours rather than wait for orders from above. They think locally and act locally but their collective action produces global behaviour. Take the relationship between foraging and colony size (and thus mouths needed to be fed); amount of food stored in the nest; amount of food available in the surrounding area; even the presence of other colonies in the nearby vicinity. No individual ant can assess any of these variables on her own. (Johnson 2001: 74)

Apparently ants are able to maintain a high level of efficiency because they communicate with each other through pheromone signals. Each ant emits pheromones that indicate to the other ants what she is doing. The key to the successful functioning of the system is communication between the ants. The communication and interaction between ants must be thought of as reciprocal. In an emergent system, therefore, interaction is a process of feedback by which each actor adjusts its own behaviour based on that of the other actors. Information has to flow at least two ways. This aspect of a complex emergent system creates an analytical challenge:

> A complex system is defined more by relationships than its constituent parts ... Understanding and tracing the relationships of a single entity is difficult, while tracing the relationships of an entire system verges on the impossible. (Manson 2001: 409)

The relationships in any given system are not only hard to trace because there are so many of them, but also because they are non-linear:

> Given the number and variety of these relationships, they extend beyond simple feedback into higher order, non-linear processes not amenable to modelling with traditional techniques. (Manson 2001: 409, citing Costanza et al. 1993)

A complex emergent system arises not because one actor, or set of actors, determines that it should be so. Rather it comes from each and every actor playing its own role in communication with other actors:

> Self-organisation is ... at the heart of complexity theory in biological sciences and social life ... bottom-up processes in which simple beginnings lead to complex entities, without there being any master plan or central intelligence planning it ... emergence [is] when the actions of multiple agents interacting dynamically and following local rules rather than top-down commands result in some kind of visible macro-behaviour or structure ... Emergent behaviour ... usually shows a mix of order and anarchy, self-organising networks and hierarchies. (Escobar 2004: 351)

Here we can see some of the other concepts associated with complexity theory which reflect the alterglobalisation movement's practices. Concepts like 'bottom-up process', 'self-organisation' and 'networks and hierarchies' are where the potentially unique contribution of complexity theory lies.

More is Different

The idea of *emergence* – that local actors create, maintain and transform the structure they function within – already has its precedents in social theory. Anderson (1972), however, points to a unique principle in complexity theory referred to as 'more is different'. Complexity theory builds on notions of communication and claims that the more actors there are, and the more communication there is between the actors, the more effective the system will be – the more the system will learn and be able to respond to and affect change. This is the principle that underlies the approach taken by movement actors to knowledge and decision-making which I outlined in Chapters 3 and 4. In this framework of decision-making, the best decisions are assumed to be reached collectively and the more people involved in making the decision, the more intelligent the decision will be because knowledge is a collective process of construction, relation and interaction.

The 1999 protests against the WTO in Seattle are often cited as the starting point of this movement. Although the search for genesis is a false search, complexity theory does add another interesting way to think about the role Seattle plays in the creation myth of the alterglobalisation movement. If we take the rhizome metaphor offered to us by Deleuze and Guattari (1987) to understand that social movements build metaphorical underground networks to subsequently emerge into visibility above ground, complexity theory would lead us to conclude that emergence occurs when reciprocal communication, or connectivity, increases sufficiently. Within this framework Seattle was the beginning of this movement not because so many people suddenly became activists and the numbers increased (although this did happen to a certain degree), nor because the media splashed images of the protests all over the TV (although that did help to make the movement visible and expand the networks), nor because the protests were successful at shutting down the conference (although this was enormously energising), but because Seattle represented a moment of reciprocal communication/contamination on an unprecedented scale. Various actors, agents, movements came together that had never come together before and they entered into communication, they connected whether they intended to or not, and created what none of those actors intended to create, a new movement system known as the alterglobalisation movement.

In the alterglobalisation movement, however, more actors does not necessarily make different. Unlike ants, the rules that govern local behaviour are not fixed, and if communication does not increase with more actors, or if communication only flows one way, or reinforces existing behaviour, then more does not necessarily make different. In the case of the alterglobalisation movement, more is only different if connectivity increases. The suggestion that more is different only begins to have its significance when it is combined with other principles of emergence. Johnson's remaining four principles are: (1) ignorance is useful; (2) encourage random encounters; (3) look for patterns in the signs; and (4) pay attention to your neighbours (Johnson 2001: 78–79). All the remaining principles have to do with communication and interaction, where communication is reciprocal, attentive and open. These principles refer to the role random encounters play in helping the individuals to accurately alter the 'macrostate of the system itself'. Through coming into contact with unfamiliar situations and information, the ants in a system become more 'adaptive' (Johnson 2001: 79). This is surprisingly similar to the idea that horizontality must come into contact with new spaces and different relations to remain open and could be adopted literally as the rationale behind the WSF.

Ignorance is Useful

The principle of 'ignorance is useful' is a unique conceptual contribution of complexity theory and has intriguing implications when applied to the alterglobalisation movement. Ignorance is useful posits that:

> Having individual agents capable of directly assessing the overall state of the system can be a real liability in swarm logic, for the same reason that you don't want one of the neurons in your brain to suddenly become sentient. (Johnson 2001: 79)

Although at first this principle seems problematic when applied to human systems, and especially to the alterglobalisation movement which is characterised by a high level of reflexivity, learning and knowledge building, the principle actually captures movement approaches to knowledge quite aptly. In Chapter 3, I described the movement actors' reluctance to make claims to *know better* in diverse and unfamiliar situations, choosing instead to perceive knowledge as at least partially context-specific. This approach to knowing mirrors the principle of 'ignorance is useful'. There is no meta-narrative about social change, no claim to predictive knowledge. There is only continuous rebellion which takes a slightly different shape from one context to the next, in which no one, or rather everyone, is deemed to have expertise. Using one movement practice, that of carnival, the Notes from Nowhere collective (2003: 178) claims that:

> carnival denies the existence of experts, or rather, insists that everyone is one – that each person possesses something unique and essential, and success depends on freeing that in all of us. It demands interaction and flexibility, face-to-face contact and collective decision-making, so that dynamic and direct democracy develops – a democracy which takes place on the stage of spontaneously unfolding life.

In Chapter 3, I showed that movement actors not only reject forms of unitary knowledge because they feel it cannot be accurate, but also because they deem it oppressive. Following the principle of 'ignorance is useful' to its logical conclusion leads to an ironic twist in the case of human behaviour, as it would imply that social actors should not attempt to understand the functioning of their own social system, or that they should at least not presume to do so correctly. This idea, even though its accuracy cannot be confirmed or denied, is reassuring for a movement that resists the oppression of meta-narratives that claim to know what is and what will be at the expense of past, present and potential subjectivities.

The Limits of Complexity Theory

Every theoretical model obscures. In the act of explanation there is necessarily also obviation. So the choice we have to make is between what we highlight and what we obscure. It is this choice that leads me to complexity theory. After several years of fieldwork in the alterglobalisation movement and many more of activism, it was precisely because complexity theory chooses to highlight the same concepts as the alterglobalisation movement that I could not resist taking it up as my starting point for a conceptual framework. Nevertheless, there are some important limitations to complexity theory. These need to be addressed, and wherever possible improved upon, if a complexity framework is to be of any explanatory power. All of these limitations have in one way or another to do with underdevelopment of the notion of the actor. The first of these is the inherent systemicity in the organismic model of the system. The second concerns the idea that 'rules' govern local actors' behaviour, which leads to a complete absence of a theory of human volition. To make complexity theory useful to the analysis of social movements, a much more complex notion of the agent is required which allows for both 'dividuals' (Strathern 1988) and compound agents. The complexity theory model of a decentralised network of dynamic interaction and communication cannot be utilised in a social system context without a discussion of agency.

Systemicity

Biological complexity theory posits an internally coherent system, where 'the behaviour of individual agents is less important than the overall system' (Johnson 2001: 145). When this approach is applied to social systems, it creates a systemic conception of society that resembles a Parsonian functionalism in which 'the society as a whole is regarded as a complex system with its own autopoietic strategy and exerting downward causation' (Stewart 2001: 333). There has been a great deal of literature criticising the idea of a social system as a coherent deterministic entity and this aspect of complexity theory can easily be moderated. Bourdieu and Wacquant (1992: 103) use the notion of 'field' to argue that:

> The products of a given field may be systematic without being the products of a system, and especially of a system characterized by common functions, internal cohesion and self-regulation.

For now, the problem of systemicity will be addressed by adjusting the understanding of the relationship between the 'local rules' and the 'macrobehaviour' that lies at the heart of emergence. Complexity theory claims that the macrobehaviour of a system arises out of the decentralised autonomous actions of 'local' actors.

In complexity theory the concept at the heart of determining local actors' practices is 'local rules'. In biological complexity theory, even though the exact outcome of interactions between individual agents remains unpredictable, the rules that govern local behaviour are predictable and static. We can say of ant communication that there are ten different pheromone signals, which are fixed and easy to decipher, but it would bring us no closer to understanding human behaviour to argue that human beings follow a set of fixed rules through which they create their social system. A social complexity theory needs a much more complex notion of what constitutes 'rules' as a conceptual approach to understanding local behaviour.

The Individual and Agency

Local Rules

The idea that local rules govern individual behaviour is an aspect of complexity theory that needs adjustment when examining human systems. It is here that we can reinsert a notion of agency into an otherwise overly totalised systemic theory. Agency can be found at two levels in an adjusted application of complexity theory to the alterglobalisation movement. The first kind of agency we find is the role that the actors themselves play in constructing the rules that govern the decision-making procedures and the dynamics of the network.[8] In particular, movement actors negotiate the degree and kind of engagement they have with the network and the decision-making procedures. They can also voice their ideas, thoughts and interests. They have the agency to communicate – in word and action. However, whether or not this communication, the voicing of ideas, becomes agency depends on the interaction between the actors and the particular circumstances. As actors establish rules and links, a second type of agency takes over and the communication and interaction between actors itself becomes an agent of change. In the case of the alterglobalisation movement, of these two types of agency, communication takes precedence. The individual uses her agency to communicate and connect and these connections produce social effects. The environmental activist Joanna Macy (1991: 58) sums up the nature of this agency in her claim that things and people:

> do not produce each other or make each other happen, as in linear causality; they *help* each other happen by providing occasion or locus or context. And in so doing, they in turn are affected. There is a mutuality here, a reciprocal dynamic. Power inheres not in any entity, but in the relationship between entities.

One type of agency the individual has, then, is to help facilitate communication and to actively build links. One of the ways this agency is exercised is through the continuous discussion of process. Movement actors play an active role in the construction of some of the rules that come to govern their behaviour. The discussions about process are of such importance to movement actors not only because the result of these negotiations becomes the framework within which the actors get to (or do not get to) express themselves, but also because the rules determined through the process are symbolic of the world within which movement actors hope to eventually live. Poor process creates rules that limit connectivity and centralise power, which is perceived to threaten the potential for 'another world'. We therefore need a better understanding of 'rules' than the vacuous one complexity theory offers us.

Both Giddens and Bourdieu offer insights into the idea that rules govern human behaviour.[9] In Giddens' theory of structuration the definition of structure is similar to the notion of system in complexity theory. Giddens (1994: 80) distinguishes between structure and system, where structure is 'rules and resources' and social systems 'comprise the situated activities of human agents reproduced across time and space' (1994: 86) and the relationship between them is that structure refers to 'the structural properties allowing the binding of time-space in social systems' (1994: 80). Giddens (1994: 83) understands the term 'rules' to refer to a diverse set of structures that are both constraining and enabling. With the idea of a formula as the backdrop, he defines rules of social life as 'techniques of generalizable procedures applied in the enactment/reproduction of social practices' and uses this conception of rules in a way that is surprisingly similar to complexity theory in his theory of structuration:

> One of the main propositions of structuration theory is that rules and resources drawn upon in the production and reproduction of social action are at the same time the means of system reproduction. (Giddens 1994: 81)[10]

So the rules (and resources) that govern the individual's actions are the means through which the social system is reproduced and maintained. This idea is what Giddens refers to as the 'duality of structure', where the constitution of actor behaviour and systems behaviour are not two separate processes, but a duality, because structure is not external to the individuals. He uses the term 'social *praxis*' to encapsulate the process through which this internalisation is expressed:

> All social life is generated in and through social *praxis*; where social *praxis* is defined to include the nature, conditions and consequences of historically and spatio-temporally situated activities and interactions produced through the agency of social actors. (Cohen 1989: 2)

On this level Giddens' notion of social *praxis* does not differ a great deal from complexity theory's notion of emergence, but his notion of what constitutes 'rules' differs greatly. Through social *praxis* people become 'both rule-following and rule-creating creatures who are knowledgeable about their actions ... rules are constituted through social action' (Tucker 1998: 81).

Despite the usefulness of Giddens' work on rules, Giddens is developing a theory of the social in general, while my concern limits itself to social movements, and, more specifically, the alterglobalisation movement. Although 'social *praxis*' includes a reference to interactions and even 'involves a "decentering" of the subject in favour of a concern for the nature and consequences in which social actors engage during their participation in day-to-day life' (Tucker 1998: 11) interaction remains relatively marginalised in Giddens' theory. Complexity theory, by contrast, posits:

a profoundly relational model in which negotiated views of reality may be built where all receivers are also potential emitters, a space of truly dialogical interaction. (Escobar 2004: 350)

The distinction made in complexity theory between reciprocal and non-reciprocal interactions, where the former result in more macro-level behaviour than the latter, bears closer resemblance to notions of connectivity.

Giddens' typology of rules is a first step in bringing agency back into complexity theory, but it is far from complete. Bourdieu, who, like Giddens, believes that social relations are 'structured dispositions which are realised through social practices' (Tucker 1998: 69), creates a 'relational model of investigating social fields' (Stewart 2001: 350), but he underdevelops the importance of types of communication and interaction between actors. To explain social reproduction Bourdieu develops the notion of *habitus*. For Bourdieu (1977: 72) the *habitus* is:

a system of durable, transposable dispositions, structured structures predisposed towards acting as structuring structures, that is, as principles which generate and organize practices and representations that can be objectively adapted to their outcomes without presupposing a conscious aiming at ends or an express mastery of the operations necessary to obtain them.

Or alternatively:

The *habitus* – embodied history, internalized as a second nature and so forgotten as history – is the active presence of the whole past of which it is the product. (Bourdieu 1994: 100)

Habitus plays a similar role in Bourdieu's theory of the social as *emergence* in complexity theory. The *habitus* is the 'principle of conductorless orchestration which gives regularity, unity and systematicity to practices' (Bourdieu 1994: 103). Bourdieu's *habitus* is a theory of stability; *habitus* tends to 'confirm and reinforce', maintaining social practices over time. Gledhill (2000: 141) concludes that Bourdieu's concept of the *habitus* seems more useful for explaining reproduction than for explaining change.

But of course any social system will simultaneously reproduce and change existing relations, so *habitus* has an important role to play in explaining certain types of behaviour that complexity theory cannot. Nevertheless, in the case of social movements, having the focus primarily on change is preferable.

Bourdieu, in his analysis of gift exchange, emphasises the variation in practices from one actor to another and concludes that these differences constitute individual strategies; he suggests that '[t]o substitute *strategy* for the *rule* is to reintroduce time, with its rhythm, its orientation, its irreversibility' (Bourdieu 1977: 9). But a reintroduction of time is not all the substitution of *strategy* for *rule* would achieve; it would also reintroduce the actor as a being of conscious intent. Thinking of rules as strategy also leaves open the possibility that the rules might not be the same for all the players. Certainly, this is a crucial point in the application of complexity theory to the alterglobalisation movement, because while all ants may be created equal, all movement actors are not. As we have seen in the preceding chapters, power inequalities exist at the level of these local rules, and different political beliefs, organisational habits and general backgrounds result in actors coming to the game often with different rules. Some of these rules are better at perpetuating centralised power than at diffusing it. We have also seen that when actors act locally and think locally it sometimes leads to conflict globally. While this last point may be a more general human reality, when the movement fails to make this conflict constructive, this disparity in rules severs connectivity.

Giddens' approach to rules adds the important consideration of resources, which brings in aspects of human systems like the state and the market that are not present in the ant systems of complexity theory, and Bourdieu develops a theory of social reproduction that seems to leave very little room for social change to occur (except under conditions of dramatic political or economic change when the *habitus* is apparently shaken out of its pattern), but still offers an aspect of 'rules' that is essential to understanding the 'rules' that may govern human actors, in particular social movement actors – the role of strategy. With the help of Bourdieu, we can interpret the local rules that govern behaviours in a complex emergent system not only as partially constructed by the actors themselves, but also as a space for strategy. However, to understand this role of strategy in the case of social movements, we need a conceptual framework that can understand the negotiation that goes into the expression of collective intent. Complexity theory has potential in this regard if we combine it with a theory of agency.

Approaching Agency

In biological complexity theory all ants are assumed to be the same and to have the same potential interpretation of communications exchanged between them. Obviously this same assumption cannot be made of human actors who receive any given message differently on the basis of a complex interrelation of various factors. This diversity we attribute to humans and deny ants is only a small part of the ways in which agency has been omitted from complexity theory (and the biological metaphor more generally).[11] The agent constitutes the system, and therefore has agency vis-à-vis the system as a whole, but we are not told any more than this about how this agency is exercised or about how these agents are constituted.

Applying complexity theory to human systems leads us to take as the most basic unit of analysis not the individual but the communication between individuals. This shift away from the individual holds within it the risk that the importance of movement actors will get understated, but I hold this risk to be only a theoretical one. The actor, of course, never disappears, never ceases to have agency. The question is rather how this agency is exercised, and I suggest that in the alterglobalisation movement agency is a collective agency, exercised primarily through communication. This analytical perspective can simultaneously account for the 'partible person' (Strathern 1988) and collective agents.[12] Conceptions of agency that posit a unitary agent with a singularity of purpose at any given moment, that place that agent in a dividing relation with the 'system' or 'structure', obscure the reality that people are often at once internally divided and not acting entirely on their own. Rather than taking a unitary approach to agency where the agent and the individual are conflated, I draw on Inden (2001) to develop a model for agency that allows for the 'agent' in the alterglobalisation movement to be understood as actively constructed through the combination of parts of people into groups of people through communication. Hardt and Negri (2004: 222) argue that the:

> production of the common is neither directed by some central point of command and intelligence nor is the result of a spontaneous harmony among individuals, but rather it emerges in the space *between*, in the social space of communication. The multitude is created in collaborative social interactions.

Although Hardt and Negri are referring to the construction of the 'common' and not to agency per se, understanding the agent in this way helps to explain how conflict of interest between individual and group interests in consensus is avoided. The constructing of outcomes is part of the process of constructing agents. This approach to agency is characteristic of network analysis. Wasserman and Faust (1994: 5) write:

> Of critical importance for the development of methods for social network analysis is the fact that the unit of analysis in network analysis is not the individual, but an entity consisting of a collection of individuals and the linkages among them.[13]

To understand how social change occurs and the role of the movement actors in bringing it about, we need to understand that there are:

> both individual and dividual modalities or aspects of personhood ... It is a misunderstanding to assume either that the social emerges out of individual actions (a powerful strain in Western ideology that has seeped into much of its scientific epistemology) or that the individual ever completely disappears by virtue of indigenous forms of relational totalization ... It would seem rather that *persons emerge precisely from that tension between dividual and individual aspects/relations*. (LiPuma 2000: 131–32)

This tension introduced by the dividual, therefore, can be understood as constructive. Anzaldúa (1987: 79) writes that she copes with her own 'plural personality' (as *mestiza*) by 'developing a tolerance for contradictions and ... ambiguities' and 'turns the ambivalence into something else'. Sensing this constructive potential, Inden (2001: 22) draws on Collingwood's notion of 'complex agency' to 'introduce the metaphysics of "overlapping classes" and "scale of forms" [as] possible replacements for the metaphysics of system and essence'. Inden defines human agency as:

> the power of people to act purposively and reflectively, in more or less complex inter-relationships with one another, to reiterate and remake the world in which they live, in circumstances where they may consider different courses of action possible and desirable, though not necessarily from the same point of view. (2001: 23)

This definition of agency suits the alterglobalisation movement in that it very closely resembles the prefigurative power described in Chapter 3, while also complementing the complexity framework in that it does not 'assume that the purposes or intentions of agents consists of master plans which actions implement or even that agents are always conscious or clear about their purposes' (Inden 2001: 24). Inden argues that taking the individual as the unit of analysis leads to homogeneity. Instead of the homogeneous individual as agent, Inden argues that 'persons as agents are themselves composed of entities that *overlap* ... Not only do the parts overlap, but the relationships among them seem to undergo a process of continual change or reproduction' (2001: 25). This idea mirrors the notion of a network in complexity theory. Manson (2001: 409) argues that: 'In complexity theory through the formation of sub-systems within networks, even homogenous components can support internal diversity through realignment of relationships ... Any given component can belong to several sub-systems.' Inden (2001: 26) adds that entities of which the agent is composed – the 'content' of the agent – can also change over time in interaction with others and as a result of circumstances, and finally Inden argues that 'agents are never inherently complete'. This approach to agency, therefore, resonates with the alterglobalisation movement's decentralised network of connections that overlap, its affinity for diversity and the idea of a continuous process.

Understanding agency in this way also helps to conceptualise *what* connects when we speak of connectivity. Links made between actors are not merely links between homogeneous entities, but rather links between ideas people have and actions people take, as well as groups people make and discussions people have. Links are not made only by and through individuals into groups, but also by a part of a person (one of her many interests/ideas/skills) and by groups of people (a link between the decisions made at a meeting in Belgium and the decisions made at a meeting in India, for example). Constructing agency in this way not only allows for a more diverse set of agents to emerge (from parts to wholes to groups), but it also paints a more complex picture of how connectivity works and how networks are built and maintained. The transition away from identity politics is related to this reconceptualisation of the agent and to understanding the difference between pluralism and diversity as democratic values. Understanding the agent as divisible and complex allows for diversity to be not only:

> the constitutive matter out of which identity is formed [but also] ... that which resists or exceeds the closure of identity. It signals not a difference *from* others but a difference that troubles identity from with*in* its would-be economy of the same. (Honig 1996: 258)

Diversity therefore differs from pluralism in that it does not necessarily take the interaction between identities as homogeneous delineated groups as a starting point. Instead, all these different types of agents, interests, identities and ideas overlap with each other, even at the level of within the individual, and it is these overlappings that hold the movement together and increase connectivity.

Agency as connectivity, however, has its problems for a prefiguration of a horizontal, diverse democracy. Agency in the alterglobalisation movement is not equally distributed across the network, because some actors are more connected than others. In a network structure, one link leads to more links and not all links are created the same. Castells (2004: 33–34) argues that networks have 'programmers and switchers' who are 'those actors and networks of actors that, because of their position in the social structure, *exercise power in the network society*'.[14] Not only are some actors and networks of actors in strategically more powerful positions, but it seems to be the nature of the network that the more connected one is, the more connected one gets. This is a positive feedback loop that could have disastrous consequences for horizontality. The actors who are more familiar with the 'local rules' that govern behaviour and are better at negotiating them can also gain relative connectedness. I experienced this myself in my research. The interactions I had that were characterised by exchange and learning led (seemingly without any help from me) to more and more of these types of interactions. I also learned that I was able to take on certain roles due to my familiarity with the 'rules'. These were often the roles that led most easily to hyperconnectivity and consequently to more agency vis-à-vis the decision-making processes – roles like meeting facilitation and giving action trainings. Many movement actors are wary of this bias built into connectivity, but they rarely know how to address it. Skillshares are widespread to diffuse knowledge and explanation is given at meetings, but it may be a bias that can only be cured as actors' positions within the network shift.[15]

Individualism

The diminished importance of the individual in this approach to agency (without withdrawing agency from individuals) resonates with the alterglobalisation movement's more general resistance to individualism. I have argued throughout that the movement no longer privileges individualism in their democratic praxis, and so it is only fitting that the notions of agency and social change do not do so either. In the 1980s a critique of 1960s movements developed which accused these movements of contributing to 'accelerating the arrival of contemporary narcissistic individualism' (Lipovetsky

1986: 99). Although this view has been heavily criticised, 'the Lipovetskian view of May [1968] achieved a virtual consensus in the 1980s' (Ross 2002: 183). Ross argues that this view is more informed by the 1980s than by the movements of the 1960s and points out that those attributing individualism to the movements of the 1960s rarely actually looked at what movement actors were saying about their own practices at the time (Ross 2002: 184). Foucault (2002: 330) argues that struggles emerging in the 1960s were:

> struggles that question the status of the individual. One the one hand, they assert the right to be different and underline everything that makes individuals truly individual. On the other hand, they attack everything that separates the individual, breaks his links with others, splits up community life, forces the individual back on himself.

Marilyn Friedman (1997: 40–42) describes the feminist challenge in the 1980s and 1990s to the ideal of 'autonomy' on the grounds that it 'is overly individualistic' and 'ignores the great importance of interpersonal relationships in sustaining everyone's life'. Friedman argues that: 'Mainstream autonomy ... is allied with liberalism, and in particular with liberal abstract individualism.' She offers the concept of 'self in community' coined by Hoagland (1988), where:

> The self in community has a sense of herself as a moral agent connected to others who are also self-conscious moral agents in a communal web of relationships that permits the separateness of selves without undermining mutual concern and interaction. (Friedman 1997: 44, citing Hoagland 1988: 144–47)

And even a single 'self' 'travel[s] between different positions' (Strathern 2004: 35) and different aspects of the self, its various identities, are made visible at different moments (Strathern 1988).[16]

This feminist approach to the self is implicit in the democratic praxis of the alterglobalisation movement and in movement actors' approaches to social change. Feminism certainly played an important role in bringing about this shift, as did the general experience of identity politics, but the less individualistic notion of the self also reflects the merging of different notions of personhood from across the world that do not share entirely the same assumptions about the individual. For example, Nandy (1998: 325) asserts that the 'fluid definitions of the self with which many South Asian cultures live' contrasts with 'the modern concept of selfhood acquired partly from the Enlightenment West'. To be clear, this is not a struggle against the individual, or against methodological or ontological individualism as an analysis of society. The rejection of individualism by the alter-globalisation movement is a rejection of individualism *as an attitude* that defines human relationships. It is a rejection of individualism *as a relation* that defines collective decision-making. In this sense, individualism can be compared with connectivity; both are attitudes imbued in human relationships. For movement actors, however, connectivity is preferable.

Finally, complexity theory and connectivity are not merely valued by movement actors for their conceptual relevance and practical use. Many movement actors like the appeal of complexity theory for precisely the reason an anthropologist might eschew it – for its biological metaphor. When prefiguration is a strategy for social change, then theory, beliefs, and practices merge together and the approach taken to social change reflects the beliefs and practices of the movement actors. The Notes from Nowhere collective (2003: 73) writes:

> As networks grow more connected by webs and actions, wires and stories, many things will emerge that we, as mere neurons in the network, don't expect, don't understand, can't control, and may not even perceive. The only way to understand an emergent system is to let it run, because no individual agent will ever be able to reveal the whole. The global movement of movements for life against money, for autonomy and dignity, for the dream of distributive direct democracy, are following an irresistible logic. It is a logic as old as the hills and the forests, an eco-logic, a bio-logic, the profound logic of life.

Despite the 'irreversible' nature of this logic, it is not, however, an inevitable logic leading down a linear path to a predetermined revolution. The eventual result of this 'irresistible' logic remains permanently unpredictable, and necessarily invisible from the point of view of any one actor. What will be, movement actors do not predict, but what they do know is that change is perpetual, and if they can reconstruct the rules by which interaction occurs, and build open networks of decentralised relations, then connectivity will thrive and it becomes at least *possible* that a new system will emerge.

CONCLUSION: TAKING THEIR TIME

We walk, not run, because we are going very far. (Zapatista saying quoted in Holloway 2004)

Slowly, Slowly, Long Life

The alterglobalisation movement is a patient movement. The sense of urgency one reads in movement documents from the 1960s, or the revolution-oriented communist uprisings and many nationalist movements, has all but disappeared in the alterglobalisation movement. Activists rarely refer to the ticking of time; they do not agitate for immediate action at all costs; they are not desperately pleading for someone to save them right now. They are building a new world, and the responsibility they feel to get it right leads them to *take their time*. As Starhawk (2001: 134) puts it: 'I don't think we have the ecological and social leeway to mount another one if this one fails.' The struggle for 'another world' is a process open to everyone, and each person needs to be incorporated on their own terms. This too, takes time. When we are in a hurry, we do not look and listen, and meaningful connectivity becomes impossible. The alterglobalisation movement actors know it is a long journey, but this, so far, has not deterred. Many activists, especially in the global south, consider today's movement to be part of a 500-year-old struggle and the few years that have passed since Seattle are no cause for impatience. An activist in the UK, on the other hand, sees the struggle as new, but is equally patient: 'We are just at the beginning, but we are beginning.' In India, the adivasis I met would laugh at the impatience they thought I displayed in every single task I carried out. They would ask me why I was in such a hurry and tell me (and the other Europeans), 'slowly, slowly, long life' in a reassuring tone. As one activist in the UK put it somewhat less eloquently than my adivasi friends, 'What is the hurry here? Capitalism is not going to fuck off immediately. I'm wary of not allowing for a long consultation process.' The alterglobalisation movement seems to have abandoned the quick-fix approach to social change offered by revolutionary dreams and has opted instead for a continuous rebellion of slow but constant change. As the Clown Army (n.d.) puts it:

> We are rebels because we love life and happiness more than 'revolution'. Because no revolution is ever complete and rebellions continues [sic] forever.

Movement actors can perhaps best be understood to be in a liminal phase in which their cultural universe contains not only one mode of being, but a multiplicity. The change they desire, is being prefigured, but has not been completed, and as such they function in the 'space between'. The international nature of the movement serves to reinforce this multiplicity and the practices, experiences and rules that govern the movement are continuously brought into question. An active effort to create a world that suits many different people has been set in motion, but can never be completed; it can only be continuously improved upon. Rebellion is a perpetual process of construction.

Even if the dream of revolution may have been abandoned, the desire for revolutionary change is intense. The alterglobalisation movement is attempting, every day, to prefigure radical social change. This prefiguration is not impatiently utopian, it is patiently realistic. There seems to be an awareness that they do not yet have all the skills needed to replace capitalism or the nation-state, or both or neither, with *another world*, but they are convinced they can learn. Part of that learning process is the creation of other worlds in the here and now.

Decentralised Network Democracy

In the preceding chapters I have attempted to outline one of those 'other worlds' – the process of decision-making in the collective spaces of the alterglobalisation movement. I presented what I consider to be the key values underlying this process as well as some of the implications of this process for both our understanding of the alterglobalisation movement and of democracy. I have argued that the alterglobalisation movement confronts us with a radical democratic alternative based on a decentralised network and principles of horizontality and diversity, and it intends to turn this alternative into reality through prefiguration and connectivity. It should be clear from the picture painted in the preceding chapters, that this democratic model is far from perfect and is riddled with problems and inconsistencies at almost every turn. However, I hope I also portrayed the ability this movement has to reflect on these shortcomings and to come up with diverse sets of solutions.

The structural model being suggested in the democratic praxis of the alterglobalisation movement is not a liberal democratic model of representative democracy, but rather a decentralised network model based on collective and divisible agents who make decisions through consensus. The solution being proposed (implicitly through their practice) to the problem of scale and the crisis of representation facing nation-states in the globalised world today is not more democracy, but *different* democracy. Rather than having more representatives or improving representation, rather even than having a form of direct democracy where 'the people' get to vote for many more purposes than merely electing leaders, the alterglobalisation movement suggests a form of democracy that rejects all formal and fixed representation. This rejection of representation, however, does not lead movement actors to the unrealistic conclusion that everyone must be involved in all decisions. Instead, the movement is in the process of creating a democratic system that would potentially allow for people to be as involved as they desire at all levels of decision-making, including the global, by getting involved in decision-making at the local level. Through decentralisation and connectivity, decisions that affect an entire network of people can, in principle, be discussed at every node of that network and then decided through communication between nodes. This communication is carried out by people who act as very temporary 'representatives' (in movement lingo, 'spokes') who have no decision-making power, but transmit the necessary information to make a collective decision – even a global one – in all the affected local contexts.

The picture I have painted of this process in the preceding chapters is presumably reason enough to question how realistic this model is. The prerequisites required to make this kind of democracy possible are by no means humble. One must learn to merge the means and ends of movement activity and to understand prefiguration as a strategic and effective mode of struggle. One must abandon the assumption that conflict is destructive and realise its constructive potential to foster diversity – *and* learn how to bring out this constructive potential. One must view difference and diversity as unifying and understand interests as collectively not individually constructed. What we understand democracy to be has to be fundamentally altered to privilege consensus decision-making over voting and decentralisation instead of representation. Finally, networks must be understood to be decentralised zones of connectivity, where the most productive communication is characterised by reciprocity and learning. In short, it requires a great deal of openness to the 'other', a trait undoubtedly essential in a 'planetary world', but still far from realised.

The obstacles presented by all the above prerequisites to decentralised democracy, are perhaps not even the biggest challenge. Above all, a decentralised democratic system needs to have a constituency that is not fixed but fluid. Individuals and groups of people, entire networks even, must have the option to sever links, to leave a group and to 'stand aside', so that one does not get held to a decision when one does not agree with it; otherwise, consensus becomes much more difficult to reach, and outcomes become potentially 'oppressive'. For this fluidity of constituency to be possible, what constitutes 'the people' cannot be determined by geography. It would have to be determined by topic or issue and continuously reconstituted decision-by-decision. As challenging as this may sound, it is not impossible. The alterglobalisation movement already has such a global, fluid constituency, but there is considerable work left to be done to make these spaces accessible and especially to build the necessary links between localities.

Despite these many challenges, the alterglobalisation movement has at the very least raised questions and brought new ways of visualising democracy into the realm of possibility. Democracy has always been primarily focused on the question of 'Who rules?' and many different answers have been found to this question over the past several hundred years. The answer being proposed by many movement actors is that no one rules. The alterglobalisation movement practices even suggest that the question of who rules is the wrong question entirely. I have argued that the democratic praxis of the alterglobalisation movement privileges instead the question 'How do we rule?' Implicit in consensus decision-making and horizontality is the assumption that if there is a clear and highly structured procedure in place for *how* to decide, then there need not be an agreement on *who* decides. The central place *process* occupies in movement discussions and practices as a goal unto itself is about setting up this alternative world in which the *how* is fixed and the *who* is fluid.

Social Change

Social change for the alterglobalisation movement is not perceived as a 'traditional' revolution achieved through a sudden break with the past envisioned as happening on a glorious day in the future. Alterglobalisation movement actors choose instead to view social change as belonging to the present. It is only natural that those of us who have been trained to look backwards and forwards along a straight line to see how social change happens have missed the social change that is already happening. In the alterglobalisation movement, beliefs about social change hide in practices, and they are obscured by diversity and conflict to the eye trained to search for unity. The aim of this book has been to go behind the public image of the alterglobalisation movement, to examine some of those practices and to explore the implications of these practices for our understanding of the alterglobalisation movement and our understanding of what constitutes democracy.

Movement actors are acutely aware that the purported unity of the nation-state is today a unity based on exclusion and conformity, in which immigrants and 'minorities' are deeply discriminated against. Furthermore, the imbalance of power between states in a 'global' world renders democracy at the state level impossible for all but the richest and most powerful countries and within those most powerful countries, movement actors argue, the leaders represent only the richest echelons of 'the people' and, in particular, corporate interests. The 'planetary world' in which movement actors find themselves, is characterised by unequal flows of people and things in a way that simultaneously opens new horizons and possibilities, while also rendering visible all that is still out of reach. The combination of the awareness that boundaries are shifting, but only in certain ways and only for certain people, with the lessons learned from the era of identity politics – namely that representation on the basis of identity is impossible in light of multiple and conflicting identities – has resulted in the need for a democracy based on more fluid and indeterminate social constituencies, but how to achieve this ideal is still an open question. For now, bringing about another world rests in the realm of *possibility*. The creation of this possibility was by no means a small feat, but the problem with creating primarily *possibility*, is that possibility exists, as always, only in the future. However, it is a future with a link to the present, and it is this link which prefiguration exploits, bringing the future possibility ever more into the present, one lesson at a time.

Other Worlds

It has not been my aim to answer the question 'Will the alterglobalisation movement succeed?' Even if we define success very broadly, it is impossible to say. Certainly there is reason enough to assume that it will not. The challenges it continuously sets for itself are great, and the obstacles are many. A critical reader will have found both theoretical and practical problems with every single value and practice described in the preceding pages. It does not seem, however, that movement actors have any intention of being deterred by these criticisms; in fact, movement actors tend to be among the most critical. If the open ethos of perpetual learning can be maintained and connectivity continuously increased, then at least the *possibility* for another world exists. And, for now, movement actors seem to be satisfied with their ability to turn possibility into reality, and realistic about how long it might take.

I have not attempted to present a comprehensive theory of social change nor of democracy. Determining whether the alter-globalisation movement will eventually be 'successful' at bringing about another world would require a deeper exploration of the material and political reality outside of movement practices and is beyond the scope of this book. It would require an analysis of the nation-state, global capitalism and the state of democracy across the world, to mention only a few lines of inquiry. Much such analysis exists already; alterglobalisation movement actors spend the majority of their time producing such analysis, and academics are not far behind them. Rather than re-articulating all this literature here, I chose to focus on an area that has thus far been relatively silent in research on the alterglobalisation movement. Ethnography, and anthropology in general, I felt, were more suited to exploring and trying to understand what the actors themselves were *doing* and what these practices meant to them. In the end, what I learned has led me to believe this was a wise choice. In order that form may follow content, perhaps it is preferable, at this juncture, not to transform movement practices into a blueprint for social change, even in the presence of tempting possibilities. Instead, I choose to let the reader put the pieces together in the hopes that a multiplicity of ideas may emerge. Why take this approach? I leave you with a clown's answer:

> Because ideas can be ignored but not suppressed and an insurrection of the imagination is irresistible. Because whenever we fall over we rise up again and again and again, knowing that nothing is lost for history, that nothing is final. Because history doesn't move in straight lines but surges like water, sometimes swirling, sometimes dripping, flowing, flooding – always unknowable, unexpected, uncertain. Because the key to insurgency is brilliant improvisation, not perfect blueprints.

NOTES

Introduction: The Unglamorous Side of Glory

1. I choose the term 'alterglobalisation movement' to refer to the global social movement that emerged at the turn of the twenty-first century. This is not a neutral choice; this movement has been notoriously hard to define. After having been dubbed the 'anti-globalisation' movement by the media, movement actors adopted various titles. Outside of the English language the movement tends to be satisfied with terms like *mouvement altermondialist, altermondialismus, movimientos alterglobalización*. Movement actors in all languages, however, often refer to the alterglobalisation movement as 'the movement' or the 'movement of movements' and often I adopt these terms. For an activist perspective on the label see Kingsnorth (2003: 71).

2. I use the term 'movement actors' because it is more inclusive than alternatives like 'activists'. I have met many people who reject the title of 'activist' because they feel it represents a division and a privileged category similar to that of a 'vanguard'. Also, the alterglobalisation movement includes many people who do not self-identify as activists and whose engagement with the movement is temporary. These people get involved, for example, because the G8 comes to their home town and they do not agree with what the G8 does, but they do not always think that this makes them 'activists'. At times, however, when I am sure the label is appropriate, I do use the term 'activist'.

3. Peoples' Global Action (PGA), for example, is a collective space of movement decision-making that has five guidelines widely adopted by activists. Only the fifth guideline addresses internal decision-making procedures, and follows intentionally *after* other principles like taking a confrontational attitude and an uncompromising attitude towards capitalism. See http://www.nadir.org/nadir/initiativ/agp/free/pga/hallm.htm.

4. This dilemma is not limited to, although it may be exaggerated in, the alterglobalisation movement. Kitschelt (1991: 340) claims: 'Concepts such as "the" women's movement, "the" student movement, "the" workers' movement or "the" environmental movement make little theoretical sense ... the great organizational, strategic, and

ideological differences within "the" women's movement render the notion of a single movement questionable.'

5. Significant here is the decrease in the central importance of 'identity as the first step in explaining strategic decisions' (Foweraker 1995: 12). This is not to say that 'identity' does not play an important role for individuals or for movements within the 'movement of movements' (and indeed identities are often used strategically in the sense of Spivak 1989, 1990, 1993), but it is to say that 'identity' as a unifying force between these various movements is negligible because these identities are too multiple, diverse and shifting.

6. This is nothing new. Dalton et al. (1990: 6) argue about New Social Movements that 'One can find evidence of nearly every conceivable political philosophy within these movements, and the behaviour of movement activists covers an equal range.'

7. Khasnabish (2004: 256), writing on the Zapatistas, found a similar phenomenon and dubbed these 'moments of coincidence', highlighting 'the capacity of diverse social movements, each with their own tactics, agendas and goals, to "coincide" or intersect with one another without sacrificing their individual autonomy'.

8. Much has been written about the transformative role of the Internet in the alterglobalisation movement, and it is not my intention to underestimate the Internet's importance. The Internet is essential to the functioning of the alterglobalisation movement, despite the obvious limits of computer access (see Juris 2008a, 2008b, de Jong et al. 2005). However, many movement actors I met expressed concern about the Internet, arguing that it was good for disseminating information but was 'dangerous' for discussion and not useful for making decisions. When I pressed for more detail, I was told that 'dangerous' meant people were more likely to disagree, misunderstand each other, and argue over the Internet than in person, and that it biased discussion to those who had time to sit in front of a computer. Graeber (forthcoming 2009) has also pointed out that the Internet and email are not useful decision-making tools because:

> listserves do seem to combine the worst aspects of speech and writing: the casual thoughtlessness of one, the permanence of the other ... debate on listserves tends towards everything that consensus meetings try to avoid: posturing, grandiose claims, sarcasm, insults, grand accusations of sexism, racism, stupidity reformism, hypocrisy.

9. See also Fields (1984, 1988), Linhart (1978) and Manceaux (1972) on the influence of Maoism and the concept of the 'people's war' as a radical democratic ideal guiding activists in France in the context of a discredited Stalinism.

10. When I mentioned to a well-informed activist/journalist in 2004 that I had met a small group of Stalinists, the reaction I got was, 'Really? I didn't think there were any more of those.' In the 'global South', however, there are still Maoist and Stalinist movements, but whether they can be considered to be part of the alterglobalisation movement is debatable.

11. Flacks, a member of SDS, wrote: 'Participatory democracy did not mean abandoning organizational structures of the usual sort ... We were thinking of participatory democracy at that time as a concept of social change. Not as a set of principles for guiding the internal organizational life of SDS' (quoted in Miller 1994: 143). Interestingly, a similar circumstance has arisen in the WSF. Even though the WSF has an International Council (IC) and an Organising Committee (OC) of 'representatives', the Charter of Principles has been interpreted by movement actors to reject the very notion of representation. Even the OC, 'perceives itself as a facilitator of a horizontal process, rather than the executive leadership of the forum' (Schönleitner 2003: 131). On the setting up of the WSF see Schönleitner (2003: 128–30), Whitaker (2001) and Leite (2004: 97–105, 2005: 77–102).

12. Daum (1988: 144) translated in Ross (2002: 77).

13. See also Mouvement du 22 Mars (2001) and Mai '68 par eux-mêmes (1989).

14. Despite my focus on the North here, identity was an important category of resistance in the North and the South (Escobar 1992: 62–85). These struggles took very different forms, however, from one context to the next. Benhabib (1996: 4) argues that identity/difference politics in liberal capitalist democracies 'focuses on the negotiation, contestation, and representation of difference within the public sphere', while in communist countries, North Africa and the Middle East, 'ethnonationalisms seek to redefine the constituents of the body politic, and aim at creating new politically sovereign bodies'. The alterglobalisation movement seems to employ an inconsistent but creative mix of these two (and other) approaches to identity.

15. The term 'essentialist' is linked to 'post-modern deconstructive critiques' which have been challenged by anthropologists who argue that 'Grassroots political organizing ... requires a homogeneous identity, a strategic essentialism, a constituency that is visible and capable of being counted' (Stephen 2005: 75, see also Nash 2005a: 11). Still, despite the strategic usefulness of certain 'essentialist' identities like 'Mayan', especially in dealings with external audiences and authorities (see Nelson 1999), the divisiveness of these identities remains very real within movement networks. Stephen (2005: 75) has called this the 'double-edged sword of identity'. Strategic essentialism

is not addressed at length here because insofar as it is used as a tactic in the alterglobalisation movement, it is used only at the level of constituent movements within the 'movement of movements' and therefore beyond the scope of this book.

16. See Checker (2001) for an ethnography of overcoming racial and environmental identities in search of 'common ground' in an environmental coalition in New York City in the 1990s. Checker, however, interprets this transition not as a decline in the central importance of identity, but as a construction of a new multi-ethnic environmental identity as a 'superseding identity'. Della Porta (2005) also maintains the importance of identity in her analysis of the alterglobalisation movement, arguing that openness and diversity can be understood in terms of 'tolerant identities'. And Smith (2008: 216), despite acknowledging that 'the international invitation to be a Zapatista ... is a moral solidarity around a political economic critique, not any kind of claim about interiority or essence (Starr 2006: 167)', writes of forging new 'global collective identities' which are 'more expansive and inclusive'. But these reinterpretations of the meaning of 'identity' make little sense when it becomes necessary to speak of 'flexible identities and multiple belongings' (della Porta 2005: 237–40) which are so broad as to encompass almost everything. In the case of the alterglobalisation movement we would have to create so many of these 'new' identities, be they superseding, tolerant or global, that their analytical significance *as a form of unity* would become negligible.

17. This shift is not without its implications in terms of inclusion and exclusion, and may be partially responsible for why the alterglobalisation movement in Europe and North America is so white. Although we can claim that 'identity' is always constructed, situational (Danforth 2000: 87), a process rather than an essence (Gupta and Ferguson 1997b: 37), some 'identities' (especially those rooted in history, race, ethnicity or sex) appear very real to those who hold them (Cowan and Brown 2000: 3) and even 'fictions of identity ... are no less powerful for being fictions' (Fuss 1989: 104).

18. The centrality of 'identity' to new social movements is debatable (see Cohen and Arato 1992: ch. 10, Calhoun 1993, Polletta and Jasper 2001). There are also some precedents to understanding *process* in social movement theory, namely Resource Mobilization Theory and Political Process Theory, but these theories are concerned with the 'emergence and development of insurgency' (McAdam et al. 1988: 697), particularly how resources and political opportunity structures influence this process of emergence (see McCarthy and

Zald 1973, 1977, Olson 1965, Tilly 1973, 1978; for a critique see Kitschelt 1991).

19. All translations of discussions, texts and emails are mine unless otherwise specified, as are any possible mistakes. For discussions and interviews carried out in Hindi, Prakash Lakra interpreted as we spoke, but I recorded the conversations to check exact wording of quotes afterwards.

20. A 'street medic' (US), or 'action medic' (UK), is an activist who provides emergency first aid care for injured protesters on the street. Being able to offer medical care from within the movement is part of the prefiguration of an alternative society. The medics, the kitchen crews, the translators/interpreters, the techies, etc. provide essential skills that help to make the autonomous zones and camps self-sufficient.

21. This shift was expressed through personal dynamics. Certain people stopped being friendly to me and stopped including me in informal discussions. They were not able to exclude me from the formal spheres, however, and I still took on active roles in the organising of the ESF. In fact, these same people who treated me as an outsider to their inner circle would ask me to chair meetings of the Organising Committee.

22. The choice for me was never one between engaging or not engaging. I was always already engaged. In my case the dilemma was how to write academically about a process that was so close to my heart in a way that was both academically rigorous and politically engaged.

23. This entrance of liberal democracy into the field of anthropology has occurred in two ways: (1) 'western' liberal democracy has itself become a subject of study and (2) the democratic imperative at the turn of the twenty-first century has brought these democratic ideals to all the 'far-off' locations of anthropology.

24. See Abu-Lughod (1990) on the tendency within anthropology to 'romanticise resistance' and Keesing (1992: 6–10) for a discussion of some conceptual problems linked to this term.

1   Horizontal Armies and Vertical Networks

1. This desire to connect with many different groups and the consequent diminishing importance of friendship in movement praxis, including decision-making, becomes politically significant when we compare it to previous social movements. See Polletta's (2002: 55–87) description of the SNCC, and the crucial role that trust and friendship played in their democratic decision-making.

2. Gathering perfectly edible food that is being thrown away by supermarkets or businesses.

3. Some of the other reasons for the small size of the protests include: the FTAA protests in Miami that had recently been very violently policed; the decentralised nature of the mobilisation with protests in Savannah, Brunswick and San Francisco; the poor organisation and outreach; the 'terror alert' and the declaration of a 'state of emergency' that accompanied the G8 summit; the police, military and national guard troops that this terror alert brought to the coast of Georgia turning it into a military zone; and finally, it was no longer considered 'cool' to go 'summit hopping'.

4. According to the 'Fix Shit Up!' collective (2004), citing Goodwine (2001), the Gullah/Geeche are the descendants of West African slaves, 'Gullah refers to the language, and Geeche is derived from "Gidzi", an ethnic group from Africa.'

5. I have not been able to confirm these facts, but for the purpose of this chapter, it is only important to understand the image activists were receiving and (re)producing of Brunswick and the relationship between the 'global activists' and the 'local people'.

6. In the US, the presence of communist and socialist tendencies is smaller. The role of these groups tends to be carried out by groups like UFPJ, which although not overtly communist, is co-chaired by Leslie Cagan, an active member of the Communist Party USA.

7. Juris (2008b: 59–60) identifies four movement sectors, 'institutional reformists, critical sectors, including Marxists and Trotskyists, radical network-based movements and militant anticapitalists' (2008b: 301). These categories overlap with the three I have outlined here. The NGOs could be considered institutional reformists, the socialist and communist groups could be considered critical sectors and the autonomous networks could also be called radical network-based movements with some militant anti-capitalists thrown in.

8. Due to the fact that political parties are banned from the ESF and WSF, some of the social movement organisations are synonymous with the communists. For example, 'Globalise Resistance', which was often used by the SWP to intervene during EPAs.

9. The IST is the international face of the UK-based SWP.

10. The term 'delegate' is often used in the ESF context. However, it does not signify official representation, only association.

11. This is a far more important point than it may seem at first glance because it represents the slow shift from building unity not on the basis of a shared identity but on the basis of *doing*, on common actions – where the actions reflect (and prefigure) a political ideal.

12. In contrast to 'autonomous', 'independent' was an ideology-free label. The rise of the term 'independent' as a label for activists within the ESF stems from the need for each actor to have a group to which she belongs. It is a way for the movement actors to demonstrate (quickly in an unfamiliar environment) that they are involved in some sort of activism outside of the ESF, that they are *doing* something on a daily basis. Many movement actors interpreted this as a type of representation. This latter group opted to refer to themselves instead as 'independents'. In this way they had the necessary proof that they were active, while at the same time criticising the practice of de facto representation. The group labels also help movement actors place each other in the web of social relations. The group labels display belonging, to both the transnational space and sometimes to a particular 'local' space. These labels become more important in the global disembedded spaces of movement activity because, as Krohn-Hansen (2003: 86) has argued about kinship relations, 'they give form to belonging in a world of flows'.

13. The term 'adivasi' means 'original dwellers' and is considered a more accurate word to describe indigenous peoples in the Indian context (Baviskar 1995: 44).

14. The NBA has been criticised for having this overtly anti-dam stance on the grounds that it does not represent the interests of the adivasis (Baviskar 1995: 222, Centre for Science and Environment 1984: 101, Dwivedi 1999: 17).

15. *Satyagraha* refers to bearing witness to the truth and protest tactics of Gandhian non-violence.

16. In this case *Dharna* was a sit/sleep in.

2   Turning Dreams into Reality

1. Weissman (2005) outlines many of these prefigurative acts in his article 'Everyday Revolutions'. He lists among others: waste recovery ('dumpster diving' or 'skipping'), free markets and free stores, squatting, alternative media, infoshops, and holistic medicine.

2. Much debate occurred between April and June 2001 in the process of rewriting the Charter of Principles. For a brief description of the rewriting process see Sen (2004).

3. For a similar discussion of process within the autonomous inspired PGA network, see Juris (2008b: 209–17, 222–31).

4. He is referring not to the London ESF, but to the local London Social Forum which had recently been launched and which his political party boycotted.

5. On the role of anarchism in the alterglobalisation movement see Bowen and Purkis (2004), Chesters (2003), Chesters and Welsh (2005b), Day (2004, 2005), Epstein (2001), Finnegan (2000), Franks (2003), Goaman (2004), Graeber (2000, 2002, 2004, 2009), Graeber and Grubacic (2004), Juris (2008b), Kaplan (2002), Morland (2004), Yuen et al. (2001).

6. For examples of prefiguration within right-wing social movements see Franks (2003: 26), Futrell (2004), Lucas (1999), MacDonald (1980). On communist prefiguration among anabaptists see O'Neil (1994).

7. Marshall (1992: 263–64) has already outlined in detail the extent to which the characterisation of anarchism as 'violent' is or is not true. Although Marshall takes the distinction between violence and non-violence to be given, my ethnography leads me to avoid doing the same. Furthermore, many acts in the alterglobalisation movement that are dubbed 'violent', are also strongly prefigurative (of a society without private property for example) (see ACME Collective 1999).

8. Consequentialism has many variants; for my purposes it suffices to take consequentialism in its most basic form as a philosophy that holds the consequences of actions to be more important that the acts themselves. Although the focus here is on *Leninist* consequentialism, the classic examples would be the utilitarianism of John Stuart Mill and Jeremy Bentham.

9. It should be mentioned, however, that this is partly May's (1994: 119) point and he sets the argument up in this way in order to argue that anarchism is based on the 'strategic' philosophy of post-structuralism, but due to the way he has defined strategy above, this leads him to call for a post-structural anarchistic practice of ethics that is 'universal in scope', which keeps him within the line of reasoning outlined here.

10. Although this bears some similarities to Habermas' (1984 [1981]) distinction between conflicts over 'systemic control' versus conflicts over the 'life world', and consequently to Rucht's (1990) division between instrumental and expressive logic of action, my point here is rather that the alterglobalisation movement merges these two approaches. The perfect example of this is the Clown Army – a literal merger between the expressive element of clowning and the instrumentality of an army. Prefiguration and horizontality are also both at once – instrumental in that the logic of action is 'power-oriented', concerned with the outcomes of political decision-making and the distribution of political power (albeit perhaps in a different sense than Rucht meant) and expressive because this redistribution of

political power is enacted partly by changing cultural codes through the construction of alternative lifestyles (see Doherty et al. 2000: 13, cf. Stammers and Eschle 2005: 59).

11. Although prefigurative politics is necessarily combined with other kinds of politics, and the movement is diverse, this is not to say that there are no linear theories of social change within the movement.

3   Creating Conflictive Spaces

1. The GLA continuously threatened to withdraw all funding for the ESF if these discussions did not stop and if the ESF was not organised on their terms. The SWP, therefore, felt that anyone who insisted on altering the terms of the ESF organising process through these discussions was placing the entire ESF in jeopardy and was therefore not 'serious'.
2. The German mobilisation against the G8 in 2007, by contrast, was permeated with *inhältliche diskussionen*.
3. For an excellent description of a less reserved and polite approach to conflict, see Alberto on the benefits of heated conflict in community assemblies during the Argentinian uprising in December 2001 (in Sitrin 2006: 43–44) and Caruso (2004) on conflict in the Mumbai WSF, where I too was repeatedly surprised at how much yelling was involved in the average more-or-less amicable meeting.
4. Here I mean that the involvement must be literally *both* real and perceived – that neither physical involvement without a sense of involvement, nor a sense of involvement without any actual involvement would suffice for the network to consider itself horizontal.
5. Despite this comment escalating tensions, most people took the comment more as an expression of exacerbation than as a personal insult. This less volatile interpretation was possible because the person who made the comment was one of the main organisers of the Hori-Zone camp. This position simultaneously gave him the necessary credentials to be respected, to be given the benefit of the doubt that his motivations for what he said were only to ensure horizontality, while paradoxically giving him the status as someone who had been involved in the 'bureaucracy bloc' at the centre of the organisation of the camp, for which he had been at the receiving end of accusations of non-horizontality himself. Consequently, his comment was not interpreted as an accusation against others, putting himself above them as more-horizontal-than-thou, because on the one hand, his horizontal intentions were not questioned, and on the

other hand, his actions (although never the intentions) had already been accused of being non-horizontal.

6. This power of 'institutions', of centralised hierarchy, should not be confused with structural power, where the latter 'shapes the social field of action so as to render some kinds of behaviour possible, while making others less possible or impossible' (Wolf 1990: 587, drawing on Foucault's sense of 'to govern'). As we shall see below, horizontal movement actors are not opposed to the power of structure when this structure is neither centralised nor hierarchical.

7. This idea of power necessitating a responsibility to resist underscores a confusion that often arises between movement approaches to power and academic approaches to power, where the latter assume that depicting 'structure' or, even worse, 'institutions' as omnipotent obviates the actor and consequently any potential for agency. Movement actors on the other hand, seem to *stress* the omnipotence of institutions precisely in order to incite people to act, in order to *create* agency. The fact that this latter tactic does seem to work, rests, I believe, on the fact that the actor never ceases to act, no matter how blurred she may be in an analysis of power. As Popkewitz and Brennan (1998: 30) argue, 'we can point to no instance of people being incapacitated to act because of intellectual knowledge. Nor have social movements been disbanded when the identification of the actors is intellectually blurred.'

8. This third approach to power resonates with feminist approaches to power that view power primarily as a capacity (see V. Held 1993, Hoagland 1988, Miller 1992, Morriss 2002, Pitkin 1972) and raises the power-over/power-to, or power-as-domination vs power-as-capacity distinction. The first two types of power described here could be considered power-over while the last could be considered power-to, but the relationship between these two concepts is ambiguous. For an interpretation of both power-over and power-to as 'capacity', see Habermas (1977), Hindess (1996), Lukes (2005). For an interpretation of power-to as a form of power-over see Wartenberg (1990) and on the interdependency of these two powers see Ortner (2006). Some have adopted the term 'power-with' to emphasise the collective, constructive and horizontal nature of what I have dubbed *prefigurative power* (see McFarland 2006, Sitrin 2006: 3, cf. Follet 1942). Holloway's (2002) discussion of power-to and power-over in relation to the separation of the 'doing'/'doer' from the 'done' is relevant here, however, in that he argues that power-over separates the 'doing' and the 'doer' from the 'done'. This is certainly an interesting proposition considering the movement's rejection of representation and emphasis on prefiguration, where we

could argue that representation is a form of separation between the 'doer' and the 'done', where they 'do' for us, and prefiguration is a reclaiming of the 'doing', of the right to be the 'doer', the power to 'take control' of the collective self. In this way, prefiguration as a merging of the means and the ends, the 'doing' and the 'done', could be understood as a direct challenge to power-over.

9. This is not to say that if centralised power were to be disguised or unidentifiable that it would somehow become legitimate. On the contrary, part of the movement's strategy is to expose much of this disguised power as illegitimate. The significant point here is that when power is centralised in the hands of the few, and therefore not a collective form of power, it is rejected (and confronted) by horizontal movement actors.

10. An interesting thing happens to 'intent' here. 'Intent' ends up being not in what one does, but in what one fails to do: The *absence* of intent to decentralise is equated to a *presence* of intent to centralise. This rests on the assumption mentioned above that, although centralisation is not inevitable, it nevertheless requires active resistance to be avoided.

11. This movement principle should not be confused with Mill's Liberty Principle that holds that man should act as he likes, so long as he does not harm the interests of another person (1962 [1859]: 136). The individualism implied in Mill's 'acting as you like' and 'interests of persons' is not present in the movement practices being described here. Individuals and groups find their unique mode of expression within the framework of collectively determined interests. See Chapter 4.

4   Reinventing Democracy

1. Many movement actors posit state-based solutions to immediate problems. The respect shown for the popular/participatory/direct democracy practiced in Porto Alegre, Brazil is a good example of movement support for state-based alternative democracy (see Wainwright 2003). Nevertheless, there is surprisingly little movement discussion about how states should rule, and a considerable amount of aversion to the state as an institution.

2. This shift away from the individual does not imply that alterglobalisation movement actors do not believe that there is such a thing as an individual or do not support individual rights. It means that interests are not perceived to be the property of individuals and cannot be constructed or acted upon outside of social interaction. This shift in focus is not an attack on the individual, but on individualism. As

Andy, an activist quoted in Losson and Quinio (2002: 24), said: 'on veut reconquérir nos rues, repousser symboliquement les voitures et au-delà faire barrage a l'individualisme érigé en mode de vie'.

3. On the influence of Montesquieu on the American republicans, see Ball (1988) and Manin (1994).

4. The rejection of the normative principle of singular unity, or univocity, does not imply that its opposite applies (difference without limits or commonality) nor does it imply lack of unity. Hardt and Negri (2004: 105) argue that the movement 'need not choose between unity and plurality'. The normative principles that guide interactions and relationships between movement actors (like consensus and anti-oppression principles) help to avoid forms of 'difference [that] are constructed as relations of subordination' (Mouffe 1996: 247).

5. For an excellent discussion of the role this rational communication style played in the WSF in India, see Caruso (2004).

6. This distinction is not the same as the institutional/non-institutional divide in much of social movement theory. Although it is a structural matter, it is not institutional because the 'official' loci of power only constitute power in a transitory and fleeting way, while institutions are characterised by their fixed and long(er)-term nature.

7. 'Unofficial' should not be confused with unaccountable or hidden. These are clearly identifiable but fluid loci of power.

8. Although activist camps as prefiguration of social alternatives have their roots in anti-nuclear movements and the Earth First! and anti-roads movements in the UK, the barrio structure was first used in Europe at the No Border camp in Strasbourg in 2002 (see Juris 2008b: 217–21).

9. The EPA differs from the IC in that it is an official decision-making body while the IC is only a consulting body. This official 'openness' of the ESF is in contrast to the WSF, where membership in the Brazilian Organising Committee (BOC) was originally closed to all except the eight founding member organisations. The Indian Organising Committee (IOC) was opened up to include 57 affiliated organisations, and an Indian General Council (IGC) was created which consisted of over 250 organisations. This more open structure was mimicked by other WSF organising committees, including the Brazilian OC of 2005, which had 24 organisations, and the three 'polycentric' WSF organising committees of 2006.

10. By way of contrast, in Mumbai during the WSF, there was a finance committee responsible for releasing funds. The members of the finance committee were also members of the Indian Organising Committee and therefore decisions were taken with full knowledge

of the budget and funds were released for decisions taken by the IOC by those responsible within the IOC.

11. Officially one can voice an opinion from afar on the e-lists, and through other people who are attending the meeting when one cannot attend. This theoretical possibility would have considerable potential were it to be put into practice. However, opinions voiced on email are almost categorically ignored or forgotten about in most movement spaces, and even where they are included, they are often overridden or postponed at meetings because the person who wrote the email is not there to defend her position.

12. The power of 'those who are there' can be understood to be equivalent to the power of the administrators in most democratic theory. The democratic praxis of the alterglobalisation movement has no official administrators (except in social forum offices) and, more importantly, no way to ensure administration happens in congruence with the decisions taken. Often no one is identified as responsible for the implementation of a decision and it does not get implemented. Other times, even when there is a vague sense of who should be implementing the decision, this link is weak enough to be ignored. When the responsibility of administration is clearly identified it is usually a highly temporary responsibility delegated on a task-by-task basis.

13. This shift in definition has a slightly undesirable consequence: if democracy is understood only as a decision-making system, it is at risk of being relegated to the realm of pure instrumentality. This movement does not privilege the instrumental value of democracy over its intrinsic value.

14. This distinction is similar to Aristotle's assertion that 'democratic equality is equality of condition and outcome' (Held 1996: 19, cf. Aristotle, 1992 [1962]: 195–98). However, the movement places the emphasis on equality of outcome and process, rather than condition, because it is assumed that equality of condition is impossible, where horizontality is the means through which this inequality of condition is limited.

15. This would be possible in certain kinds of networks made up of fixed groups, where each group has a fixed membership. The networks examined here are not fixed, structured or determinable. Even if there were a clear set of groups affiliated to the Dissent! network or to the ESF Organising Committee, there would be no limit to the number of people who could attend meetings or associate themselves with the affiliated groups. This unboundedness arises in a static analysis but becomes infinitely more complex and indeterminate in a dynamic analysis. Who is involved and in which capacity changes

considerably over time, even who is *present* changes from one meeting to the next.

16. At the anti-G8 mobilisation in Brunswick, Georgia, in the USA in 2004, the group of activists I worked with had the most restrictive use of vocabulary I have encountered. This was made clear to me when I used the words 'we should' and was told, very respectfully and helpfully, that words like 'should' and 'must' and 'have to' were authoritarian (and presumably 'should' therefore not be used).

17. This adversarial nature of democracy has been challenged most famously by Rousseau in *The Social Contract* (1968 [1762]), who argued that democracy would not need to be adversarial once the people were raised to 'will nothing contrary to the will of society' (Book 3: 265). Rousseau put forth the notion of the common good, but did so on the basis of the potential that 'the people' could function as a unitary single actor (Wiser 1983: 267). For Rousseau the common good was 'a unitary concept, which he opposed to the "contradictory views and debates" of adversary democracy' (Mansbridge 1983: 19). The alterglobalisation movement rejects this univocity and challenges the adversarial nature of democracy through the assertion of difference. This rejection of the 'common good' also brings into question the applicability of theories of 'deliberative democracy', often used to explain democracy in the alterglobalisation movement (see della Porta 2003, 2004). Although deliberative democracy understands 'that decisions about state power are collective' (Cohen 1996: 101) and is 'premised on the fact of disagreement' and therefore in tune with the central role of conflict in movement practices, it assumes 'that the pursuit of agreement is the only way forward, that conflict must be resolved through mechanisms of collective deliberation' (Knowles 2001: 334).

18. Many democratic theorists have acknowledged 'the people' to be highly diverse, with conflicting interests, and some have concluded from this that the common good does not and cannot ever exist. Schumpeter (1976 [1942]: 251), for example, argues that 'There is no such thing as a uniquely determined common good that all people could agree on or be made to agree on by the force of rational argument.' Schumpeter further argues that people's wants and needs are heavily influenced by consumerism and the media. According to Schumpeter (described in Held 1996: 187): 'What one confronts in politics is largely a "manufactured" not a "genuine" popular will. The *volonté générale* of "classic democracy" is, in reality today, "the product and not the motive power of the political process".' Considering this observation about the contemporary nature of the general will, Rousseau's notion of the common good becomes even

less desirable in the context of the alterglobalisation movement, certain sections of which have spurned both consumerism and the mainstream media. We can even understand activists' shift towards diversity and decentralised democratic structure as an act of resistance that creates spaces *now*, within which movement actors can break free from this 'manufactured product' that is the general will and express a variety of other unique and creative wills.

19. The WSF does employ a type of representation. The Organising Committee is made up of people who represent different movements, organisations and networks that have affiliated to the WSF – a structure for which it has been criticised (see Albert 2004).

20. This point requires me to highlight again the context to which I am referring, which is the global network spaces of movement activity. It is here that we find this rejection of representation. Although this rejection is certainly more widespread than in just these global network spaces, it is not universal, and many organisations use representation and hierarchy internally. This in no way challenges or contradicts the rejection within the collective spaces of the global networks.

21. The Climate Camp sprang out of the UK Dissent! network.

22. This version of the 'tyranny of the majority' could be worse than that under representative democracy if attached to geographical locations, because it could make (almost) forced evictions possible. This is why the distinction between force and *volonté* is so important. If withdrawal is voluntary, this system would be liberating because it would leave room for those who do not agree to create alternatives and take control in a way that suits them, rather than be forced to live under a regime they do not support.

5 Resisting Unity Through Networks

1. For some examples of literature on the alterglobalisation movement and complexity theory see Chesters (2004b), Chesters and Welsh (2005b), Escobar (2004), Hardt and Negri (2004), Notes from Nowhere (2003).

2. This idea of communication characterised by reciprocal contamination is similar to Habermas's theory of communicative action (1984 [1981]) and Hall's (1985) work on 'articulation'. Habermas (1984 [1981]: 249) views communication as an agent and defines communicative action as, 'the type of interaction in which all participants harmonize their individual plans of action and thus pursue their illocutionary aims without reservation'. Harmonisation involves an 'intersubjective recognition of criticizable

validity claims' and those communicating are expected to be capable of 'mutual criticism' (1984 [1981]: 119). The idea of mutual criticism bears clear resemblance to that of reciprocal contamination, but in Habermas it is unclear to what extent criticism is competitive and to what extent it involves cooperation. While reciprocal contamination is a process of merging two conflicting beliefs (or finding a solution that allows two conflicting beliefs that cannot be merged to coexist), mutual criticism seems to be aimed at the accepting or rejecting of one 'validity claim' in favour of another. Habermas (1984 [1981]: 100) uses competitive language and tends towards univocity as the ideal, but communicative action is at times described similarly to reciprocal contamination, where 'the interpretive task consists in incorporating the other's interpretation of the situation into one's own'. Hall (1985: 113–14) uses the term 'articulation', by which he refers to:

> a connection or link which is not necessarily given in all cases, as a law or a fact of life, but which requires particular conditions of existence to appear at all, which has to be positively sustained by specific processes, which is not 'eternal' but has constantly to be renewed, which can under some circumstances disappear or be overthrown, leading to the old linkages being dissolved and new connections – re-articulations – being forged. It is also important that an articulation between different practices does not mean that they become identical or that the one is dissolved into the other. Each retains its distinct determinations and conditions of existence. However, once an articulation is made, the two practices can function together, not as an 'immediate identity' ... but as 'distinctions within a unity'.

See also Laclau and Mouffe (1985: 105).

3. This ideal interaction is similar to Habermas's 'Ideal Speech Situation' and could be understood as a counterfactual model against which to measure actual communication (with an element of anticipation). Although this ideal interaction rests upon reciprocity, it does not mirror Habermas's stipulation that in ideal speech situations the best argument will win. The ideal interaction in the alterglobalisation movement is the merging of ideas to facilitate reciprocal contamination, but without the individualist assumption that this merging can occur through an equality of inputs as required by Habermas's ideal (see Habermas 1984 [1981]: 177–80).

4. This approach implies an understanding of networks similar (but not identical) to that of Castells (2004: 10–11), who argues that networks (of digital technologies) 'recombine information on

the basis of recurrent, interactive communication' and that this 'recombination is the source of innovation'.

5. An important sidenote that requires mention is that the integration and fusing of networks through connectivity does not lead to a *singluar* goal for the resulting network. This is an intentional practice, and would seem to imply that movement actors have an understanding of power generation within networks that is similar to Castells (2004: 32), who argues that, 'in a world of networks, the ability to exercise control over others depends on two basic mechanisms: the ability to programme/reprogramme the networks in terms of goals assigned to the network; and the ability to connect different networks to ensure their cooperation by sharing common goals and increasing resources', but that movement actors therefore define their network less by a singular goal, in contrast to Castells, but rather by the refusal to create a single goal, which in turn is a refusal to create such sources of power.

6. Munro (2005: 262) writes: 'connections for Strathern are "provisional" as well as "partial"'. Connectivity too, is necessarily always only partial, and often provisional and the displacement of identity may also be only partial and provisional from the actors point of view. As Santos (2006: 132) writes: 'the WSF underwrites the idea that the world is an exhaustible totality, as it holds many totalities, all of them partial'.

7. Somewhat paradoxically, the other element that makes this centralisation of power impossible is the potential for splitting the network. The option to leave a group ensures that power which is exercised without the authority of the group as a whole cannot ever grow out of proportion, and will always be counterbalanced.

8. I use the term 'actor' and 'agent' interchangeably in this section but, as will become clear below, the two are not synonymous.

9. Latour (1999) and Law (1999) also contribute to the discussion of 'rules' through actor-network theory. In actor-network theory actors would not so much follow rules as perform them. Actor-network theory 'is a theory that says that by following circulations we can get more than by defining entities, essences or provinces' (Latour 1999: 20) and 'it tells us that entities take their form and acquire their attributes as a result of their relations with other entities ... it also tells us that [entities] are *performed* in, by, and through those relations' (Law 1999: 3–4, cf. Strathern 1988).

10. Although Giddens uses the term himself, he warns against the possible connotations of 'rules': 'To speak of structure as "rules" and resources, and of structures as isolable sets of rules and resources,

runs a distinct risk of misinterpretation because of certain dominant uses of "rules" in the philosophical literature' (Giddens 1994: 80).

11. As Inden (2001: 12) writes of the use of a biological metaphor: 'it is all the more deadly because of the silence it imposes on the subject'.

12. See also Evans (1995) on the 'fragmented self' and Daniel (1984) and Busby (1997) on the 'permeable' person. These notions are similar but not identical to 'partible person' (see Munro 2005).

13. This is similar to 'the premise of actor-network theory (ANT) that agency is a property of heterogeneous networks of human and non-human actors', which:

> has profound implications for our understanding of identity. Like Haraway's cyborgs, the hybrid assemblages of bodies, things, and representations that constitute persons do not end at the skin. It is not enough to assert that identity is reflected or communicated by material culture, nor even that individuals are constituted within the material structures of a social field. (Whitridge 2004)

14. Juris (2008b: 326) drawing on Castells (2000: 16) writes:

> the most important network nodes are not centres but rather 'switchers,' which receive, interpret, and circulate information … I further distinguish between 'relayers,' who process and distribute information within a single network, and 'switchers' who occupy key nodal positions within multiple movement networks.

15. Considering this positive feedback loop, activist 'burn-out' can be viewed as a potentially positive and necessary element to horizontality because it leads to the pulling back of central figures and the opening up of space for new people to take on these critical roles of 'switchers' and 'relayers'.

16. Here it must be mentioned that Strathern argues that for Melanesians these identities are made visible through relations with others, where 'agents are not the authors of their own acts' (Strathern 1988: 273). Here (and in several other ways) the comparison halts. Movement actors are often intentional about what they make visible.

BIBLIOGRAPHY

Abu-Lughod, L. 1990. 'The Romance of Resistance: Tracing Transformations of Power Through Bedouin Women', *American Ethnologist* 17(1): 41–55.

ACME Collective. 1999. 'N30 Black Bloc Communiqué', in E. Yuen, G. Katsiaficas and B.D. Rose (eds) *The Battle of Seattle: New Challenges to Capitalist Globalization*. New York: Soft Skull Press.

Ahern, L. 2001. 'Language and Agency', *Annual Review of Anthropology* 30: 109–37.

Albert, M. 2004. 'The WSF: Where to Now?', in J. Sen, A. Anand, A. Escobar and P. Waterman (eds) *The World Social Forum: Challenging Empires*. New Delhi: The Viveka Foundation. Also available at: http://www.choike.org/nuevo_eng/informes/1557.html. Accessed October 2008.

Alvares, C. and Billorey, R. 1988. *Damming the Narmada*. Third World Network/APPEN.

Anderson, P. 1972. 'More is Different', *Science* 177: 393–96.

Anzaldúa, G. 1987. *Borderlands: La Frontera*. Berkeley: University of California Press.

Appadurai, A. 1991. 'Global Ethnoscapes: Notes and Queries for a Transnational Anthropology', in R. Fox (ed.) *Recapturing Anthropology*. Santa Fe: School of American Research Press.

Appadurai, A. 1996. *Modernity at Large: Cultural Dimensions of Globalization*. Minneapolis: University of Minnesota Press.

Appiah, K.A. 1994. 'Identity, Authenticity, Survival: Multicultural Societies and Social Reproduction', in A. Gutmann (ed.) *Multiculturalism*. Princeton, NJ: Princeton University Press.

Arendt, H. 1970. *On Violence*. London: Allen Lane.

Aretxaga, B. 1999. 'A Fictional Reality: Paramilitary Death Squads and the Construction of State Terror in Spain', in J.A. Sluka (ed.) *Death Squads: The Anthropology of State Terror*. Philadelphia, PA: University of Pennsylvania Press.

Aristotle (1992 [1965]) *The Politics*, trans. T.A. Sinclair. Harmondsworth: Penguin.

Bakunin, M. 1984. *Marxism, Freedom and the State*. London: Freedom Press.

Balandier, G. 2004 [1967]. *Anthropologie politique*. Paris: Presses Universitaires de France.

Ball, T. 1988. *Transforming Political Discourse: Political Theory and Critical Conceptual History.* Oxford: Blackwell.

Barber, B. 1984. *Strong Democracy.* Berkeley: University of California Press.

Barth, F. 1969. *Ethnic Groups and Boundaries.* Boston, MA: Little, Brown.

Baviskar, A. 1995. *In the Belly of the River.* Oxford: Oxford University Press.

Benhabib, S. 1996. 'The Democratic Moment and the Problem of Difference', in S. Benhabib (ed.) *Democracy and Difference.* Princeton, NJ: Princeton University Press.

Berman, P. 1996. *A Tale of Two Utopias.* New York: W.W. Norton.

Bey, H. 1990. 'The Temporary Autonomous Zone', URL: http://www.hermetic.com/bey/taz_cont.html. Accessed May 2007.

Bodie, A. 2004. 'Autonomous Spaces: AS an alternative ESF experience', *Euromovements*, URL: http://www.euromovements.info/upload/autonomous_spaces.doc. Accessed March 2009.

Boéri, J. and Hodkinson, S. 2005. 'Social Forums after London: The Politics of Language', *Red Pepper* January, URL: http://www.redpepper.org.uk/Jan2005/x-Jan2005-ESF.html. Accessed December 2006.

van Boeschoten, R. 2000. 'When Difference Matters: Sociopolitical Dimensions of Ethnicity in the District of Florina', in J.K. Cowan (ed.) *Macedonia: The Politics of Identity and Difference.* London: Pluto Press.

Bourdieu, P. 1977. *Outline of a Theory of Practice.* Cambridge: Cambridge University Press.

Bourdieu, P. 1994. 'Structures, Habitus and Practices', in *The Polity Reader in Social Theory.* Cambridge: Polity Press.

Bourdieu, P. and Wacquant, L. 1992. *An Invitation to Reflexive Sociology.* Cambridge: Polity Press.

Bowen, J. and Purkis, J. 2004. 'Introduction: Why Anarchism Still Matters', in J. Purkis and J. Bowen (eds) *Changing Anarchism.* Manchester: Manchester University Press.

Braungart, R. and Braungart, M. 1990. 'Youth Movements in the 1980s: A Global Perspective', *International Sociology* 5(2): 157–81.

Breines, W. 1989. *Community and Organization in the New Left 1962–1968: The Great Refusal.* New Brunswick, NJ: Rutgers University Press.

Bressan, A. 2003. 're: LSF report'. Email. Sent to 'esf-uk-info' e-list, posted 11 October.

Busby, C. 1997. 'Permeable and Partible Persons: A Comparative Analysis of Gender and Body in South India and Melanesia', *Journal of the Royal Anthropological Institute* 3(2): 261–78.

Calderia, T. 1996. 'Fortified Enclaves: the New Urban Segregation', *Public Culture* 8(2): 303–28.

Calderón, F., Piscitelli, A. and Reyna, J.L. 1992. 'Social Movements: Actors, Theories, Expectations', in A. Escobar and S. Alvarez (eds) *The Making of Social Movements in Latin America: Identity, Strategy and Democracy*. Boulder, CO: Westview Press.

Calhoun, C. 1993. 'New Social Movements of the Early Nineteenth Century', *Social Science History* 17(3): 385–427.

Callinicos, A. 2003. 're: LSF report'. Email. Sent to 'esf-uk-info' e-list, posted 11 October.

Callinicos, A. 2005. Email. Sent to 'ESF-FSE' e-list. Posted 8 February.

Caruso, G. 2004. 'Conflict Management and Hegemonic Practices in the World Social Forum 2004', *International Social Science Journal* 56(182): 577–89. Also online: http://www.openspaceforum.net/twiki/tiki-read_article.php?articleId=20. Accessed October 2008.

Castells, M. 1997. *The Power of Identity: The Information Age. Economy, Society and Culture*, vol. 2. Oxford: Blackwell.

Castells, M. 2004. 'Informationalism, Networks, and the Network Society: A Theoretical Blueprint', in M. Castells (ed.) *The Network Society: A Cross-cultural Perspective*. Cheltenham: Edward Elgar.

Caute, D. 1988. *The Year of the Barricades: A Journey Through 1968*. New York: Harper and Row.

Centre for Science and Environment. 1984. *The Second Citizens Report*. New Delhi: Centre for Science and Environment.

Chatterjee, P. 1993. *The Nation and its Fragments*. Princeton, NJ: Princeton University Press.

Checker, M. 2001. '"Like Nixon Coming to China": Finding Common Ground in a Multi-ethnic Coalition for Environmental Justice', *Anthropological Quarterly* 74(3): 135–46.

Chesters, G. 2003. 'Shapeshifting: Civil Society, Complexity and Social Movements', *Anarchist Studies* 11(1): 42–65.

Chesters, G. 2004a. 'ESF: Encounter or Representation'. Online: www.nadir.org/nadir/initiativ/agp/free/wsf/london2004/1022encounter.htm. Accessed December 2006.

Chesters, G. 2004b. 'Global Complexity and Global Civil Society', *Voluntas: International Journal of Voluntary and Nonprofit Organizations* 15 (4): 323–42.

Chesters, G. and Welsh, I. 2005a. 'Complexity and Social Movement(s): Process and Emergence in Planetary Action Systems', *Theory, Culture & Society* 22(5): 187–211.

Chesters, G. and Welsh, I. 2005b. *Complexity and Social Movements: Acting on the Edge of Chaos*. London: Routledge.

Climate Camp. n.d. 'How We Work'. Online: http://www.climatecamp.org.uk/archive/howwework.htm. Accessed December 2006.

Clown Army. CIRCA. (n.d.) 'About The Army'. Online: www.clownarmy.org/about/about.html. Accessed October 2006.

Cohen, I. 1989. *Structuration Theory: Anthony Giddens and the Constitution of Social Life*. London: Macmillan.

Cohen, J. 1983. 'Rethinking Social Movements', *Berkeley Journal of Social Movements* 28: 97–113.

Cohen, J. and Arato, A. 1992. *Civil Society and Political Theory*. Cambridge, MA: MIT Press.

Cohen, J. 1993. 'Moral Pluralism and Political Consensus', in D. Copp, J. Hampton and J. Roemer (eds) *The Idea of Democracy*. Cambridge: Cambridge University Press.

Cohen, J. 1996. 'Procedure and Substance in Deliberative Democracy', in S. Benhabib (ed.) *Democracy and Difference*. Princeton, NJ: Princeton University Press.

Comaroff, J. and Comaroff, J.L. 1991. *Of Revelation and Revolution: Christianity, Colonialism and Consciousness in South Africa*, vol. 1. Chicago, IL: Chicago University Press.

Comaroff, J. and Comaroff, J.L. 1992. *Ethnography and the Historical Imagination*. Boulder, CO: Westview Press.

Cooke, B. and Kothari, U. (eds) 2001. *The Tyranny of Participation*. London: Zed Books.

Coombe, R.J. 1998. *The Cultural Life of Intellectual Properties: Authorship, Appropriation and the Law*. Durham, NC: Duke University Press.

Cooper, F. and Packard, R. 1997. *International Development and the Social Sciences*. Berkeley, CA: University of California Press.

Corr, A. 1999. *No Trespassing! Squatting, Rent Strikes, and Land Struggles Worldwide*. Boston, MA: South End Press.

Corr, A. 2005. 'Anarchist Squatting and Land Use in the West: Direct Action and the Critique of Real Estate'. Online: http://squat.net/archiv/anders/anarchist_squatting.html. Accessed June 2005.

Cowan, J.K. and Brown, K.S. 2000. 'Introduction: Macedonian Inflections', in J.K. Cowan (ed.) *Macedonia: The Politics of Identity and Difference*. London: Pluto Press.

Crewe, E. and Harrison, E. 1998. *Whose Development? An Ethnography of Aid*. London: Zed Books.

Crosby, C. 1992. 'Dealing with Difference', in J. Butler and J. Scott (eds) *Feminists Theorize the Political*. London: Routledge.

Crouch, C. 2004. *Post-Democracy*. Cambridge: Polity Press.

Crozier, M., Huntington, S. and Watanuki, J. 1975. *The Crisis of Democracy*. The Trilateral Commission. Online: http://www.trilateral.org/library/crisis_of_democracy.pdf. Accessed December 2006.

D'Souza, D. 1995. 'You Need a Thorn to Remove a Thorn', Online: www.narmada.org/articles/dsouza.interview.html. Accessed October 2006.

Dahl, R. 1989. *Democracy and its Critics*. New Haven, CT: Yale University Press.

Dahl, R. 1998. *On Democracy*. New Haven, CT: Yale University Press.

Dahl, R. 2000. 'A Democratic Paradox?', *Political Science Quarterly* 115(1): 35–40.

Dalton, R., Kuechler, M. and Bürklin, W. 1990. 'The Challenge of New Movements', in R. Dalton and M. Keuchler (eds) *Challenging the Political Order*. Oxford: Polity Press.

Danforth, L. 2000. '"How Can a Woman Give Birth to One Greek and One Macedonian?" The Construction of National Identity among Immigrants to Australia from Northern Greece', in J.K. Cowan (ed.) *Macedonia: The Politics of Identity and Difference*. London: Pluto Press.

Daniel, E. 1984. *Fluid Signs: Being a Person the Tamil Way*. Berkeley, CA: University of California Press.

Daniels, R.V. 1989. *Year of the Heroic Guerrilla: World Revolution and Counterrevolution in 1968*. New York: Basic Books.

Daum, N. 1988. *Des révolutionnaires dans un village parisien*. Paris: Londreys.

Davis, M. 1990. *City of Quartz: Excavating the Future in Los Angeles*. London: Verso.

Day, R.J.F. 2004. 'From Hegemony to Affinity: The Political Logic of the Newest Social Movements', *Cultural Studies* 18(5): 716–48.

Day, R.J.F. 2005. *Gramsci is Dead – Anarchist Currents in the Newest Social Movements*. London: Pluto Press.

De Angelis, M. 2003a. 'The 1st LSF: What Have We Achieved?'. Email. Posted 11 October. Also available at: http://www.commoner.org. uk/01-10groundzero.htm. Accessed March 2009.

De Angelis, M. 2003b. 'Democracy'. Email. Sent to 'esf-uk-info' e-list. Posted 14 October.

de Certeau, M. 1984. *The Practice of Everyday Life*. Berkeley: University of California Press.

de Certeau, M. 1988. *The Writing of History*. New York: Colombia University Press.

de Jong, W., Shaw, M. and Stammers, N. (eds) 2005. *Global Activism, Global Media*. London: Pluto Press.

de Tocqueville, A. 2000 [1835–40]. *Democracy in America*. Indiana, IN: Hackett.

Dean. 2004. 'Response' to 'Overview of Preparation for ESF in London'. 26 January. Online: http://www.indymedia.org.uk/en/2004/01/284413. html?c=on#c85707. Accessed August 2007.

Deleuze, G. and Guattari, F. 1987. *A Thousand Plateaus*. London: Continuum.

della Porta, D. 2003. 'Democracy in Movement: Organizational Dilemma and Globalization from Below', *Colloque 'Les mobilisations alter-mondialistes'* 3–5 December. Online: http://www.afsp.mshparis. fr/activite/groupe/germm/collgermm03txt/germm03dellaporta.pdf. Accessed August 2007.

della Porta, D. 2004. 'Making the Polis: Social Forums and Democracy in the Global Justice Movement', revised version of the paper 'Deliberation in Movement: Why and How to Study Deliberative Democracy and Social Movements', presented at the conference 'Empirical Approaches to Deliberative Politics', European University Institute, Florence, 21–22 May. Online: http://falcon.arts.cornell.edu/ sgt2/contention/documents/4-1-05%20della%20Porta.doc. Accessed August 2007.

della Porta, D. 2005. 'Multiple Belongings, Tolerant Identities, and the Construction of "Another Politics": Between European Social Forum and the Local Social Fora', in D. della Porta and S. Tarrow (eds) *Transnational Protest and Global Activism*. Lanham, MD: Rowman and Littlefield.

Derrida, J. 1982. 'Différance', in *Margins of Philosophy*, trans. A. Bass. Chicago: University of Chicago Press. Online: http://www.stanford. edu/class/history34q/readings/Derrida/Differance.html. Accessed December 2006.

Diani, M. 1992. 'The Concept of Social Movement', *Sociological Review* 40(1): 1–25.

Dillon, M.C. 1993. 'The Metaphysics of Presence: Critique of a Critique', in G. Madison (ed.) *Working Through Derrida*. Evanston, IL: Northwestern University Press.

Dissent! 2004a. 'Introduction to the Dissent! network'. Online: http:// dissent.org.uk/content/view/62/52/. Accessed October 2006.

Dissent! 2004b. 'PGA Call Out for Action in Solidarity with 2004 G8'. Posted by 'Reverend Chuck0'. Online: http://www.infoshop.org/inews/ article.php?story=04/04/27/2119242. Accessed October 2006.

Dissent! Reconvergence Working Group. 2005a. 'DISSENT –RECONVERGENCE 2006 call-out and consulta [V1.0]'. Email. Sent to 'resistg82005' e-list. Posted 13 November.

Dissent! Reconvergence Working Group. 2005b. 'Minutes of Dissent! Reconvergence/Consulta WG, Leeds 4 Dec'. Email. Sent to 'dissent-process' e-list. Posted 7 December 2005.

Doane, M. 2005. 'The Resilience of Nationalism in a Global Era: Megaprojects in Mexico's South', in J. Nash (ed.) *Social Movements: An Anthropological Reader*. Oxford: Blackwell.

Doherty, B., Paterson, M. and Seel, B. 2000. 'Direct Action in British Environmentalism', in B. Doherty, M. Paterson and B. Seel (eds) *Direct Action in British Environmentalism*. London: Routledge.

Dolgoff, S. 1970. 'The Relevance of Anarchism to Modern Society', *Libertarian Analysis*. Minneapolis, MN: Soil of Liberty. Also available online: http://flag.blackened.net/liberty/spunk/Spunk191.txt. Accessed October 2008.

Douglas, N. 2003. 're: LSF report'. Email. Sent to 'esf-uk-info' e-list. Posted 9 October.

Dowding, K. 2006. 'Three-dimensional Power: A Discussion of Steven Lukes' *Power: A Radical View*', *Political Studies Review* 4: 136–45.

Dunn, J. 1980. *Political Obligation in its Historical Context: Essays in Political Theory*. Cambridge: Cambridge University Press.

Dwivedi, R. 1999. 'Displacement, Risks and Resistance: Local Perceptions and Actions in the Sardar Sarovar', *Development and Change* 30(1): 43–78.

Dyson, M. 1994. 'Essentialism and the Complexities of Racial Identity', in D. Goldberg (ed.) *Multiculturalism*. Cambridge, MA: Blackwell.

Edelman, M. 2002 [1999]. 'Peasants Against Globalization', reproduced in J. Vincent (ed.) *The Anthropology of Politics: A Reader in Ethnography, Theory and Critique*. Oxford: Blackwell. Originally from M. Edelman, 1999. *Peasants Against Globalization: Rural Social Movements in Costa Rica*. Stanford, CA: Stanford University Press.

Eisenstadt, S.N. 1999. *Paradoxes of Democracy: Fragility, Continuity and Change*. Baltimore, MD: Johns Hopkins University Press.

Eisenstein, Z. 1988. *The Female Body and the Law*. Berkeley: University of California Press.

Eley, G. 2002. *Forging Democracy: The History of the Left in Europe, 1850–2000*. Oxford: Oxford University Press.

Epstein, A.L. 1958. *Politics in an Urban African Community*. Manchester: Manchester University Press.

Epstein, B. 1991. *Political Protest and Cultural Revolution*. Berkeley: University of California Press.

Epstein, B. 2001. 'Anarchism and the Anti-globalization Movement', *Monthly Review* 54(4): 1–14.

Eriksen, T.H. 2003. 'Introduction', in T.H. Eriksen (ed.) *Globalisation: Studies in Anthropology*. London: Pluto Press.

Eschle, C. 2001. *Global Democracy, Social Movements and Feminism*. Boulder, CO: Westview Press.

Escobar, A. 1992. 'Culture, Economics, and Politics in Latin American Social Movements: Theory and Research', in A. Escobar and S. Alvarez (eds) *The Making of Social Movements in Latin America: Identity, Strategy, and Democracy*. Boulder, CO: Westview Press.

Escobar, A. 2001. 'Culture Sits in Places: Reflections on Globalism and Subaltern Strategies of Localization', *Political Geography* 20: 139–74.

Escobar, A. 2004. 'Other Worlds Are (Already) Possible: Self-organization, Complexity and Post-capitalist Culture', in J. Sen, A. Anand, A. Escobar and P. Waterman (eds) *The World Social Forum: Challenging Empires*. New Delhi: The Viveka Foundation. Also available online: http://www.choike.org/nuevo_eng/informes/1557.html. Accessed April 2009.

Escobar, A. and Alvarez, S. 1992a. 'Introduction: Theory and Protest in Latin America Today', in A. Escobar and S. Alvarez (eds) *The Making of Social Movements in Latin America: Identity, Strategy and Democracy*. Boulder, CO: Westview Press.

Evans, J. 1995. *Feminist Theory Today: An Introduction to Second-Wave Feminism*. London: SAGE.

Evans, S. 1980. *Personal Politics: The Roots of Women's Liberation in the Civil Rights Movement and the New Left*. New York: Vintage Books Edition, Random House.

Fabian, J. 1983. *Time and the Other*. New York: Columbia University Press.

Facilitation/Process Group of the Stirling Hori-Zone Convergence Space. 2005. 'decision-making at horizone'. Email. Sent to 'resistg82005' e-list. Posted 24 July 2005.

Fields, A. 1984. 'French Maoism', in S. Sayres, A. Stephanson, S. Aronowitz and F. Jameson (eds) *The 60s Without Apology*. Minneapolis: University of Minnesota Press.

Fields, A. 1988. *Trotskyism and Maoism: Theory and Practice in France and the United States*. New York: Autonomedia.

Findji, M.T. 1992. 'From Resistance to Social Movement: The Indigenous Authorities Movement in Colombia', in A. Escobar and S. Alvarez (eds) *The Making of Social Movements in Latin America: Identity, Strategy and Democracy*. Boulder, CO: Westview Press.

Finnegan, W. 2000. 'After Seattle: Anarchists get Organized', *The New Yorker* 17 April: 40–51.

Fix Shit Up! Collective. 2004. 'Fix Shit Up!' Pamphlet.

Flores, R. (and Tanka, G.) 2001. 'Autonomy and Participatory Democracy: An Ongoing Discussion on the Application of Zapatista Autonomy in the United States', interview by P. McLaren *International Journal of Educational Reform* 10(2). Online: http://www.inmotionmagazine. com/qanda/qanda.html. Accessed June 2005.

Follett, M.P. (1942) 'Power' in Dynamic Administration: The Collected Papers of Mary Parker Follett, ed. H.C. Metcalf and L. Urwick. New York: Harper.

Foucault, M. 1980. Power/Knowledge: Selected Interviews and Other Writings, ed. by C. Gordon. Brighton: Harvester Press.

Foucault, M. 1983. 'Afterword: The Subject and Power', in H. Dreyfus and P. Rabinow (eds) Michel Foucault: Beyond Structuralism and Hermeneutics. Chicago IL: University of Chicago Press.

Foucault, M. 2002. 'The Subject and Power', in J. Faubion (ed.) Michel Foucault: Power. Essential Works of Foucault 1954–1984, vol. 3. London: Penguin.

Foweraker, J. 1995. Theorizing Social Movements. London: Pluto Press.

Franks, B. 2003. 'The Direct Action Ethic from 59 Upwards', Anarchist Studies 11(1): 13–41.

Freeman, J. 1970. 'The Tyranny of Structurelessness.' Online: http://struggle.ws/pdfs/tyranny.pdf. Accessed December 2006.

Friedman, M. 1997. 'Autonomy and Social Relationships: Rethinking the Feminist Critique', in D. Meyers (ed.) Feminists Rethink the Self. Boulder, CO: Westview Press.

Fukuyama, F. 1992. The End of History and the Last Man. London: Hamish Hamilton.

Fuller, A. 1989. 'The Structure and Process of Peace Movement Organizations: Effects on Participation', Conflict Resolution Consortium. Online: http://www.colorado.edu/conflict/full_text_search/AllCRCDocs/89-8.htm. Accessed December 2006.

Furnivall, J.S. 1948. Colonial Policy and Practice: A Comparative Study of Burma and Netherlands India. Cambridge: Cambridge University Press.

Fuss, D. 1989. Essentially Speaking: Feminism, Nature and Difference. New York: Routledge.

Futrell, R. 2004. 'Free Spaces, Collective Identity and the Persistence of U.S. White Power Activism', Social Problems 51(1): 16–42.

George, S. 2004. Another World is Possible If ... London: Verso.

Gerlach, L. 1983. 'Movements of Revolutionary Change: Some Structural Characteristics', in J. Freeman (ed.) Social Movements of the Sixties and Seventies. New York: Longman.

Giddens, A. 1994. 'Elements of the Theory of Structuration', in The Polity Reader in Social Theory. Cambridge: Polity Press.

Gitlin, T. 1993 [1987]. The Sixties: Years of Hope, Days of Rage. New York: Bantam Books.

'Give Up Activism'. n.d. Online: http://www.eco-action.org/dod/no9/activism.htm. Accessed December 2006.

Gledhill, J. 2000. Power and Its Disguises. Sterling, VA: Pluto Press.

Gluckman, M. 1954. *Rituals of Rebellion in South-East Africa*. Manchester: Manchester University Press.

Gluckman, M. 1965. *Politics, Law and Ritual in Tribal Society*. Oxford: Blackwell.

Goaman, K. 2004. 'The Anarchist Travelling Circus: Reflections on Contemporary Anarchism, Anti-capitalism and the International Scene', in J. Purkis and J. Bowen (eds) *Changing Anarchism*. Manchester: Manchester University Press.

Gould, C. 1996. 'Diversity and Democracy: Representing Differences', in S. Benhabib (ed.) *Democracy and Difference*. Princeton, NJ: Princeton University Press.

Graeber, D. 2000. 'Anarchy in the USA', *In These Times* 10 January. Online: http://www.inthesetimes.com/issue/24/03/graeber2403.html. Accessed June 2005.

Graeber, D. 2001. *Fragments of an Anarchist Anthropology*. Chicago: Prickly Paradigm Press.

Graeber, D. 2002. 'The New Anarchists', *New Left Review* 13: 61–73.

Graeber, D. 2004. 'The Twilight of Vanguardism', in J. Sen, A. Anand, A. Escobar and P. Waterman (eds) *The World Social Forum: Challenging Empires*. New Delhi: The Viveka Foundation. Also available online: http://www.choike.org/nuevo_eng/informes/1557.html. Accessed April 2009.

Graeber, D. 2008. 'There Never was a West: Or, Democracy Emerges from the Spaces in Between', in *Possibilities: Essays on Hierarchy Rebellion and Desire*. Oakland, CA: AK Press.

Graeber, D. forthcoming 2009. *Direct Action: An Ethnography*. Oakland, CA: AK Press.

Graeber, D. and Grubacic, A. 2004. 'Anarchism, Or the Revolutionary Movement of the Twenty-first Century'. Online: http://www.zmag. org/content/showarticle.cfm?ItemID=4796. Accessed June 2005.

Granovetter, M. 1973. 'The Strength of Weak Ties', *American Journal of Sociology* 78(6): 1360–80.

Granovetter, M. 1983. 'The Strength of Weak Ties: A Network Theory Revisited', *Sociological Theory* 1: 201–33.

Grauwacke, A.G. 2004. *Autonome in Bewegung: Aus den Ersten 23 Jahren*. Berlin: Assoziation A.

Grubacic, A. 2003. 'Towards Another Anarchism'. Online: http://www. zmag.org/grubanar.htm. Accessed June 2005.

Gupta, A. and Ferguson, J. 1997a. 'Discipline and Practice: "The Field" as Site, Method, and Location in Anthropology', in A. Gupta and J. Ferguson (eds) *Anthropological Locations: Boundaries and Grounds of a Field Science*. Berkeley: University of California Press.

Gupta, A. and Ferguson, J. 1997b. 'Beyond "Culture": Space, Identity, and the Politics of Difference', in A. Gupta and J. Ferguson (eds)

Culture, Power, Place: Explorations in Critical Anthropology. Durham, NC: Duke University Press.

Gutmann, M. 2002. *The Romance of Democracy: Compliant Defiance in Contemporary Mexico.* Berkeley: University of California Press.

Habermas, J. 1977. 'Hannah Arendt's Communications Concept of Power', *Social Research* 44(1): 3–24, reprinted in S. Hinchman and L. Hinchman (eds) 1994. *Hannah Arendt: Critical Essays.* Albany: SUNY Press.

Habermas, J. 1984 [1981]. *The Theory of Communicative Action: Reason and the Rationalization of Society* (vol. 1). Boston, MA: Beacon Press.

Habermas, J. 1996. 'Three Normative Models of Democracy', in S. Benhabib (ed.) *Democracy and Difference.* Princeton, NJ: Princeton University Press.

Hale, C. 1997. 'Cultural Politics of Identity in Latin America', *Annual Review of Anthropology* 26: 567–90.

Hale, C. 2002. 'Does Multiculturalism Menace? Governance, Cultural Rights and the Politics of Identity in Guatemala', *Journal of Latin American Studies* 34: 485–524.

Hale, C. 2006. 'Activist Research v. Cultural Critique: Indigenous Land Rights and the Contradictions of Politically Engaged Anthropology', *Cultural Anthropology* 21(1): 96–120.

Hall, S. 1985. 'Signification, Representation, Ideology: Althusser and the Post-Structuralist Debates', *Critical Studies in Mass Communication* 2(2): 91–113.

Hannerz, U. 1992. 'The Global Ecumene as a Network of Networks', in A. Kuper (ed.) *Conceptualizing Society.* London: Routledge.

Hannerz, U. 2003. 'Several Sites in One', in T.H. Eriksen (ed.) *Globalisation: Studies in Anthropology.* London: Pluto Press.

Hardt, M. and Negri, A. 2004. *Multitude.* London: Hamish Hamilton.

Harvey, N. 1998. 'The Zapatistas, Radical Democratic Citizenship and Women's Studies', *Social Politics* 5: 158–87.

Hayden, R. 1992. 'Constitutional Nationalism in the former Yugoslav Republics', *Slavic Review* 51(4): 654–73.

Hegedus, Z. 1989. 'Social Movements and Social Change in Self-creative Society: New Civil Initiatives in the International Arena', *International Sociology* 4(1): 19–36.

Held, D. 1994. 'Democracy: From City-states to a Cosmopolitan Order?', in *The Polity Reader in Social Theory.* Cambridge: Polity Press.

Held, D. 1996. *Models of Democracy.* Stanford, CA: Stanford University Press.

Held, V. 1993. *Feminist Morality: Transforming Culture, Society and Politics.* Chicago, IL: University of Chicago Press.

Hernandez, M.T. 2002. *Delirio.* Austin: University of Texas Press.

Hindess, B. 1996. *Discourses of Power: From Hobbes to Foucault.* Oxford: Blackwell.

Hirsch, J. 1988. 'The Crisis of Fordism, Transformations of the "Keynesian" Security State, and New Social Movements', in L. Kriesberg (ed.) *Research in Social Movements, Contexts and Change*, vol. 10. Greenwich, CT: JAI Press.

Hoagland, S.L. 1988. *Lesbian Ethics: Toward a New Value.* Palo Alto, CA: Institute of Lesbian Studies.

Hobart, M. 1993. *An Anthropological Critique of Development: The Growth of Ignorance.* London: Routledge.

Hobbes, T. 1968 [1660]. *Leviathan*, ed. C. Macpherson (ed.) Harmondsworth: Penguin.

Hoedeman, O. 2005. 'Corporate Power', in D. Miller and G. Hubbard (eds) *Arguments Against the G8.* London: Pluto Press.

Hogden, M. 1973. *Early Anthropology in the Sixteenth and Seventeenth Century.* Philadelphia: Pennsylvania University Press.

Holloway, J. 2002. *Change the World Without Taking Power: The Meaning of Revolution Today.* London: Pluto Press.

Holloway, J. 2004. '"Walking We Ask Questions" an interview with John Holloway', interviewer M. Sitrin. Online: http://www.anarchist-studies.org/article/articleprint/78/-1/9/. Accessed June 2005.

Holston, J. and Caldeira, T. 1998. 'Democracy, Law and Violence: Disjunctions of Brazilian Citizenship', in F. Agüero and J. Stark (eds) *Fault Lines of Democracy in Post-transition Latin America.* Miami, FL: North-South Center.

Honig, B. 1996. 'Difference, Dilemmas and the Politics of Home', in S. Benhabib (ed.) *Democracy and Difference.* Princeton, NJ: Princeton University Press.

Horizontals. 2003. 'Horizontals Statement: The Horizontals Come to Town'. Email. Posted 19 October 2003. Also online: http://esf2004.net/en/tiki-index.php?page=HorizontalsStatement. Accessed February 2004.

Horizontals. 2004. 'European Social Forum (ESF) in UK in 2004; What's Happening? Log of Evidence'. Email. Posted 7 February 2004. Also online. http://esf2004.net/en/tiki-index.php?page=LogOfProcess. Accessed February 2004.

Inden, R. 2001. *Imagining India.* London: Hurst and Co.

International Working Group on Resistance Against the G8 2007. 'A Global Call Written at Anti-G8 "Camp Inski", Northern Germany, August 2006'. Online: http://dissentnetzwerk.org/node/119. Accessed October 2008.

Irigaray, L. 1985. *This Sex Which is Not One.* Ithaca, NY: Cornell University Press.

Johnson, S. 2001. *Emergence.* London: Penguin.

Juris, J. 2004. 'The London ESF and the Politics of Autonomous Space', *Euromovements*. Online: http://www.euromovements.info/newsletter/. Accessed November 2006.

Juris, J. 2008a. 'The New Digital Media and Activist Networking within Anti-Corporate Globalization Movements', in J. Inda and R. Rosaldo (eds) *The Anthropology of Globalization*, 2nd edn. Malden, MA: Blackwell.

Juris, J. 2008b. *Networking Futures: The Movements against Corporate Globalization*. Durham, NC: Duke University Press.

Kaplan, E. 2002. 'Keepers of the Flame', *Village Voice* 29 January. Online: http://www.villagevoice.com/issues/0205/kaplan.php. Accessed June 2005.

Katsiaficas, G. 1987. *The Imagination of the New Left*. Boston, MA: South End Press.

Katsiaficas, G. 2001. 'Seattle was not the Beginning', in E. Yuen, G. Katsiaficas, B.D. Rose (eds) *The Battle of Seattle: New Challenges to Capitalist Globalization*. New York: Soft Skull Press. Also online: http://www.eroseffect.com/articles/battleofseattle.pdf. Accessed April 2009.

Katsiaficas, G. 2006. *The Subversion of Politics*. Oakland, CA: AK Press.

Kearney, M. 1991. 'Borders and Boundaries of State and Self at the End of the Empire', *Journal of Historical Sociology* 41: 52–74.

Keesing, R. 1992. *Custom and Confrontation: The Kwaio Struggle for Cultural Autonomy*. Chicago, IL: University of Chicago Press.

Khasnabish, A. 2004. 'Moments of Coincidence: Exploring the Intersection of Zapatismo and Independent Labour in Mexico', *Critique of Anthropology* 24(3): 256–76.

Kingsnorth, P. 2003. *One No, Many Yeses: A Journey to the Heart of the Global Resistance Movement*. London: Free Press.

Kitschelt, H. 1989. *The Logics of Party Formation: Ecological Politics in Belgium and West Germany*. Ithaca, NY: Cornell University Press.

Kitschelt, H. 1991. 'Resource Mobilization Theory: A Critique', in D. Rucht (ed.) *Research on Social Movements – The State of the Art in Europe and the USA*. Frankfurt am Main: Campus Verlag/Boulder, CO: Westview Press.

Klein, N. 2000. *No Logo*. New York: Picador USA.

Klein, N. 2005. 'Reclaiming the Commons', in T. Mertes (ed.) *The Movement of Movements: Is Another World Really Possible?* London: Verso.

Knowles, D. 2001. *Political Philosophy*. London: Routledge.

Krohn-Hansen, C. 2003. 'Into Our Time: The Anthropology of Political Life in the Era of Globalisation', in T.H. Eriksen (ed.) *Globalisation: Studies in Anthropology*. London: Pluto Press.

Kropotkin, P. 1927. *Revolutionary Pamphlets*. New York: Vanguard Press.

Kruks, S. 2001. *Retrieving Experience: Subjectivity and Recognition in Feminist Politics*. Ithaca, NY: Cornell University Press.

Kuper, A. 1995. 'Comments', *Current Anthropology* 36(3): 424–26.

Laclau, E. 1985. 'New Social Movements and the Plurality of the Social', in D. Salter (ed.) *New Social Movements and the State in Latin America*. Dordrecht: CEDLA.

Laclau, E. and Mouffe, C. 1985. *Hegemony and the Socialist Strategy: Towards a Radical Democratic Politics*. London: Verso.

Lang, S. and Schneider, F. 2003. 'The Dark Side of Camping'. Online: http://makeworlds.org/node/44. Accessed December 2006.

Latour, B. 1999. 'On recalling ANT', in J. Law and J. Hassard (eds) *Actor Network Theory and After*. Oxford: Blackwell.

Law, J. 1999. 'After ANT: Complexity, Naming and Topology', in J. Law and J. Hassard (eds) *Actor Network Theory and After*. Oxford: Blackwell.

Leite, J.C. 2004. 'WSF (a Brief History): A New Method of Doing Politics', in special issue on 'World Social Forum: A Debate on the Challenges for Its Future', *Transform! Newsletter* 1.

Leite, J.C. 2005. *The World Social Forum: Strategies of Resistance*. Chicago: Haymarket Books.

Levidow, L. 2004. 'European Social Forum: Making Another World Possible?', *Radical Philosophy* 28. Online: www.nadir.org/nadir/initiativ/agp/free/wsf/london2004/0908another_world.htm. Accessed November 2006.

Leys, C. 2005. 'Democracy', in D. Miller and G. Hubbard (eds) *Arguments Against the G8*. London: Pluto Press.

Li, T. 1999. 'Compromising Power: Development, Culture and Rule in Indonesia', *Cultural Anthropology* 14(3): 295–322.

Linhart, R. 1978. *Division du travail*. Paris: Galilée.

Lipovetsky, G. 1986. '"Changer la vie" ou l'irruption de l'individualisme transpolitique', *Pouvoirs* 39: 91–100.

LiPuma, E. 2000. *Encompassing Others: The Magic of Modernity in Melanesia*. Ann Arbor: University of Michigan Press.

Llewellyn, K. and Hoebel, E.A. 1941. *The Cheyenne Way: Conflict and Case Law in Primitive Jurisprudence*. Norman: University of Oklahoma Press.

Lloyd, G. 1982. *The Man of Reason*. London: Methuen.

Lorenzano, L. 1998. 'Zapatismo: Recomposition of Labour, Radical Democracy and Revolutionary Project', in J. Holloway and E. Pelaez (eds) *Zapatista! Reinventing Revolution in Mexico*. London: Pluto Press.

Losson, C. and Quinio, P. 2002. *Géneration Seattle: Les Rebelles de la mondialisation*. Paris: Grasset.

Lucas. 1999. 'New Alliances on the Right', *Animal* 3.

Lukes, S. 2005. *Power: A Radical View*. New York: Palgrave Macmillan.

Lynd, S. 1969. 'Towards a History of the New Left', in P. Lang (ed.) *The New Left*. Boston, MA: Porter Sargent Publisher.

Lyon-Callo, V. and Hyatt, S.B. 2003. 'The Neoliberal State and the Depoliticization of Poverty: Activist Anthropology and "Ethnography from Below"', *Urban Anthropology and Studies of Cultural Systems and World Economic Development* 32: 47–79.

McAdam, D., McCarthy, J.D. and Zald, M.N. 1988. 'Social Movements', in N. Smelser (ed.) *Handbook of Sociology, Part IV: Social Process and Change*. Newbury Park, CA: SAGE.

McCarthy, J.D. and Zald, M.N. 1973. *The Trend of Social Movements in America*. New York: Morristown.

McCarthy, J.D. and Zald, M.N. 1977. 'Resource Mobilization and Social Movements: A Partial Theory', *American Journal of Sociology* 82(6): 1212–41.

MacDonald, A. 1980. *The Turner Diaries*. Arlington, VA: National Vanguard Books.

McFarland, A. 2006. 'Comment: Power-Over, To, and With', *City and Culture* 5(1): 39–41.

McGrane, B. 1989. *Beyond Anthropology: Society and the Other*. New York: Columbia University Press.

McKay, G. 1998. *DIY Culture: Party and Protest in Nineties Britain*. London: Verso.

Macy, J. 1991. *World as Lover, World as Self*. Berkeley: Parallax Press.

Mai '68 par eux-mêmes. 1989. Paris: Editions du monde libertaire.

Manceaux, M. 1972. *Les Maos en France*. Paris: Gallimard.

Manin, B. 1994. 'Checks, Balances and Boundaries: The Separation of Powers in the Constitutional Debate of 1787', in B. Fontana (ed.) *The Invention of the Modern Republic*. Cambridge: Cambridge University Press.

Mansbridge, J. 1983. *Beyond Adversary Democracy*. Chicago: University of Chicago Press.

Manson, S. 2001. 'Simplifying Complexity: A Review of Complexity Theory', *Geoform* 32: 405–14.

Marcus, G. 1995. 'Ethnography in/of the World System: The Emergence of Multi-sited Ethnography', *Annual Review of Anthropology* 24: 95–117.

Marglin, F. and Marglin, S. 1990. *Dominating Knowledge: Development, Culture and Resistance*. Oxford: Clarendon Press.

Marriott, M. and Cohn, B. 1958. 'Networks and Centres in the Integration of Indian Civilization', *Journal of Social Research* 1(1): 1–9.

Marshall, P. 1992. *Demanding the Impossible: A History of Anarchism*. London: Fontana Press.

May, T. 1994. *The Political Philosophy of Poststructuralist Anarchism*. University Park, PA: Pennsylvania State University Press.

Melucci, A. 1989. *Nomads of the Present*. London: Hutchison.

Melucci, A. 1992. 'Liberation or Meaning? Social Movements, Culture and Democracy', *Development and Change* 23(3): 43–77.

Mill, J.S. 1962 [1859]. 'On Liberty', in M. Warnock (ed.) *Utilitarianism: On Liberty*. London: Collins.

Miller, E. 2005. 'The Gang of 8: The Good Governance Roadshow', in D. Miller and G. Hubbard (eds) *Arguments Against the G8*. London: Pluto Press.

Miller, J. 1994. *Democracy is in the Streets*. Cambridge, MA: Harvard University Press.

Miller, J.B. 1992. 'Women and Power', in T. Wartenberg (ed.) *Rethinking Power*. Albany: SUNY Press.

Mintz, S. 1985. *Sweetness and Power: The Place of Sugar in Modern History*. New York: Penguin.

Mirza, H.S. 1997. 'Introduction: Mapping a Genealogy of Black British Feminism', in H.S. Mirza (ed.) *Black British Feminism: A Reader*. London: Routledge.

Mitchell, J.C. 1960. *Tribalism and the Plural Society*. Oratie: University College of Rhodesia and Nyasaland/London: Oxford University Press.

Moore, D. 2000. 'The Crucible of Cultural Politics: Reworking "Development" in Zimbabwe's Eastern Highlands', *American Ethnologist* 26(3): 654–89.

Morland, D. 2004. 'Anti-capitalism and Poststructuralist Anarchism', in J. Purkis and J. Bowen (eds) *Changing Anarchism*. Manchester: Manchester University Press.

Morriss, P. 2002. *Power: A Philosophical Analysis*. Manchester: Manchester University Press.

Mosse, D. 2002. 'The Making and Marketing of Participatory Development', in P. Quarles van Ufford and A. Giri (eds) *A Moral Critique of Development: In Search of Global Responsibilities*. London: Routledge. Page numbers cited here are from the online version available at: http://www.kus.uu.se/Mosse.pdf. Accessed April 2009.

Mouffe, C. 1988. 'Hegemony and New Political Subjects: Toward a New Concept of Democracy', in C. Nelson and L. Grossberg (eds) *Marxism and the Interpretation of Culture*. Urbana: University of Illinois Press.

Mouffe, C. 1996. 'Democracy, Power and the "Political"', in S. Benhabib (ed.) *Democracy and Difference*. Princeton, NJ: Princeton University Press.

Mouffe, C. 2000. *The Democratic Paradox*. New York: Verso.

Mouvement du 22 Mars. 2001. *Ce n'est qu'un début, continuons le combat*. Paris: [Re]découverte.

Mueller, T. 2001. 'Empowering Anarchy'. Online: http://www.infoshop. org/library/EmpoweringAnarchy.pdf. Accessed June 2005.

Munro, R. 2005. 'Partial Organization: Marilyn Strathern and the Elicitation of Relations', *Sociological Review* 53(Supp. 1): 245–66.

Mushaben, J. 1989. 'The Struggle Within: Conflict, Consensus, and Decision-making among National Coordinators and Grass-roots Organizers in the West German Peace Movement', in B. Klandermans (ed.) *International Social Movement Research, vol. II: Organizing for Change: Social Movement Organizations in Europe and the United States*. Greenwich, CT: JAI Press.

Nandy, A. 1998. 'The Politics of Secularism and the Recovery of Religious Tolerance', in R. Bhargava (ed.) *Secularism and its Critics*. Oxford: Oxford University Press.

Nash, J. 1997. 'The Fiesta of the World: The Zapatista Uprising and Radical Democracy in Mexico', *American Anthropologist* 99(2): 261–74.

Nash, J. 2001. *Mayan Visions*. London: Routledge.

Nash, J. 2005a. 'Introduction: Social Movements and Global Processes', in J. Nash (ed.) *Social Movements: An Anthropological Reader*. Oxford: Blackwell.

Nash, J. 2005b. 'Defying Deterritorialization: Autonomy Movements against Globalization', in J. Nash (ed.) *Social Movements: An Anthropological Reader*. Oxford: Blackwell.

Negri, A. 1996. 'Constituent Republic', in P. Virno and M. Hardt (eds) *Radical Thought in Italy, A Potential Politics*. Minnesota: University of Minnesota Press.

Nelson, D. 1999. *A Finger in the Wound*. Berkeley: University of California Press.

Nelson, N. and S. Wright 1995. *Power and Participatory Development: Theory and Practice*. London: Intermediate Technology Publications.

Nomadlab. 2002. 'Breaking Free of the Protest Mentality'. Online: http://info.interactivist.net/print.pl?sid=02/04/25/1946259. Accessed December 2006.

Notes from Nowhere collective (ed.) 2003. *We Are Everywhere*. London: Verso.

'Nouvelles d'Amerique Latine'. 2005. Email. Sent 23 February 2005.

Nunes, R. 2004. 'Territory and Deterritory: Inside and Outside the ESF 2004, New Movement Subjectivities', *Euromovements*. Online: http://www.euromovements.info/newsletter/. Accessed November 2006.

Nunes, R. 2005. 'Nothing is What Democracy Looks Like: Openness, Horizontality, and the Movement of Movements', in D. Harvie, K. Milburn, B. Trott and D. Watts (eds) *Shut Them Down!* Leeds: Autonomedia/Dissent! Also online: www.shutthemdown.org/contents. html.

Olson, M. 1965. *The Logic of Collective Action: Public Goods and the Theory of Groups*. Cambridge, MA: Harvard University Press.

O'Neil, D.J. 1994. 'Communist Prefiguration: The Munster Anabaptists', *International Journal of Social Economics* 24(10): 116–32.

Ortner, S. 2006. *Anthropology and Social Theory: Culture, Power and the Acting Subject*. Durham, NC: Duke University Press.

Pagden, A. 1982. *The Fall of Natural Man: The American Indian and the Origin of Comparative Ethnography*. Cambridge: Cambridge University Press.

Paley, J. 2001. *Marketing Democracy: Power and Social Movements in Post-Dictatorship Chile*. Berkeley: University of California Press.

Paley, J. 2002. 'Toward an Anthropology of Democracy', *Annual Review of Anthropology* 31: 469–96.

'Paris: May 1968'. Online: http://www.geocities.com/cordobakaf/maya. html. Accessed December 2006. Originally printed in *Solidarity* 1968.

Pateman, C. 1988. *The Sexual Contract*. Stanford, CA: Stanford University Press.

PGA (Peoples' Global Action). n.d. 'Hallmarks of Peoples' Global Action'. Online: http://www.nadir.org/nadir/initiativ/agp/free/pga/hallm.htm. Accessed October 2006.

Pharr, S. and Putnam, R. (eds) 2000. *Disaffected Democracies: What's Troubling the Trilateral Countries?* Princeton, NJ: Princeton University Press.

Pitkin, H.F. 1972. *Wittgenstein and Justice: On the Significance of Ludwig Wittgenstein for Social and Political Thought*. Berkeley: University of California Press.

Poldervaart, S. 2004. "Over Ya Basta! en Verzet als Scheppende Kracht'. Online: http://www.yabasta.be/spip.php?article61. Accessed May 2007.

Polletta, F. 2002. *Freedom is an Endless Meeting*. Chicago: University of Chicago Press.

Polletta, F. and Jasper, J. 2001. 'Collective Identity and Social Movements', *Annual Review of Sociology* 27: 283–305.

Ponniah, T. and Fisher, W. 2004. 'Under a Tree in Porto Alegre 2003: Democracy in its Most Radical Sense', in J. Sen, A. Anand, A. Escobar and P. Waterman (eds) *The World Social Forum: Challenging Empires*. New Delhi: The Viveka Foundation. Also online: http://www.choike. org/nuevo_eng/informes/1557.html. Accessed April 2009.

Popkewitz, T. and Brennan, M. 1998. *Foucault's Challenge: Discourse, Knowledge and Power in Education*. New York and London: Teacher's College Press.

Povinelli, E. 2002. 'The State of Shame: Australian Multiculturalism and the Crisis of Indigenous Citizenship', *Critical Inquiry* 24: 575–610.

Pratt, J. 2003. *Class, Nation and Identity: The Anthropology of Political Movements*. London: Pluto Press.

Proudhon, P. 1923. *General Idea of the Revolution in the 19th Century*. London: Freedom Press.

Reyes, O. 2004a. Email. Sent to 'Rede de Resistencias Global', e-list. Posted 25 March 2004.

Reyes, O. 2004b. Email. Sent to 'democratisetheESF' e-list. Posted 14 December 2004.

Robertson, R. 1995. 'Globalization', in M. Featherstone, S. Lash and R. Robertson (eds) *Global Modernities*. London: SAGE.

Rochon, T. 1988. *Culture Moves: Ideas, Activism, and Changing Values*. Princeton, NJ: Princeton University Press.

Rootes, C. 1982. 'Student Activism in France: 1968 and After', in P.G. Cerny (ed.) *Social Movements and Protest in France*. London: Frances Pinter.

Rose, N. 1996. 'Governing "Advanced" Liberal Democracies', in A. Barry, T. Osborne and N. Rose (eds) *Foucault and Political Reason: Liberalism, Neo-liberalism and Rationalities of Government*. Chicago, IL: University of Chicago Press.

Ross, K. 2002. *May '68 and its Afterlives*. Chicago: University of Chicago Press.

Ross, R. 1983. 'Generational Change and Primary Groups in a Social Movement', in J. Freeman (ed.) *Social Movements of the Sixties and Seventies*. New York: Longman.

Rousseau, J.J. 1968 [1762]. *The Social Contract*. Harmondsworth: Penguin.

Rucht, D. 1990. 'The Strategies and Action Repertoires of New Movements', in R. Dalton and M. Keuchler (eds) *Challenging the Political Order*. Oxford: Polity Press.

Said, E. 1991. 'The Politics of Knowledge', *Raritan* 41(1): 17–31.

Sale, K. 1973. *SDS*. New York: Random House.

Santos, B. de Sousa. 2004. 'The World Social Forum: Toward a Counter-hegemonic Globalization (Part I)', in J. Sen, A. Anand, A. Escobar and P. Waterman (eds) *The World Social Forum: Challenging Empires*. New Delhi: The Viveka Foundation. Also available online: http://www. choike.org/nuevo_eng/informes/1557.html. Accessed April 2009.

Santos, B. de Sousa. 2006. *The Rise of the Global Left*. London: Zed Books.

Scheper-Hughes, N. 1995. 'The Primacy of the Ethical: Propositions for a Militant Anthropology', *Current Anthropology* 36(3): 409–20.

Schirmer, J. 1998. *The Guatemalan Military Project: A Violence Called Democracy*. Philadelphia: University of Pennsylvania Press.

Schönleitner, G. 2003. 'World Social Forum: Making Another World Possible?', in J. Clark (ed.) *Globalizing Civic Engagement*. London: Earthscan Publications.

Schöpflin, G. 2003. 'Identities, Politics and Post-Communism in Central Europe', *Nations and Nationalism* 9(4): 477–90.

Schumpeter, J. 1976 [1942]. *Capitalism, Socialism and Democracy*. London: Allen and Unwin.

Scott, J. 1985. *Weapons of the Weak: Everyday Forms of Peasant Resistance*. New Haven, CT: Yale University Press.

Scott, J. 1998. *Seeing Like a State: How Certain Schemes to Improve the Human Condition have Failed*. New Haven, CT: Yale University Press.

SDS. 1962. 'Port Huron Statement of the Students for a Democratic Society, 1962'. Online: http://coursesa.matrix.msu.edu/~hst306/documents/huron.html. Accessed December 2006.

Sellwood, M. 2003. 're: LSF report'. Email. Sent to 'esf-uk-info' e-list. Posted 12 October 2003.

Sen, A. 1999. 'Democracy as a Universal Value', *Journal of Democracy* 10(3): 3–17. Also online: http://muse.jhu.edu/demo/jod/10.3sen.html. Accessed June 2009.

Sen, A. 2006. *Identity and Violence: The Illusion of Destiny*. New York: W.W. Norton.

Sen, J. 2004. 'A Tale of Two Charters', in J. Sen, A. Anand, A. Escobar and P. Waterman (eds) *The World Social Forum: Challenging Empires*. New Delhi: The Viveka Foundation. Also online: http://www.choike.org/nuevo_eng/informes/1557.html. Accessed April 2009.

Shapiro, I. 2003. *The State of Democratic Theory*. Princeton, NJ: Princeton University Press. Also online: http://www.pupress.princeton.edu/chapters/i7672.html.

Sheth, P. 1991. *Sardar Sarovar Project: Dynamics of Development*. Ahmedabad: Vikas Bharati.

Sitrin, M. 2006. *Horizontalism: Voices of Popular Power in Argentina*. Oakland, CA: AK Press.

Slowcode. 2006. 'Consulta? thoughts on stu's mail, back and beyond'. Email. Sent to 'dissentprocess' e-list. Posted on 13 February 2006.

Smith, J. 2008. *Social Movements for Global Democracy*. Baltimore, MD: Johns Hopkins University Press.

Soldatenko, M. 2005. 'México '68: Power to the Imagination', *Latin American Perspectives* 32(4): 111–32.

Speed, S. 2006. 'At the Crossroads of Human Rights and Anthropology: Toward a Critically Engaged Activist Research'. *American Anthropologist* 108(1): 66.

Spelman, E. 1988. *Inessential Woman*. Boston, MA: Beacon Press.

Spivak, G. 1989. 'In a Word: An Interview', *Differences* 1: 124–56.

Spivak, G. 1990. *Postcolonial Critics: Interviews, Strategies, Dialogues*. New York: Routledge.

Spivak, G. 1993. *Inside the Teaching Machine*. New York: Routledge.

Stammers, N. and Eschle, C. 2005. 'Social Movements and Global Activism', in W. de Jong, M. Shaw and N. Stammers (eds) *Global Activism, Global Media*. London: Pluto Press.

Starhawk. 2001. 'Staying on the Streets', in *On Fire: The Battle of Genoa and the Anti-Capitalist Movement*. Edinburgh: One-Off Press.

Stephen, L. 2005. 'Gender, Citizenship and the Politics of Identity', in J. Nash (ed.) *Social Movements: An Anthropological Reader*. Oxford: Blackwell.

Stewart, P. 2001. 'Complexity Theories, Social Theory, and the Question of Social Complexity', *Philosophy of the Social Sciences* 31(3): 323–60.

Stoler, A. 1995. *Race and the Education of Desire: Foucault's History of Sexuality and the Colonial Order of Things*. Durham, NC: Duke University Press.

StopG8. 2006. 'Verslag Vergadering Dissent-Gent'. Email. Sent to 'stopdeg8' e-list. Posted 26 October.

Strathern, M. 1988. *The Gender of the Gift: Problems with Women and Problems with Society in Melanesia*. Berkeley: University of California Press.

Strathern, M. 2004. *Partial Connections: Updated Edition*. Walnut Creek, CA: AltaMira Press.

Sturgeon, N. 1995. 'Theorizing Movements: Direct Action and Direct Theory', in M. Darnovsky, B. Epstein and R. Flacks (eds) *Cultural Politics and Social Movements*. Philadelphia, PA: Temple University Press.

Subcomandante Marcos. 1996. 'First Declaration Against Neoliberalism and for Humanity'. 30 January 2006. Online: http://struggle.ws/mexico/ezln/ccri_1st_dec_real.html Accessed July 2007.

Swartz, M.J., Turner, V. and Tuden, A. 2002 [1966]. Originally 'Introduction' in *Political Anthropology*. Chicago: Aldine Publishing Company. Reproduced in J. Vincent (ed.) 2002. *The Anthropology of Politics: A Reader in Ethnography, Theory and Critique*. Oxford: Blackwell.

Sylvain, R. 2005. '"Land, Water and Truth": Sen, Identity and Global Indigenism', in J. Nash (ed.) *Social Movements: An Anthropological Reader*. Oxford: Blackwell.

Tambiah, S. 1996. *Levelling Crowds: Ethnonationalist Conflicts and Collective Violence in South Asia*. Berkeley: University of California Press.

Taussig, M. 1993. 'The Colour of Alterity', in A. Taussig (ed.) *Mimesis and Alterity*. London: Routledge.

Tilly, C. 1973. 'Does Modernization Breed Revolution?', *Comparative Politics* 5: 425–47.

Tilly, C. 1978. *From Mobilization to Revolution*. Reading, MA: Addison-Wesley.

Todorov, T. 1985. *The Conquest of America and the Question of the Other*. New York: Harper Perennial.

Touraine, A. 1985. 'An Introduction to the Study of Social Movements', *Social Research* 52(4): 749–87.

Touraine, A. 1997. *What is Democracy?* Boulder, CO: Westview Press.

Trott, B. 2005. 'Gleneagles, Activism and Ordinary Rebelliousness', in D. Harvie, K. Milburn, B. Trott and D. Watts (eds) *Shut Them Down!* Leeds: Autonomedia/Dissent! Also online: http://www.shutthemdown.org/Resources/Ch%2019.pdf.

Tucker, K. 1998. *Anthony Giddens and Modern Social Theory*. London: Sage.

UK Local Social Forum Network. 2004. 'A Different ESF is Possible'. Online: http://209.85.129.104/search?q=cache:MeMc6enGwuQJ:www.moviments.net/euromovements/tiki-download_file.php%3FfileId%3D50+A+Different+ESF+is+Possible&hl=fr&ct=clnk&cd=2&client=safari. Accessed December 2004.

Verdery, K. 1998. 'Transnationalism, Nationalism, Citizenship, and Property: Eastern Europe since 1989', *American Ethnologist* 25(2): 291–306.

Wade, P. 1999. 'Working Culture: Making Cultural Identities in Cali, Colombia', *Current Anthropology* 40(4): 449–71.

Wainwright, H. 2003. *Reclaim the State*. London: Verso.

Wainwright, H. 2004. 'Change the World by Transforming Power – Including State Power!', *Red Pepper*, November 2004. Also online: http://www.redpepper.org.uk/Nov2004/x-Nov2004-Holloway(HW).html.

Walter, L. 1995. 'Feminist Anthropology?', *Gender and Society* 9(3): 272–88.

Warren, K. 1998. *Indigenous Movements and Their Critics: Pan-Mayan Activism in Guatemala*. Princeton, NJ: Princeton University Press.

Warren, K. 2002. 'Voting Against Indigenous Rights in Guatemala: Lessons from the 1999 Referendum', in K. Warren and J. Jackson (eds)

Indigenous Movements, Self-Representation, and the State. Austin: University of Texas Press.

Warren, M. 1996. 'What Should We Expect from More Democracy: Radically Democratic Responses to Politics', *Political Theory* 24(2): 241–70.

Wartenberg, T. 1990. *The Forms of Power: From Domination to Transformation.* Philadelphia, PA: Temple University Press.

Wasserman, S. and Faust, K. 1994. *Social Network Analysis: Methods and Applications.* Cambridge: Cambridge University Press.

Watts, D. 2003. *Six Degrees: The Science of a Connected Age.* New York: W.W. Norton.

Weber, M. 1978. *Economy and Society: An Outline of Interpretive Sociology*, trans. E. Fischoff et al. Berkeley: California University Press.

Weissman, A. 2005. 'Everyday Revolutions: Practices and Institutions for Living Beyond Capitalism in Everyday Life'. Online: http://freegan. info/?page=EvRev. Accessed December 2006.

Welsh, I. and Purkis, J. 2003. 'Redefining Anarchism for the Twenty-first Century: Some Modest Beginnings', *Anarchist Studies* 11(1): 5–12.

Whitaker, C. 2001. 'World Social Forum: Origins and Aims'. Online: http://www.fsmt.org.co/eng-origen.htm. Accessed December 2006.

Whitaker, C. 2004. 'The WSF as Open Space', in J. Sen, A. Anand, A. Escobar and P. Waterman (eds) *The World Social Forum: Challenging Empires.* New Delhi: The Viveka Foundation. Also online: http://www. choike.org/nuevo_eng/informes/1557.html. Accessed April 2009.

Whitridge, P. 2004. 'Cyborgs, Chimeras and other Hybrid Selves: An Actor-network Perspective on the Construction of Identity', Theoretical Archaeology Group conference, University of Glasgow. 17–19 December 2004. Online: http://www.gla.ac.uk/archaeology/ news/conferences/tag/sessions/1.html#B. Accessed December 2006.

Wilson, G. 1968 [1942]. *The Economics of Detribalization in Northern Rhodesia.* Manchester University Press for Institute for Social Research, Rhodes-Livingstone Papers nos 5–6, 1968 reprint of 1942 edition.

Wiser, J. 1983. *Political Philosophy, A History of the Search for Order.* Englewood Cliffs, NJ: Prentice-Hall Inc.

Wolf, E.R. 1990. 'Facing Power – Old Insights, New Questions', *American Anthropologist* 92: 586–96.

Wolff, J. 1996. *An Introduction to Political Philosophy.* Oxford: Oxford University Press.

Wolin, S. 1996. 'Fugitive Democracy', in S. Benhabib (ed.) *Democracy and Difference.* Princeton, NJ: Princeton University Press.

Wood, G.D. 1998. 'Consultant Behaviour: Projects as Communities: Consultants, Knowledge and Power', *Project Appraisal* 16(1): 54–64.

WSF Brazilian Organizing Committee and International Council. 2001. 'The WSF Charter of Principles'. Online: http://www.forumsocial-mundial.org.br/main.php?id_menu=4_2&cd_language=2. Accessed December 2006.

WSF Brazilian Organizing Committee and International Council. 2002. 'Note from the Organizing Committee on the Principles that Guide the WSF'. Online: http://www.lfsc.org/wsf/wsf2006info.htm. Accessed July 2007.

Yuen, E., Katsiaficas, G., Rose, B.D. (eds) 2001. *The Battle of Seattle: New Challenges to Capitalist Globalization*. New York: Soft Skull Press.

Young, I.M. 1990. *Justice and the Politics of Difference*. Princeton, NJ: Princeton University Press.

Young, I.M. 2000. *Inclusion and Democracy*. Oxford: Oxford University Press.

Z, K and T. 2006. 'Consulta?' email. Sent to 'dissentprocess' e-list. Posted 9 February.

INDEX